CHRISTIAN INITIATION

1552-1969

ALCUIN CLUB COLLECTIONS
No. 52

Christian Initiation 1552-1969

RITES OF
BAPTISM AND CONFIRMATION
SINCE THE
REFORMATION PERIOD

Peter J. Jagger

Published for the Alcuin Club

LONDON
S · P · C · K
1970

First published in 1970
by S.P.C.K.
Holy Trinity Church
Marylebone Road
London N.W.1

Made and printed in Great Britain by
William Clowes and Sons, Limited
London and Beccles

© Peter J. Jagger, 1970

SNB 281 02597 5

A. RAYMOND GEORGE

A patient and encouraging teacher

Contents

ACKNOWLEDGEMENTS   xi

ABBREVIATIONS   xv

PREFACE   xvii

Part 1
Common Forms

TWENTY COMMON FORMS   3

Part 2
The Revisions of the Anglican Communion

1   THE CHURCH OF ENGLAND RITES 1552   11
WITH NOTES ON THE REVISIONS OF 1559, 1604,
AND THE SCOTTISH LITURGY OF 1637

The Ministration of Baptism   12
Confirmation   19

2   THE CHURCH OF ENGLAND RITES 1662   22
WITH NOTES ON THE ALTERATIONS PROPOSED IN 1689

The Ministration of Publick Baptism of Infants   22
The Order of Confirmation   30

3   THE CANADIAN RITES 1918   34
The Ministration of Publick Baptism of Infants   34
The Order of Confirmation   36

4   THE IRISH RITES 1926   39
The Ministration of Public Baptism of Infants   39
The Order for Confirmation   42

5   THE CHURCH OF ENGLAND PROPOSED RITES 1928   45
An Alternative Order of the Ministration of Publick Baptism of Infants   46
An Alternative Order of Confirmation   51

6   THE AMERICAN RITES 1928   54
The Ministration of Holy Baptism   54
The Order of Confirmation   59

7 THE SCOTTISH EPISCOPAL RITES 1929   61

   The Ministration of Public Baptism of Infants   61
   The Order of Confirmation   64

8 THE CHURCH OF INDIA, PAKISTAN,
   BURMA, AND CEYLON RITES 1951   67

   The Ministration of Holy Baptism   67
   The Order of Confirmation   73

9 THE SOUTH AFRICAN RITES 1954   77

   The Ministration of Publick Baptism of Infants   77
   The Order of Confirmation   82

10 THE CANADIAN RITES 1959   86

   The Ministration of Holy Baptism to Children   86
   The Order of Confirmation   92

11 THE CHURCH OF INDIA, PAKISTAN,
   BURMA, AND CEYLON RITES 1960   95

   The Ministration of Holy Baptism   95
   The Permissive Ceremonies   98
   The Order of Confirmation   99

12 THE WEST INDIAN RITES 1964   103

   The Order for the Administration of Holy Baptism   103
   The Order for Confirmation   109

13 THE SOUTH AFRICAN RITES 1967   113

   The Administration of Baptism to Children   113
   The Administration of Confirmation   119
   The Administration of Baptism and Confirmation   122

14 THE AUSTRALIAN RITES 1967   125

   The Administration of Baptism   125
   A Service of Confirmation   129
   A Rite of Baptism and Confirmation   132

15 THE SCOTTISH EPISCOPAL RITE 1967   134

   Permissive Rite for the Baptism of Infants   134

16 THE CHURCH OF ENGLAND RITES 1968   138

   The Baptism of those who are not old enough to Answer for Themselves 138
   The Confirmation of those who have already been Baptized and are
     now old enough to Answer for Themselves   142
   The Baptism and Confirmation of those who are old enough to
     Answer for Themselves   145

17 THE WELSH RITES 1968   148

   Public Baptism of Infants   148
   The Order of Confirmation   152

18 THE IRISH RITES 1969   155
    The Order for the Baptism of Children   155

Part 3
The Non-Anglican Revisions

1 THE BOOK OF COMMON ORDER 1611   163
   WITH NOTES ON THE GENEVAN SERVICE BOOK 1556
   The Order of Baptism   163

2 THE WESTMINSTER DIRECTORY 1644   173
   The Administration of Baptism   173

3 THE METHODIST RITES 1936   177
   The Order of Service for the Baptism of Infants   177
   The Order of Service for the Public Reception of New Members   180

4 THE CONGREGATIONALIST RITES 1936   185
   The Baptism of Children   185
   The Reception of Church Members   188

5 THE CHURCH OF SCOTLAND RITES 1940   191
   Order for the Administration of the Sacrament of Baptism to Infants   191
   Order for the Confirmation of Baptized Persons   194

6 THE PRESBYTERIAN RITES 1948   198
   The Order for the Administration of the Sacrament of Baptism   198
   Order for the Confirmation of Baptismal Vows   202

7 THE BAPTIST RITES 1960   205
   The Baptism of Believers   205
   The Laying on of Hands with Prayer upon those who have been
     Baptized   209

8 THE MORAVIAN RITES 1960   211
   The Baptism of Infants   211
   The Baptism of Adults and the Confirmation of such as have been
     Baptized in Infancy   214

9 THE LUTHERAN RITES 1962   218
   Order for the Baptism of Infants   218
   Order for Confirmation   221

10 THE ROMAN CATHOLIC RITES 1964   224
   The Rite of Infant Baptism   224
   The Rite of Confirmation   229

CONTENTS

11 THE METHODIST RITES 1967   232
    The Baptism of Infants   233
    Public Reception into Full Membership   239
    The Baptism of those who are able to Answer for Themselves with
        the Public Reception into Full Membership   243

12 THE PRESBYTERIAN RITES 1968   249
    Order for the Administration of the Sacrament of Baptism   249
    Act of Confirmation   253

13 THE CHURCH OF SCOTLAND RITES 1968   257
    Order for the Administration of Holy Baptism   257
    Confirmation and Admission to the Lord's Supper   262
    Holy Baptism, Confirmation and Admission to the Lord's Supper   266
    Vows of Church Membership   269

14 THE CONGREGATIONALIST RITES 1969   270
    The Baptism of Children   270
    The Reception of Church Members on Profession of Faith   272

15 THE ROMAN CATHOLIC RITE 1969   275
    Rite of Baptism   275

Part 4
Appendixes

1 THE IGLESIA FILIPINA INDEPENDIENTE RITES 1961   291
   The Administration of Holy Baptism   291
   The Sacrament of Confirmation   297

2 THE CHURCH OF SOUTH INDIA RITES 1962   301
   The Baptism of Infants   304
   An Order of Service for the Reception of Baptized Persons into the
       Full Fellowship of the Church   310

3 THE CHURCH OF THE PROVINCE OF EAST AFRICA   315
   PRESBYTERIAL CONFIRMATION: EPISCOPAL LAYING ON OF HANDS   315

4 THE EAST AFRICAN CHURCH UNION   317
   An Infant Baptismal Liturgy   317

Acknowledgements

I am indebted to the following for permission to reproduce copyright material.

PART 2

1. *The Scottish Liturgy 1637.* William Blackwood & Sons Ltd.
2. *The Book of Common Prayer 1662.* Material is Crown Copyright and is reproduced by permission.
3. The General Synod of the Anglican Church of Canada.
4. The General Synod of the Church of Ireland.
5. *The Book of Common Prayer with the Additions and Deviations Proposed in 1928.* Material is copyright and is reproduced by permission.
6. The Custodian of the Standard Book of Common Prayer, New York. (This material is not copyright.)
7. The Publications Committee of the Episcopal Church in Scotland.
8. The Indian Society for Promoting Christian Knowledge.
9. *The Book of Common Prayer set forth by authority for use in the Church of the Province of South Africa 1954.* Material is copyright and is reproduced by permission.
10. The General Synod of the Anglican Church of Canada.
11. The Indian Society for Promoting Christian Knowledge.
12. The Provincial Authorities of the West Indies.
13. The Liturgical Committee of the Church of the Province of South Africa.
14. The Liturgical Commission of the Church of England in Australia. All rights reserved.
15. The Publications Committee of the Episcopal Church in Scotland.
16. The Registrars of the Convocations of Canterbury and York.
17. The Church in Wales Publications.
18. The Standing Committee of the General Synod of the Church of Ireland.

PART 3

1. William Blackwood & Sons Ltd.
   Liturgical Portions of the Genevan Service Book, The Faith Press Ltd.
2. William Blackwood & Sons Ltd.
3. The Epworth Press.
4. The Congregational Church in England and Wales.
5. *The Book of Common Order* by permission of the Committee on Public Worship and Aids to Devotion of the Church of Scotland.

6. Presbyterian Church of England Committee on Publications and Publicity.
7. The Baptist Union of Great Britain and Ireland.
8. The Moravian Church in Great Britain and Ireland.
9. *The Lutheran Service Book and Hymnal*, by permission of the Commission on the Liturgy and Hymnal.
10. *The Small Ritual*, Burns, Oates.
    Confirmation, the Catholic Truth Society.
11. The Epworth Press.
12. Presbyterian Church of England Committee on Publications and Publicity.
13. *Holy Baptism and Confirmation and the Admission to the Lord's Supper*, by permission of the Committee on Public Worship and Aids to Devotion of the Church of Scotland.
14. The Congregational Church in England and Wales.
15. English translation of the new Roman Catholic *Rite of Baptism for Children*, copyright © 1969, International Committee on English in the Liturgy, Inc. All rights reserved.

PART 4

1. The Most Reverend Isabelo de los Reyes, Jr (Obispo Maximo, Iglesia Filipina Independiente).
2. *The Book of Common Worship of the Church of South India*, by permission of the Synod of the Church of South India.
3. *Minutes of the Provincial Liturgical Panel*, the Archbishop of East Africa.
4. The East Africa Church Union Consultation.

I am indebted to a large number of people who have helped me with this work. The following gladly supplied me with information:

The Most Reverend L. J. Beecher (Archbishop of East Africa); the Most Reverend F. H. Moncrieff (Primus of the Episcopal Church in Scotland); the Most Reverend Isabelo de los Reyes, Jr (Obispo Maximo, Iglesia Filipina Independiente); the Right Reverend R. G. Arthur (Bishop of Grafton); the Right Reverend E. G. Munn (Bishop of Caledonia); the Right Reverend K. A. Viall (Assistant Bishop of Tokyo); the Right Reverend H. A. J. Witt (Bishop of North-West Australia); the Reverend B. Beck; the Reverend J. S. Brown; the Reverend C. O. Buchanan; the Reverend J. M. G. Carey; the Reverend E. E. Chandlee; the Reverend G. Davies; the Reverend R. E. Davies; the Reverend Dr C. Rand; the Reverend T. J. Raphael; the Reverend Dr M. H. Shepherd, Jr; the Reverend G. J. Sigler; the Reverend J. Wilkinson; Mr F. N. D. Kelly; Miss D. Fraser.

ACKNOWLEDGEMENTS

Three members of the Community of the Resurrection, Mirfield, gave me their enthusiastic help and encouragement: the Reverend H. Benedict Green, C.R., Vice-Principal of the College of the Resurrection; the Reverend Gordon Arkell, C.R., Librarian of the Community Library, who traced and made available a large number of books; and the Reverend H. Edward Symonds, C.R., who helped with proof reading the first draft of the manuscript.

Four ladies of my parish, Mrs J. Murphy and the Misses H. Norfolk, B. Granger, and K. Hind, helped with the long process of typing and retyping until the final copy of the manuscript was complete.

The Reverend Canon R. C. D. Jasper gave help, assistance, and advice, over the past three years, both as a liturgical expert and in his capacity as Editorial Secretary of the Alcuin Club.

I must express my thanks to the Reverend A. Raymond George who, while having no hand in this work, a number of years ago guided my first faltering footsteps in the field of Liturgiology. To him this work is dedicated as a sign of my lasting gratitude.

Finally, my thanks are due to the Alcuin Club for their interest in this work and their acceptance of it as an addition to their Liturgical Collections.

PETER J. JAGGER

Abbreviations

ABBREVIATIONS OF RITES

1662 B	The Ministration of Publick Baptism of Infants, 1662.
1662 C	The Order of Confirmation, 1662.
1928 IB	An Alternative Order of the Ministration of Publick Baptism of Infants, 1928.
1928 C	An Alternative Order of Confirmation, 1928.
A IB	The Church of England in Australia: A Rite of Baptism of Infants.
A C	The Church of England in Australia: A Service of Confirmation.
IPBC 51 B	The Church of India, Pakistan, Burma, and Ceylon: The Ministration of Holy Baptism, 1951.
IPBC 51 C	The Church of India, Pakistan, Burma, and Ceylon: The Order of Confirmation, 1951.
S C	The Church of Scotland: Confirmation and Admission to the Lord's Supper.
W IB	The Church in Wales: Public Baptism of Infants.
SA IB	The Church of the Province of South Africa: The Administration of Baptism to Children.
SA C	The Church of the Province of South Africa: The Administration of Confirmation.
S2 IB	Alternative Services Second Series: 1968: The Baptism of those who are not old enough to answer for Themselves.
S2 C	Alternative Services Second Series: 1968: The Confirmation of those who have already been Baptized and are now old enough to answer for Themselves.
M	The Methodist Church: Public Reception into Full Membership.

GENERAL ABBREVIATIONS

CF	Common Form.
BCP	Book of Common Prayer.
MHB	Methodist Hymn Book.
AV	Authorized Version.
RV	Revised Version.
RSV	Revised Standard Version.
NEB	New English Bible.

GENERAL DIRECTIONS

The following points should be noted in using this book:

COMMON FORMS

Information as to the use of the Common Forms is given as the Introduction to Part 1—Common Forms.

SCRIPTURE PASSAGES

When the opening words of a passage are given, followed by a reference to the book, chapter, and verse, this indicates that in the original text the passage is given in full. Where only book, chapter, and verse are given, the full passage is not reproduced in the original text.

NUMBERS

These are inserted in the margin in order to give easy reference to any part of any text. They do not reproduce numbers given in the original texts.

RUBRICS

Rubrics are printed in sans serif type, thus:

Then shall the Bishop say,

except in the footnotes and in the variations where italic is used.

VARIATIONS

When a text varies from a Common Form or from a rite listed in Abbreviations of Rites on page xiii, the variation is printed in the same type size as the commentary followed by the original wording within angled brackets $\langle \; \rangle$.

Preface

The revision, or rather the enlargement of the Prayer Book, is a work which cannot be much longer delayed. When once the subject is fairly brought before English Churchmen, they will see that the cautious conservatism of merely working up old materials into new services is one which can satisfy nobody and will equally offend those who would be offended by any change.

Such were the views expressed a hundred years ago by the great Anglican liturgist J. M. Neale.[1]

In the past many liturgists have been inclined to work along the lines condemned by Neale. They have merely worked over "old material" and, with a few additions and alterations, have reproduced the liturgy they sought to revise. There is no doubt that past liturgies, both ancient and modern, are of immense value in the creation of new liturgies, if the material is used wisely and creatively, and not for purely anti-quarian reasons. In the collection of rites which follow there are examples of both types of liturgical revision as these methods have been applied in the revision of the rites of Christian initiation.

It is only in recent years that interest in the revision of the initiatory rites has come to the fore in liturgiology. As this interest is still very much in its infancy, much more work needs to be carried out on the subject. While there are innumerable volumes which provide texts of the eucharistic liturgy, and information about the attempts in many Churches to revise this rite, this is by no means the case with regard to the initiatory rites. Until recent years little has been done to provide a useful collection of baptism and confirmation liturgies. However, this omission has now been partly rectified, for with the publication of this work three volumes of such texts will be available to the English reader: *Documents of the Baptismal Liturgy*, by E. C. Whitaker; *Christian Initiation: The Reformation Period*; *Some early Reformed Rites of Baptism and Confirmation and other Contemporary Documents*, by J. D. C. Fisher. This present volume completes the survey up to the time of publication, 1969.

While this work has been compiled from within the Anglican Church, which fact has influenced its order and contents, the wide range of rites

---

[1] *Essays in Liturgiology and Church History*, J. M. Neale (1863), p. 225.

in Part 3 and the Appendixes will, I hope, give the work a catholic appeal. But, however catholic an edited work claims to be, it must be acknowledged that in the work of compiling and editing personal interests and ultimate aims cannot be completely obviated. A number of factors have influenced the order and selection of the rites contained in this work. While, no doubt, even within the limits set, many other rites could have been included in this selection, boundaries must be fixed somewhere, and this decision inevitably depends upon the editor. The following factors have helped to determine these boundaries. The work continues where Canon Fisher's book leaves off, i.e.: 1552, and follows the same pattern of historical development. All the texts reproduced are printed and used in the English language. But for a few exceptions all the rites of baptism are those used for the baptism of infants. In the case of complete rites of initiation only some of the rites available have been included. Available evidence, from various parts of the world, indicates that the general practice regarding Christian initiation is still the baptism of infants followed by confirmation at the "age of discretion". The contents of Part 2 reflect the editor's Anglican position, and, if carefully studied, give a detailed account of the revision of the initiatory rites as it has been carried out in the Anglican Communion in different parts of the world.

The first two rites in Part 3 are included because of their historic value, the remaining rites of this section give a fairly full picture of the theological and liturgical position, in the field of Christian initiation, in a number of major Christian communions which exist in the British Isles. The Appendix contains a small number of interesting rites from overseas. The Iglesia Filipina Independiente Rites are conservative revisions but of interest because of their origin and the historic background of that Church. While infant baptism–confirmation is not practised in the Western Church the proposals from East Africa offer interesting possibilities for the future.

Where a Church has an authorized rite, or rites, in general use, and other experimental rites which have been issued for permissive use, both are reproduced, thus giving some indication of changes in position and emphasis, and also some idea of the line of future liturgical revision.

Because of their theological and liturgical importance introductory rubrics are given in full. Inevitably their inclusion increases both the size and the cost of the book, but they are essential if the texts they introduce are to be of any real or lasting value.

Introductory comments which prefix each rite have been kept to a minimum. These comments give details of the date of the revision and the authority for its use; the date and source of the text here reproduced; and, where it is thought necessary, brief notes on the history of the rite.

While the main purpose behind this work is to provide liturgical scholars and students with a comprehensive collection of initiatory rites, it is also hoped that the work may be of some ecumenical value. Since the birth of the Liturgical Movement there has been a growing interest in liturgical study, which has drawn together liturgical scholars and students of many denominations. In every Church there are those who are seeking to compose the ideal liturgical expression of the various rites used in their Church. As yet there is no common agreement as to the number of the sacraments, or their underlying theology, but Baptism and the Eucharist do find a place in the life of all orthodox branches of the Church. And, in spite of all the theological differences which divide Christendom, the dominical sacrament of Baptism is the basis of communion among all Christians as a sacramental bond of unity. This belief finds support in all branches of the divided Church. Cardinal Bea, the late President of the Secretariat for Promoting Christian Unity, always emphasized that the unity of Christian baptism binds all Christians together, in spite of their divisions, and provides a secure basis for real brotherhood in Christ. It is now generally agreed that wherever and by whomsoever baptism is duly administered, the recipient is received into the one, holy, Catholic, Apostolic Church. The ideal of a common rite of Christian initiation, baptism–confirmation, is no longer an ideal confined to the minds and files of a few liturgical scholars; it is a possibility for the foreseeable future, and the desire of many at local level.

It is my hope and prayer that the study of the texts contained in these pages may assist this pursuit and thus hasten the drawing together of the many members of the One Body.

The Feast of Saint Andrew, 1969   PETER J. JAGGER

Part 1
COMMON FORMS

Twenty Common Forms

To avoid repetition in the various texts which follow, reference will be made to the following "Common Forms" printed below; with the exception of the texts given in Part 2, chapters 1 and 2, where the texts are given in full. Common Forms numbers 1–10 are from "The Ministration of Publick Baptism of Infants to be used in the Church"; numbers 13–19 are from "The Order of Confirmation"—the texts contained in the Book Annexed to the Act of Uniformity of 1662. The Common Form 11 is the Lord's Prayer with concluding doxology; number 12 is the standard text of the Apostles Creed; number 20 is from "An Alternative Order of Confirmation", 1928.

In the liturgies which follow reference to these Common Forms will be given thus (CF6). Variations within the text are noted; but alterations in style, for example, the use of capital letters, and punctuation, are not recorded. Where a Common Form is used, but with several variations, the full text is then given. It should be noted that variations in the use of capital letters, and punctuation, are also to be found in different editions of the 1662 Book of Common Prayer.

1 Dearly beloved, forasmuch as all men are conceived and born in sin; and that our Saviour Christ saith, None can enter into the Kingdom of God, except he be regenerate and born anew of Water and of the Holy Ghost; I beseech you to call upon God the Father, through our Lord Jesus Christ, that of his bounteous mercy he will grant to *this Child* that thing which by nature *he* cannot have; that *he* may be baptized with Water and the Holy Ghost, and received into Christ's holy Church, and be made *a lively member* of the same.

2 Almighty and immortal God, the aid of all that need, the helper of all that flee to thee for succour, the life of them that believe, and the resurrection of the dead; We call upon thee for *this Infant*, that *he*, coming to thy holy Baptism, may receive remission of *his* sins by spiritual regeneration. Receive *him*, O Lord, as thou hast promised by thy well-beloved Son, saying, Ask, and ye shall have; seek and ye shall find; knock, and it shall be opened unto you: So give now unto us that ask; let us that seek find; open the gate unto us that knock; that *this Infant* may enjoy the everlasting benediction of thy heavenly washing, and may come to the eternal kingdom which thou hast promised by Christ our Lord. *Amen.*

3 They brought young children to Christ, that he should touch them; and his disciples rebuked those that brought them. But when Jesus saw it,

he was much displeased, and said unto them, Suffer the little children to come unto me, and forbid them not; for of such is the kingdom of God. Verily I say unto you, Whosoever shall not receive the kingdom of God as a little child, he shall not enter therein. And he took them up in his arms, put his hands upon them, and blessed them.

4   Almighty and everlasting God, heavenly Father, we give thee humble thanks, for that thou hast vouchsafed to call us to the knowledge of thy grace and faith in thee: Increase this knowledge, and confirm this faith in us evermore. Give thy Holy Spirit to *this Infant*, that *he* may be born again, and be made *an heir* of everlasting salvation; through our Lord Jesus Christ, who liveth and reigneth with thee and the Holy Spirit, now and for ever. *Amen.*

5a   O merciful God, grant that the old Adam in *this child* may be so buried, that the new man may be raised up in *him. Amen.*

5b   Grant that all carnal affections may die in *him*, and that all things belonging to the Spirit may live and grow in *him. Amen.*

5c   Grant that *he* may have power and strength to have victory, and to triumph against the devil, the world, and the flesh. *Amen.*

5d   Grant that whosoever is here dedicated to thee by our office and ministry may also be endued with heavenly virtues, and everlastingly rewarded, through thy mercy, O blessed Lord God, who dost live, and govern all things, world without end. *Amen.*

6   Almighty, everliving God, whose most dearly beloved Son Jesus Christ, for the forgiveness of our sins, did shed out of his most precious side both water and blood; and gave commandment to his disciples, that they should go teach all nations, and baptize them in the Name of the Father, and of the Son, and of the Holy Ghost; Regard, we beseech thee, the supplications of thy Congregation; sanctify this Water to the mystical washing away of sin; and grant that *this Child*, now to be baptized therein, may receive the fulness of thy grace, and ever remain in the number of thy faithful and elect children; through Jesus Christ our Lord. *Amen.*

7   We receive this Child into the Congregation of Christ's flock (*here the Priest shall make a Cross upon the Child's forehead*), and do sign *him* with the sign of the Cross in token that hereafter *he* shall not be ashamed to confess the faith of Christ crucified, and manfully to fight under his banner, against sin, the world, and the devil; and to continue Christ's faithful soldier and servant unto *his* life's end. Amen.

8 Seeing now, dearly beloved brethren, that *this Child is* regenerate, and grafted into the body of Christ's Church, let us give thanks unto Almighty God for these benefits; and with one accord make our prayers unto him, that *this Child* may lead the rest of *his* life according to this beginning.

9 Our Father, which art in heaven, Hallowed be thy Name. Thy kingdom come, Thy will be done, in earth as it is in heaven. Give us this day our daily bread; And forgive us our trespasses, As we forgive them that trespass against us; And lead us not into temptation, But deliver us from evil. Amen.

10 We yield thee hearty thanks, most merciful Father, that it hath pleased thee to regenerate *this Infant* with thy Holy Spirit, to receive *him* for thine own *Child* by adoption, and to incorporate *him* into thy holy Church. And humbly we beseech thee to grant, that *he*, being dead unto sin, and living unto righteousness, and being buried with Christ in his death, may crucify the old man, and utterly abolish the whole body of sin; and that, as *he is* made *partaker* of the death of thy Son, *he* may also be *partaker* of his resurrection; so that finally, with the residue of thy holy Church, *he* may be *an inheritor* of thine everlasting kingdom, through Christ our Lord. Amen.

11 Our Father, which art in heaven, Hallowed be thy Name, Thy kingdom come, Thy will be done, in earth as it is in heaven. Give us this day our daily bread; And forgive us our trespasses, As we forgive them that trespass against us; And lead us not into temptation, But deliver us from evil. For thine is the kingdom, the power, and the glory, For ever and ever. Amen.

12 I believe in God the Father Almighty, Maker of heaven and earth:
 And in Jesus Christ his only Son our Lord, Who was conceived by the Holy Ghost, Born of the Virgin Mary, Suffered under Pontius Pilate, Was crucified, dead, and buried: He descended into hell; The third day he rose again from the dead; He ascended into heaven, And sitteth on the right hand of God the Father Almighty; From thence he shall come to judge the quick and the dead.
 I believe in the Holy Ghost; The holy Catholic Church; The Communion of Saints; The Forgiveness of sins; The Resurrection of the body; And the life everlasting. Amen.

13 Do ye here, in the presence of God, and of this Congregation, renew the solemn promise and vow that was made in your name at your Baptism; ratifying and confirming the same in your own persons, and acknowledging yourselves bound to believe and to do all those things, which your Godfathers and Godmothers then undertook for you?

14 The Bishop.

Our help is in the Name of the Lord;
Answer. Who hath made heaven and earth.
Bishop. Blessed be the Name of the Lord;
Answer. Henceforth world without end.
Bishop. Lord, hear our prayers;
Answer. And let our cry come unto thee.

15 Bishop.

Let us pray.

Almighty and everliving God, who hast vouchsafed to regenerate these thy servants by Water and the Holy Ghost, and hast given unto them forgiveness of all their sins: Strengthen them, we beseech thee, O Lord, with the Holy Ghost the Comforter, and daily increase in them thy manifold gifts of grace; the spirit of wisdom and understanding; the spirit of counsel and ghostly strength; the spirit of knowledge and true godliness; and fill them, O Lord, with the spirit of thy holy fear, now and for ever. Amen.

16 Defend, O Lord, this thy Child (or *this thy Servant*) with thy heavenly grace, that *he* may continue thine for ever; and daily increase in thy Holy Spirit, more and more, until *he* come unto thy everlasting kingdom. Amen.

17 Almighty and everliving God, who makest us both to will and to do those things that be good and acceptable unto thy divine Majesty; We make our humble supplications unto thee for these thy servants, upon whom (after the example of thy holy Apostles) we have now laid our hands, to certify them (by this sign) of thy favour and gracious goodness towards them. Let thy fatherly hand, we beseech thee, ever be over them; let thy Holy Spirit ever be with them; and so lead them in the knowledge and obedience of thy Word, that in the end they may obtain everlasting life; through our Lord Jesus Christ, who with thee and the Holy Ghost liveth and reigneth, ever one God, world without end. *Amen.*

18 O almighty Lord, and everlasting God, vouchsafe, we beseech thee, to direct, sanctify, and govern both our hearts and bodies, in the ways of thy laws, and in the works of thy commandments; that through thy most mighty protection, both here and ever, we may be preserved in body and soul; through our Lord and Saviour Jesus Christ. *Amen.*

19 The Blessing of God Almighty, the Father, the Son, and the Holy Ghost, be upon you, and remain with you, for ever. *Amen.*

20 Dearly beloved in the Lord, in ministering Confirmation the Church doth follow the example of the Apostles of Christ. For in the eighth chapter of the Acts of the Apostles we thus read:

They therefore that were scattered abroad went about preaching the word. And Philip went down to the city of Samaria, and proclaimed unto them the Christ. When they believed Philip preaching good tidings concerning the kingdom of God and the name of Jesus Christ, they were baptized, both men and women. Now when the apostles which were at Jerusalem heard that Samaria had received the word of God, they sent unto them Peter and John: who, when they were come down, prayed for them, that they might receive the Holy Ghost: for as yet he was fallen upon none of them: only they had been baptized into the name of the Lord Jesus. Then laid they their hands on them, and they received the Holy Ghost.

The Scripture here teacheth us that a special gift of the Holy Spirit is bestowed through laying on of hands with prayer. And forasmuch as this gift cometh from God alone, let us who are here present pray to Almighty God, that he will strengthen with his Holy Spirit in Confirmation those who in Baptism were made his children.

You, then, who are to be confirmed must now declare before this congregation that you are stedfastly purposed, with the help of this gift, to lead your life in the faith of Christ and in obedience to God's will and commandments; and must openly acknowledge yourselves bound to fulfil the Christian duties to which your Baptism hath pledged you.

Part 2
THE
REVISIONS
OF THE
ANGLICAN
COMMUNION

1. The Church of England Rites 1552
with notes on the revisions of 1559, 1604 and the Scottish Liturgy of 1637

THE RITES OF 1552

These texts are from *The Boke of Common Prayer, and Administracion of the Sacramentes, and other rites and Ceremonies in the Churche of Englande.* The Book, commonly called *The Second Prayer-Book of Edward VI*, was a revision of the 1549 BCP, and was authorized for use from All Saints' Day 1552, as a result of the Act of Uniformity passed over the period 9 March to 14 April 1552.

The rites which follow reproduce those of the Whitchurch edition, as found in the Parker Society volume, *The Two Liturgies, A.D. 1549 and A.D. 1552, with other Documents set forth by authority in the Reign of King Edward VI* (Cambridge University Press 1844).

THE RITES OF 1559

Revision on the 1552 BCP began soon after Elizabeth's accession to the throne in 1558. The modified Book was presented to Parliament; and a new Act of Uniformity passed on 28 April 1559 enacted that it should be used from and after the Feast of the Nativity of St John Baptist.

THE RITES OF 1604

The next revision of the Prayer Book was occasioned by the Millenary Petition of the Puritans to King James I. At the Hampton Court Conference in January 1604 a number of issues were discussed and certain changes promised. The alterations agreed to by the King and the Bishops were authorized when, on 9 February 1604, the King issued Letters Patent to the members of the Ecclesiastical Commission in accordance with the provision at the end of the Uniformity Act of 1559. The Letters specified the alterations to be carried out and ordered the publication and exclusive use of the amended Book.

THE RITES OF 1637
The Scottish Liturgy

Work on a revised Prayer Book for the Church of Scotland began in 1616 when King James procured an Act to be passed at Aberdeen for the preparation of a Service Book for the Scottish Church. The revised Book had many set-backs, and experienced a difficult and stormy passage. After an interval of twenty years the new Book of Common Prayer for the use of the Church of Scotland was ratified by Royal Proclamation in December 1636. The Book was first used on 23 July 1637, and was the cause of a riot in the Cathedral Church of St Giles, Edinburgh.

While this Book has been commonly known as *Laud's Liturgy*, this title is a misnomer. If Archbishop Laud had had his way, the Church of Scotland would have had to accept the English Book of Common Prayer without any variations. However, in spite of Laud's attitude, the Scottish bishops prevailed upon the King, who agreed that revision could take place. Once the work was undertaken, Laud did have some limited influence upon the proceedings, but only by way of preliminary suggestions and revision in the final stages. Laud said, "The Scottish bishops were commanded by his Majesty to let me see from time to time what they did in the Service Book." The revisions suggested by the Scottish bishops were carefully considered by Laud, who while rejecting some of their proposals approved of the final result.

Footnotes:

Reference to the variations in the different editions are noted as follows.

Grafton 1   refers to the variations in Richard Grafton's first edition of the 1552 BCP, as given in the Parker Society volume.

Grafton 2   refers to the variations in Richard Grafton's second edition of the 1552 BCP as given in the Parker Society volume.

1559   refers to the variations in Richard Grafton's edition of *The Boke of Common Praier, and Administration of the Sacramentes, and Other Rites and Ceremonies in the Church of England* (1559); the texts printed in *The Ancient and Modern Library*.

Keeling 59 refers to the variations in other editions of the 1559 BCP, noted by William Keeling in *Liturgiae Britannicae* (1851).

1604   refers to the variations found in the revisions authorized by King James I in 1604, and noted by William Keeling in *Liturgiae Britannicae*, and *The First Prayer Book of Edward VI compared with The Successive Revisions* (1877).

1637   refers to the variations in *The Booke of Common Prayer and Administration of the Sacraments, and other parts of divine Service for the use of the Church of Scotland*. Printed by Robert Young (Edinburgh 1637), and reproduced in *Book of Common Prayer*, Scottish Liturgy 1637, edited by James Cooper (1904).

Variations in punctuation, use of capital letters and lower case are not noted.

I   THE MINISTRATION OF BAPTISM
TO BE USED IN THE CHURCH

2   It appeareth by ancient writers, that the Sacrament of Baptism in the old time was not commonly ministered, but at two times in the year: at Easter, and Whitsuntide. At which times [1] it was openly ministered, in the presence of all the congregation. Which custom (now being grown out of use) [2] although it cannot for many considerations be well restored again,[3] yet [4] it is thought good to follow the same

[1] time it, Keeling 59.   [2] brackets omitted, 1604 and 1637.
[3] although it can . . . restored again, bracketed, 1604 and 1637.
[4] yet, omitted, 1604 and 1637.

as near as conveniently may be: wherefore the people are to be admonished, that it is most convenient that Baptism should not be ministered but upon Sundays, and other holy days, when the most number of people may come together, as well as for that the congregation there present may testify the receiving of them that be newly baptized into the number of Christ's Church, as also because in the Baptism of infants every man present may be put in rememberance of his own profession made to God in his Baptism. For which cause also, it is expedient that Baptism be ministered in the English tongue. Nevertheless (if necessity so require) children may at all times be baptized at home.

3 PUBLIC BAPTISM[1]

4 When there are children to be baptized upon the Sunday, or holy-day, the Parents shall give knowledge over-night, or in the morning, afore the beginning of Morning prayer to the Curate.[2] And then the Godfathers, Godmothers, and people, with the children, must be ready at the Font, either immediately after the last lesson at Morning prayer, or else immediately after the last lesson at Evening prayer, as the Curate[2] by his discretion shall appoint, And then standing there, the Priest[3] shall ask whether the children be baptized or no. If they answer, no: then shall the Priest[4] say thus.

Dearly beloved, forasmuch as all men be conceived and born in sin, and that our Saviour Christ saith, none can enter into the kingdom of God, except he be regenerate, and born anew of water, and[5] the Holy Ghost: I beseech you to call upon God the Father, through our Lord Jesus Christ, that of his bounteous mercy, he will grant to these children that thing which by nature they cannot have, that they may be baptized with water and the Holy Ghost, and received into Christ's holy church, and made lively members of the same.

5 Then the Priest shall say.[6,7]

Let us pray.

Almighty and everlasting God, which of thy great mercy didst save Noe[8] and his family in the Ark, from perishing by water: and also didst safely lead the children of Israel, thy people, through the Red Sea, figuring thereby thy holy Baptism; and by the Baptism of thy well-

---

[1] PUBLIC BAPTISM, omitted in 1559, 1604, and 1637. It was retained in only one edition of 1559.

[2] Presbyter or Curate, 1637.

[3] the Presbyter, 1637. Priest: Fredric Bully, in his book A Tabular View of the variations in the Communion and Baptismal Offices of the Church of England, . . . (1842), notes that two copies of the 1559 BCP and an edition dated 1606 read here and passim, Minister for Priest.
T. M. Fallow, in his book The Order of Baptism . . . (1838), notes several places where the word Minister is substituted for the word Priest; he does not, however, note the edition in which these alterations are found. Fallow also notes that in the revision in the reign of Charles I, the word Priest was substituted for Minister throughout the service.

[4] Presbyter, 1637.   [5] and of, 1604 and 1637.

[6] Then shall the Priest say, 1604.

[7] Then shall the Presbyter say, 1637. Throughout 1637 for Priest read Presbyter.

[8] Noah, 1604 and 1637.

beloved Son Jesus Christ, didst sanctify the flood Jordan, and all other waters, to the mystical washing away of sin.[1] We beseech thee for thy[2] infinite mercies, that thou wilt mercifully look upon these children, sanctify them and wash them with thy[3] Holy Ghost, that they being delivered from thy wrath, may be received into the Ark of Christ's Church, and being stedfast in faith, joyful through hope, and rooted in charity, may so pass the waves of this troublesome world, that finally they may come to the land of everlasting life, there to reign with thee, world without end: through Jesus Christ our Lord. Amen.

Almighty and immortal God, the aid of all that need, the helper of all that flee[4] to thee for succour, the life of them that believe, and the resurrection of the dead, We call upon thee for these infants, that they coming to thy holy Baptism, may receive remission of their sins by spiritual regeneration. Receive them, O Lord, as thou hast promised by thy wellbeloved Son, saying: Ask and you shall have, seek and you shall find, knock and it shall be opened unto you, So give now unto us that ask. Let us that seek find. Open the[5] gate unto us that knock, that these infants may enjoy the everlasting benediction of thy heavenly washing, and may come to the eternal kingdom, which thou hast promised by Christ our Lord. Amen.

6   Then shall the Priest say: Hear the words of the Gospel, written by Saint Mark in the tenth Chapter.[6]

At a certain time they brought[7] children to Christ that he should touch them, and his disciples rebuked those that brought them. But when Jesus saw it, he was[8] displeased, and said unto them. Suffer little children to come unto me, and forbid them not; for to such belongeth the kingdom of God.[9] Verily I say unto you: whosoever doth[10] not receive the kingdom of God as a little child, he shall not enter therein. And when he had taken them up in his arms, he put his hands upon them,[11] and blessed them. *Mark. x.*[12]

---

[1] sin: (Sanctify this fountain of baptism, thou which art the Sanctifier of all things.*) rubric added* *The water in the font shall be changed twice in the month at least: and before any child be baptized in the water so changed, the Presbyter or Minister shall say at the font the words thus inclosed ( ). continue, things*.) And further we beseech thee for . . .).
[2] thine, 1559, 1604, and 1637.   [3] the Holy Ghost, 1604 and 1637.
[4] fly, 1559.   [5] open thy, Grafton 2 and 1559.
[6] *by S. Mark in the tenth Chapter*, 1604 and 1637. 1637 adds (ver 13).
[7] young children, 1637.   [8] much displeased, 1637.
[9] for of such is the kingdom of God, 1637.   [10] shall not, 1637.
[11] And he took them up in his arms, put his hands upon them and blessed them, 1637.
[12] *Mark. x.* not in, 1559, 1604, and 1637.

7   After the Gospel is read, the Minister[1] shall make this brief exhortation upon the words of the Gospel.

Friends, you[2] hear in this Gospel the words of our Saviour Christ, that he commanded the children to be brought unto him: how he blamed those that would have kept them from him; how he exhorteth[3] all men to follow their innocency. You[4] perceive how by his outward gesture and deed he declared[5] his good will toward them. For he embraced them in his arms, he laid his hands upon them, and blessed them. Doubt not ye[6] therefore, but earnestly believe[7] that he will likewise favourably receive these present infants, that he will embrace them with the arms of his mercy, that he will give unto them the blessing of eternal life, and make them partakers of this everlasting kingdom. Wherefore we being thus persuaded of the good will of our heavenly Father, toward[8] these infants declared by his Son Jesus Christ, and nothing doubting but that he favourably alloweth this charitable work of ours, in bringing these children[9] to his holy Baptism: Let us faithfully and devoutly give thanks unto him, and say.

Almighty and everlasting God, heavenly Father, we give thee humble thanks, that thou hast vouchsafed to call us to the knowledge of thy grace and faith in thee: increase this knowledge, and confirm this faith in us evermore. Give thy holy Spirit to these infants, that they may be born again, and be made heirs of everlasting salvation, through our Lord Jesus Christ: who liveth and reigneth with thee and the Holy Spirit, now and for ever. Amen.

8   Then the Priest shall speak unto the Godfathers and Godmothers on this wise.

Wellbeloved friends, ye have brought these children here to be baptized; ye have prayed that our Lord Jesus Christ would vouchsafe to receive them, to lay his hands upon them, to bless them, to release them of their sins, to give them the kingdom of heaven, and everlasting life, Ye have heard also that our Lord Jesus Christ hath promised in his Gospel to grant all these things that ye have prayed for: which promise he for his part will most surely keep and perform. Wherefore after this promise made by Christ, these infants must also faithfully for their part promise by you that be their sureties, that they will forsake the devil and all his

---

[1] *Presbyter or Minister*, 1637.   [2] ye hear, Grafton 2 and 1559.
[3] exhorted, Grafton 2, 1559, and 1637.   [4] Ye, 1559.   [5] declare, 1604.
[6] not you, Grafton 2 and 1559; ye not, 1604 and 1637.
[7] stedfastly believe, 1637.   [8] towards, Grafton 2, 1559, and 1637.
[9] the children, 1604.

works, and constantly believe God's holy word, and obediently keep his commandments.

9　Then shall the Priest demand of the Godfathers and Godmothers these questions following.[1]

Dost thou forsake the devil and all his works, the vain pomp and glory of the world, with all[2] covetous desires of the same, the[3] carnal desires of the flesh, so that thou wilt not follow, nor be led by them? *Answer.* I forsake them all.

Minister.[4] Dost thou believe in God the Father almighty, maker of heaven and earth? and in Jesus Christ his only-begotten Son our Lord,[5] and that he was conceived by the Holy Ghost, born of the virgin Mary, that he suffered under Poncius[6] Pilate, was crucified, dead, and buried, that he went down into hell, and also did rise again the third day, that he ascended into heaven, and sitteth at the right hand of God the Father almighty, and from thence[7] shall come again at the end of the world, to judge the quick and the dead?

And dost thou believe in the Holy Ghost, the holy Catholic Church, the Communion of Saints, the remission of sins, the resurrection of the flesh, and everlasting life after death? *Answer.* All this I steadfastly believe.

Minister.[8] Wilt thou be baptized in this faith? *Answer.* That is my desire.

10　Then shall the Priest say

O merciful God, grant that the old Adam in these children may be so buried, that the new man may be raised up in them. Amen.

Grant that all carnal affections may die in them, and that all things belonging to the Spirit may live and grow in them. Amen.

Grant that they may have power and strength to have victory and to triumph against the devil, the world and the flesh. Amen.

Grant that whosoever is here dedicated to thee by our office and ministry, may also be endued with heavenly virtues, and everlastingly rewarded through thy mercy, O blessed Lord God, who dost live and govern all things world without end. Amen.

Almighty everliving God, whose most dearly beloved Son Jesus Christ, for the forgiveness of our sins, did shed out of[9] his most precious side

---

[1] following, omitted Grafton 2 and 1559.
[2] all the covetous, Grafton 2 and Keeling 59.
[3] and the carnal, Grafton 2 and 1559.　　[4] *The Minister,* 1559. *Presbyter,* 1637.
[5] our Lord? And . . . , 1604 and 1637.　　[6] Pontius Pilate, 1604 and 1637.
[7] he shall, 1637.　　[8] *Presbyter,* 1637.　　[9] of, omitted, 1559.

both water and blood, and gave commandment to his disciples that they should go teach all nations, and baptize them in the name of the Father, the Son, and of the Holy Ghost: Regard, we beseech thee, the supplications of thy congregation,[1] and grant that all thy servants which shall be baptized in this water[2] may receive the fulness of thy grace, and ever remain in the number of thy faithful and elect children, through Jesus Christ our Lord. Amen.[3]

11 Then the Priest shall take the child in his hands, and ask the name; and naming the child, shall dip it in the water, so it be discreetly and warily done, saying.

N. I baptize thee in the name of the Father, and of the Son, and of the Holy Ghost. Amen.

12 And if the child be weak it shall suffice to pour water upon it, saying the foresaid words.

N. I baptize thee in the name of the Father, and of the Son, and of the Holy Ghost. Amen.

13 Then the Priest shall make a cross upon the child's forehead saying.

We receive this child into the congregation of Christ's flock[4] and do sign him with the sign of the cross, in token that hereafter he shall not be ashamed to confess the faith of Christ crucified, and manfully[5] to fight under his banner against sin, the world, and the devil, and to continue Christ's faithful soldier and servant unto his life's end. Amen.

14 Then shall the Priest say.

Seeing now, dearly beloved brethren, that these children be regenerate and grafted[6] into the body of Christ's congregation:[7] let us give thanks unto God for these benefits, and with one accord make our prayers unto almighty God, that they may lead the rest of their life according to this beginning.

15 Then shall be said.

Our Father which[8] art in heaven, etc.

---

[1] thy Church, 1637.
[2] water (which we here bless and dedicate in thy Name to this spiritual washing) may receive . . . , 1637.
[3] *The First Prayer-Book of Edward VI Compared with The Successive Revisions*, notes that in two editions of 1559, Amen, was omitted.
[4] into the Church of Christ and do . . ., 1637.
[5] and stoutly to resist sin, the world, and the devil, 1637.
[6] graffed, 1559.
[7] body of Christ's Church, 1637.
[8] Our Father which, etc., Grafton 2; Our Father which art, etc., 1559.

16   Then shall the Priest say.

We yield thee hearty thanks, most merciful Father, that it hath pleased thee to regenerate this infant with thy Holy Spirit, to receive him for thy[1] own child by adoption, and to incorporate him into thy holy congregation.[2] And humbly we beseech thee to grant that he, being dead unto sin, and living unto righteousness, and being buried with Christ in his death, may crucify the old man, and utterly abolish the whole body of sin: that as he is made partaker of the death of thy Son, so he may be partaker of his resurrection: so that finally, with the residue of thy holy congregation,[2] he may be inheritor of thine everlasting kingdom: through Christ our Lord. Amen.

17   At the last end, the Priest calling the Godfathers and Godmothers together, shall say this short[3] exhortation following.

Forasmuch as these children have promised by you to forsake the Devil and all his works, to believe in God and to serve him, you must remember that it is your parts and duties to see that these infants be taught so soon as they shall be able to learn what a solemn vow, promise, and profession, they have made by you. And that they may know these things the better ye shall call upon them to hear sermons. And chiefly ye[4] shall provide that they may learn the Creed, the Lord's prayer, and the ten Commandments in the English tongue, and all other things which a Christian man ought to know and believe, to his soul's health: and that these children may be virtuously brought up, to lead a godly and a Christian life: remembering alway[5] that Baptism doth represent unto us our profession, which is to follow the example of our Saviour Christ, and to be made like unto him: that as he died and rose again for us, so should we which are baptized, die from sin, and rise again unto righteousness, continually mortifying all our evil and corrupt affections, and daily proceeding in all virtue, and godliness of living.

18   The Minister[6] shall command that the children be brought to the Bishop to be confirmed of him, so soon as they can say in their vulgar tongue the articles of the faith, the Lord's prayer, and the X[7] Commandments, and be further instructed in the Catechism[8] set forth for that purpose, accordingly[9] as it is there expressed.

---

[1] thine, Grafton 2, 1559, 1604, and 1637.   [2] holy Church, 1637.
[3] short, omitted, 1604 and 1637.   [4] you, 1559, 1604, and 1637.
[5] always, Grafton 2, 1559, 1604 and 1637.   [6] Presbyter or Minister, 1637.
[7] ten Commandments, 1604, and 1637.
[8] which is set forth in this book for that purpose, 1637.   [9] according, 1604 and 1637.

1 CONFIRMATION[1]
2 WHEREIN IS CONTAINED A
CATECHISM FOR CHILDREN[2]

3 To the end that Confirmation may be ministered to the more edifying of such as shall receive it (according unto[3] Saint Paul's doctrine, who teacheth that all things should be done in the Church to the edification of the same) it is thought good that none hereafter shall be confirmed, but such as can say in their mother tongue the articles of the faith, the Lord's prayer, and the X[4] commandments: and can also answer to such questions of this short Catechism, as the Bishop (or such as he shall appoint) shall by his discretion appose them[5] in. And this order is most convenient to be observed for divers considerations.

4 First, because that when children come to the years of discretion, and have learned what their Godfathers and Godmothers promised for them in baptism, they may then themselves with their own mouth, and with their own consent, openly before the Church, ratify and confirm the same: and also promise that, by the grace of God, they will[6] evermore endeavour themselves faithfully to observe and keep such things, as they by their own mouth and confession have assented unto.

5 Secondly, forasmuch as Confirmation is ministered to them that be baptized, that by imposition of hands and prayer they may receive strength and defence against all temptations to sin, and the assults of the world, and the Devil: it is most meet to be ministered when children come to that age, that partly by the frailty of their own flesh, partly by the assults of the world and the Devil, they begin to be in danger to fall into sundry kinds of sin.

6 Thirdly, for that it is agreeable with the usage of the Church in times past, whereby it was ordained that Confirmation should be ministered to them that were of perfect age, that they, being instructed in Christ's religion, should openly profess their own faith, and promise to be obedient unto the will of God.

7 And that no man shall think that any detriment shall come to children by deferring of their Confirmation, he shall know for truth, that it is certain by God's word, that children being baptized have all things necessary for their salvation, and be undoubtedly saved.

In all the texts there now follows: A CATECHISM THAT IS TO SAY, AN INSTRUCTION TO BE LEARNED OF EVERY CHILD, BEFORE HE BE BROUGHT TO BE CONFIRMED OF THE BISHOP.
1637 adds: by the Bishop, and to be used throughout the whole Church of Scotland.

8 So soon as the children can say in their mother tongue, the articles of the faith, the Lord's prayer, the X[7] Commandments: and also can answer to such questions[8] of this short Catechism, as the Bishop (or such as he shall appoint) shall by his discretion appose them in: then shall they be brought to the Bishop by one that shall be his Godfather, or Godmother, that every child may have a witness of his Confirmation.

9 And the Bishop shall confirm them on this wise.[9]

[1] THE ORDER OF CONFIRMATION, 1604 AND 1637.
[2] omitted in 1604 and 1637 and the following included: Or Laying on of Hands upon Children Baptized, and able to render an account of their Faith, according to the Catechism following.
[3] according to, Grafton 1, 1604, and 1637.
[4] Ten Commandments, 1604 and 1637.   [5] appose him in, 1604.
[6] they shall, 1559.   [7] Ten Commandments, 1604 and 1637.
[8] question, Grafton 2 and 1559.
[9] This rubric is included at the end of 8 in 1637.

CONFIRMATION[1,2]

11 Our help is in the name of the Lord.
Answer. Which hath made both[3] heaven and earth.
Minister.[4] Blessed is[5] the name of the Lord
Answer. Henceforth world without end.
Minister.[4] Lord, hear our prayer.[6]
Answer. And let our cry come to[7] thee.

12   Let us pray.

Almighty and everliving God, who[8] hast vouchsafed[9] to regenerate these thy servants by water and the Holy Ghost, and hast given unto them forgiveness of all their sins: strengthen them, we beseech thee, O Lord,[10] with the Holy Ghost the Comforter, and daily increase in them thy manifold gifts of grace: the spirit of wisdom and understanding, the spirit of counsel and ghostly strength, the spirit of knowledge and true godliness: and fulfil them, O Lord,[10] with the spirit of thy holy fear. Amen.

13 Then the Bishop shall lay his hand upon every child severally, saying.

Defend, O Lord, this child with thy heavenly grace, that he may continue thine for ever, and daily increase in thy Holy Spirit more and more, until he come unto thy everlasting kingdom. Amen.

14 Then shall the Bishop say,[11]

Almighty[12] everliving God, which makest us both to will, and to do those things that be good and acceptable unto thy Majesty: we make our humble supplications unto thee for these children, upon whom (after the example of thy holy Apostles) we have laid our hands, to certify them (by this sign) of thy favour, and gracious goodness towards them: let thy fatherly hand, we beseech thee, ever be over them: let thy Holy Spirit ever be with them; and so lead them in the knowledge and obedience of thy word, that in the end they may obtain the everlasting life, through our Lord Jesus Christ: who with thee and the Holy Ghost liveth and reigneth one God, world without end. Amen.

[1] CONFIRMATION, OR LAYING ON OF HANDS, 1604 AND 1637.
[2] This rubric follows in 1637: *The Bishop shall say,*
[3] both, omitted, 1604 and 1637.   [4] *Bishop,* 1637.
[5] Blessed be, 1604 and 1637.   [6] prayers, 1604 and 1637.
[7] unto, 1604 and 1637.   [8] which, Grafton 2 and 1559.
[9] hast vouchedsafe, Grafton 2 and 1559.   [10] (O Lord), 1559.
[11] *Bishop say.* Let us pray, Grafton 1 and 2, 1559, 1604, and 1637.
[12] and everliving, 1604 and 1637.

15 Then the Bishop shall bless the children, thus saying,[1]

The blessing of God Almighty, the Father, the Son, and the Holy
Ghost, be upon you, and remain with you for ever. Amen.

16 The Curate[2] of every Parish, or some other at his appointment, shall diligently
upon Sundays, and holy days half an hour before Evensong,[3] openly in the Church
instruct and examine so many children of his parish sent unto him, as the time will
serve, and as he shall think convenient, in some part of this Catechism.

17 And all Fathers, Mothers, Masters, and Dames,[4] shall cause their children,
servants, and prentices (which have not learned their Catechism) to come to the
church at the time appointed, and obediently to hear, and be ordered by the
Curate,[2] until such time as they have learned all that is here appointed for them
to learn. And whensoever the Bishop shall give knowledge for children to be
brought afore[5] him to any convenient place, for their Confirmation: Then shall
the Curate[2] of every parish either bring or send in writing the names of all those
children of his parish, which can say the Articles of their faith,[6] the Lord's prayer,
and the X[7] Commandments: and also how many of them can answer to the other
questions contained in this Catechism.

18 And there shall none be admitted to the holy Communion, until such time as he
can say the Catechism, and be confirmed.

[1] *saying thus*, 1604 and 1637.   [2] *Presbyter or Curate*, 1637.
[3] *Evening Prayer*, Grafton 2 and 1559.   [4] *Masters, and Mistresses*, 1637.
[5] *before him*, 1604 and 1637.   [6] *of the Faith*, 1604 and 1637.
[7] *Ten Commandments*, 1604 and 1637.

2. The Church of England Rites 1662
with notes on the alterations proposed in 1689

These texts are from THE BOOK OF COMMON PRAYER and *Administration of the Sacraments and Other Rites and Ceremonies of the Church according to the use of the Church of England*; the Book which was annexed to the Act of Uniformity of 1662.

The importance of these two rites is twofold. First, they are a link with the past, with the Anglican revisions of 1552 and 1549 and through these with the principal sources of Sarum and Hermann. Secondly, they have undoubtedly influenced the revisions and new rites of the twentieth century.

THE ALTERATIONS PROPOSED IN 1689

One of the avowed aims of William III, on his accession to the English throne, was to draw together the "Church of England and all Protestant Dissenters". His attempt to bring about such a reconciliation was the main purpose behind the issue of the "Royal Commission" to the Archbishop of York and others, on 17 September 1689. The Commission called together ten bishops and twenty divines, who were to consider the revision of the Prayer Book with a view to making it more acceptable to the Dissenters. After a period of six weeks, during which period the Committee had eighteen sessions and six sub-committees, their work was completed. Their suggested alterations amounted to 598. While their work, which was never made public, was doomed to failure, their proposed alterations are of some importance in the history of the Book of Common Prayer. In the text which follows the alterations proposed in 1689 are given as footnotes. Details of the proposed alterations are from *Alterations in the Book of Common Prayer prepared by the Royal Commissioners, for the Revision of the Liturgy, in 1689*, which was printed by order of the House of Commons, 2 June 1854. In transcribing the alterations of 1689 into the footnotes which follow, a number of orthographical changes have been carried out.

I THE MINISTRATION OF
PUBLICK BAPTISM OF INFANTS
TO BE USED IN THE CHURCH

2   The people are to be admonished, that it is most convenient that Baptism should not be administered but upon Sundays,[1] and other Holy-days, when the most number of people come together: as well for that the Congregation there-present may testify the receiving of them that be newly baptized into the number of Christ's Church; as also because in the Baptism of Infants every man present may be put in remembrance of his own profession made to God in his Baptism. For which cause

[1] Sundays, altered to, Lord's days.

also it is expedient that Baptism be ministered in the vulgar tongue. Nevertheless (if necessity so require) children may be baptized upon any other day.[1]

3   And note, that there shall be for every male child to be baptized two Godfathers and one Godmother; and for every female, one Godfather and two Godmothers.[2]

4   When there are children to be baptized, the parents shall give knowledge thereof over night, or in the morning before the beginning of Morning Prayer, to the Curate.[3] And then the Godfathers and Godmothers[4] and the people with the children must be ready at the Font, either immediately after the last Lesson at Morning Prayer, or else immediately after the last Lesson at Evening Prayer[5] as the Curate by his discretion shall appoint. And the Priest[6] coming to the Font (which is then to be filled with pure Water) and standing there, shall say,[7]

Hath this Child been already baptized, or no?

If they answer, No: then shall the Priest proceed as followeth.

5   Dearly beloved, forasmuch as all men are conceived and born in sin, and that our Saviour Christ saith, none can enter into the kingdom of God, except he be regenerate and born anew of Water and of the Holy Ghost: I beseech you to call upon God the Father, through our Lord Jesus Christ, that of his bounteous mercy he will grant to *this Child* that thing which by nature *he* cannot have; that he may be baptized with Water and the Holy Ghost, and received into Christ's holy Church, and be made *a lively member* of the same.[8]

6   Then shall the Priest say,

Let us pray.

Almighty and everlasting God, who of thy great mercy didst save

[1] Against this rubric was added the note: Q. Conc: a Cure by a Canon of Ministers Christning Children in other Ministers Parishes without their leave, & when there is no urgent Occasion?

[2] Additions to this rubric: None are to be sureties but such as either have received the Communion, or are ready to do it.

Whereas it is appointed by this Office that all Children shall be presented by Godfathers and Godmothers, to be baptized, which is still continued according to the ancient custom of the Church, that so, besides the obligation that lies on the Parents to breed up their Children in the Christian Religion, there may be likewise other Sureties to see that the Parents do their duty, and look to the Christian Education of the persons baptized, in case of the default or death of the Parents: yet there being some difficulties in observing this good and useful constitution, it is hereby provided, that if any person comes to the Minister and tells him he cannot conveniently procure Godfathers and Godmothers for his child, and yet he desires his child may be baptized upon the Engagement of the Parent or Parents only, in that case, the Minister, after discourse with him, if he persists, shall be obliged to baptize such child or children, upon the Suretiship of the Parent or Parents, or some other near Relation or Friends.

[3] *Curate*, altered to, *Minister*.   [4] *Godfathers and Godmothers*, altered to, *Sureties*.
[5] after *Evening Prayer, (if it may be)*.
[6] *Priest*, altered to, *Minister*, and so throughout, with the exception of the places noted.
[7] After, *shall say, (if the case be in the least doubtful)*.
[8] Against the Preface: Dearly beloved ... except he ..., is the following note: Q. whether this may not be the preface. Dearly Beloved forasmuch as our Saviour saith that which is born of the flesh is flesh, and that none can enter, etc. (But this passage was afterward struck through.)

Noah and his family in the ark from perishing by water; and also didst safely lead the children of Israel thy people through the Red Sea, figuring thereby thy holy Baptism; and by the Baptism of[1] thy well-beloved Son Jesus Christ, in the river Jordan, didst sanctify Water to[2] the mystical washing away of sin: We beseech thee, for thine infinite mercies, that thou wilt mercifully look upon *this Child*; wash *him* and sanctify *him* with the Holy Ghost; that *he*, being delivered from thy wrath, may be received into the ark of Christ's Church; and being stedfast in faith, joyful through hope, and rooted in charity, may so pass the waves of this troublesome world, that finally *he* may come to the land of everlasting life, there to reign with thee world without end,[3] through Jesus Christ our Lord. *Amen.*

7 Almighty and immortal God, the aid of all that need, the helper of all that flee to thee for succour, the life of them that believe, and the resurrection of the dead: We call upon thee for *this Infant*, that *he*, coming to thy holy Baptism, may receive remission of *his* sins by spiritual regeneration.[4] Receive *him*, O Lord, as thou hast promised by thy well-beloved Son, saying Ask, and ye shall have; seek, and ye shall find; knock, and it shall be opened unto you: So give now unto us that ask; let us that seek find; open the gate unto us that knock; that *this Infant* may enjoy the everlasting benediction of thy heavenly washing, and may come to the eternal kingdom which thou hast promised by Christ our Lord. *Amen.*

8 Then shall the people stand up, and the Priest shall say,

Hear the words of the Gospel, written by Saint Mark in the tenth chapter at the thirteenth verse.

They brought young children to Christ, that he should touch them; and his disciples rebuked those that brought them. But when Jesus saw it, he was much displeased, and said unto them, Suffer the little children to come unto me, and forbid them not; for of such is the kingdom of God. Verily I say unto you, Whosoever shall not receive the kingdom of God as a little child, he shall not enter therein. And he took them up in his arms, put his hands upon them, and blessed them.

---

[1] by the baptism of, struck out and finally altered to, after the Baptism of.

[2] sanctify Water to, altered to, appoint water to be used in this Sacrament for.

[3] and being stedfast ... world without end, ..., struck out, and altered thus: and persevering in Faith, hope and charity, may so pass through this present Evil world, that finally He may come to Everlasting life, through Jesus Christ our Lord. Amen.

[4] may receive remission of *his* sins by spiritual regeneration; altered to, may be regenerated and receive remission of sin.

9 After the Gospel is read, the Minister shall make this brief exhortation upon the words of the Gospel.

Beloved, ye hear in this Gospel the words of our Saviour Christ, that he commanded the children to be brought unto him; how he blamed those that would have kept them from him; how he exhorteth all men to follow their innocency. Ye perceive how by his outward gesture and deed he declared his good will toward them; for he embraced them in his arms, he laid his hands upon them, and blessed them. Doubt ye not therefore, but earnestly believe, that[1] he will likewise favourably receive *this* present *Infant*; that he will embrace *him* with the arms of his mercy; that he will give unto *him* the blessing of eternal life, and make *him partaker* of his everlasting kingdom. Wherefore we being thus persuaded of the good will of our heavenly Father towards *this Infant*, declared by his Son Jesus Christ; and nothing doubting but that he favourably alloweth this charitable work of ours in bringing *this Infant* to his holy Baptism; let us faithfully and devoutly give thanks unto him, and say,

Almighty and everlasting God, heavenly Father, we give thee humble thanks that thou hast vouchsafed to call us to the knowledge of thy grace and faith in thee: Increase this knowledge, and confirm this faith in us evermore. Give thy Holy Spirit to *this Infant*, that *he* may be born again, and be made *an heir* of everlasting salvation, through our Lord Jesus Christ, who liveth and reigneth with thee and the Holy Spirit, now and for ever. *Amen.*

10 Then shall the Priest speak unto the Godfathers and Godmothers on this wise.[2]

Dearly beloved, ye have brought *this Child* here to be baptized; ye have prayed that our Lord Jesus Christ would vouchsafe to receive *him*, to release *him* of *his* sins,[3] to sanctify *him* with the Holy Ghost, to give *him* the kingdom of heaven and everlasting life. Ye have heard also that our Lord Jesus Christ hath promised in his Gospel, to grant all these things that ye have prayed for: which promise he, for his part, will most surely keep and perform. Wherefore, after this promise made by Christ, *this Infant* must also faithfully, for *his* part, promise by you that

---

[1] earnestly believe, that ..., altered to, stedfastly believe, that according to his gracious Covenant, he will likewise ...
[2] This rubric omitted, and the following passage included: *Then shall the Minister, speaking to the Congregation, ask,*
Who are the Sureties for this child?
Then may the Parent or Parents present their Sureties, if there be any other besides Themselves.
[3] *his* sins, altered to, sin.

are *his* sureties, (until *he* come of age to take it upon *himself*,) that *he* will renounce the devil and all his works, and constantly believe God's holy Word, and obediently keep his commandments.

11 I demand therefore,

Dost thou, in the name of this Child, renounce the devil and all his works, the vain pomp and glory of the world,[1] with all covetous desires of the same, and the carnal desires[2] of the flesh, so that thou wilt not follow nor be led by them?
Answer: I renounce them all.

Minister.

Dost thou believe in God the Father Almighty, Maker of heaven and earth?

And in Jesus Christ his only-begotten Son our Lord? And that he was conceived by the Holy Ghost, born of the Virgin Mary; that he suffered under Pontius Pilate, was crucified, dead, and buried; that he went down into hell, and also did rise again the third day; that he ascended into heaven, and sitteth at the right hand of God the Father Almighty; and from thence shall come again at the end of the world, to judge the quick and the dead?

And dost thou believe in the Holy Ghost; the holy Catholick Church; the Communion of Saints; the Remission of sins; the Resurrection of the flesh; and everlasting life after death?
Answer. All this I stedfastly believe.

Minister.

Wilt thou be baptized in this faith?
Answer: That is my desire.

Minister.

Wilt thou then obediently keep God's holy will and commandments, and walk in the same all the days of thy life?
Answer: I will.[3]

12 Then shall the Priest say,

O merciful God, grant that the old Adam in *this Child* may be so buried, that the new man may be raised up in *him. Amen.*

---

[1] vain pomp and glory of the world, altered to, pomps and vanities of the wicked world.
[2] the carnal desires, altered to, all the sinful Lusts.
[3] altered to, I will, God being my helper.

Grant that all carnal affections may die in *him*, and that all things belonging to the Spirit may live and grow in *him*. *Amen*.

Grant that *he* may have power and strength, to have victory, and to triumph against the devil, the world, and the flesh. *Amen*.

Grant that whosoever is here dedicated to thee by our office and ministry may also be endued with heavenly virtues, and everlastingly rewarded, through thy mercy, O blessed Lord God, who dost live, and govern all things, world without end. *Amen*.

13 Almighty everliving God, whose most dearly beloved Son Jesus Christ, for the forgiveness of our sins, did shed out of his most precious side both water and blood; and gave commandment to his disciples, that they should go teach all nations, and baptize them in the Name of the Father, and of the Son, and of the Holy Ghost: Regard, we beseech thee, the supplications of thy Congregation; sanctify this Water to the mystical washing away of sin; and grant that *this Child*, now to be baptized therein, may receive the fulness of thy grace, and ever remain in the number of thy faithful and elect children; through Jesus Christ our Lord. *Amen*.

14 Then the Priest shall take the Child into his hands, and shall say to the Godfathers and Godmothers,[1]

Name this Child.

And then naming it after them (if they shall certify him that the Child may well endure it) he shall dip it in the Water discreetly and warily, saying,[2]

N. I baptize thee in the Name of the Father, and of the Son, and of the Holy Ghost. Amen.

15 But if they certify that the Child is weak, it shall suffice to pour Water upon it, saying the foresaid words,[3]

N. I baptize thee in the Name of the Father, and of the Son, and of the Holy Ghost. Amen.[4]

16 Then shall the Priest say.[5]

We receive this Child into the Congregation of Christ's flock,

---

[1] *Godfathers and Godmothers*, altered to, *Sureties*.

[2] the words, (*if they shall certify . . . warily, saying*, Struck out, and altered at first thus: *He shall pour water upon It and use caution according as he shall be certified of the condition of the child*. But this alteration was struck out, and the following finally substituted: *He shall pour or sprinkle water upon It; or, (if They shall certify Him that the Child may well endure It) he shall dipt It in the Water discreetly and warily, saying*, N. etc.

[3], [4] This rubric, and the baptismal formula were struck out, as they were contained in the foregoing alteration.

[5] The word, *Priest*, is left unaltered.

here the Priest[1] shall make a Cross upon the Child's forehead

and do sign *him* with the sign of the Cross, in token that hereafter he shall[2] not be ashamed to confess the faith of Christ crucified, and[3, 4] manfully to fight under his banner against sin, the world, and the devil, and continue Christ's faithful soldier and servant unto *his* life's end. Amen.

17 Then shall the Priest[5] say,

Seeing now, dearly beloved brethren, that *this Child is* regenerate[6] and grafted into the body of Christ's Church, let us give thanks unto Almighty God for these benefits, and with one accord make our prayers unto him, that *this Child* may lead the rest of *his* life according to this beginning.

18 Then shall be said (all kneeling),

Our Father which art in heaven, Hallowed by thy Name, Thy kingdom come, Thy will be done, in earth as it is in heaven. Give us this day our daily bread; And forgive us our trespasses, As we forgive them that trespass against us; And lead us not into temptation, But deliver us from evil. Amen.

19 Then shall the Priest say,

We yield hearty thanks, most merciful Father, that it hath pleased thee to regenerate *this Infant* with[7] thy Holy Spirit, to receive him for thine own *Child* by adoption, and to incorporate *him* into thy holy Church. And humbly we beseech thee to grant that *he* being dead unto sin, and living unto righteousness, and being buried with Christ in his death, may crucify the old man, and utterly abolish the whole body of sin; and that, as *he is* made *partaker* of the death of thy Son, *he* may also be *partaker* of his resurrection; so that finally, with the residue of thy holy Church, *he* may be *an inheritor* of thine everlasting kingdom; through Christ our Lord. *Amen.*

20 Then, all standing up, the Priest shall say to the Godfathers and Godmothers[8] this exhortation following.

[1] The word, *Priest*, is left unaltered.
[2] in token that hereafter he shall, struck out, and the following words inserted, to mind him hereafter.
[3] crucified, and, and, altered to, but.
[4] to manfully; the insertion of the word "to", at this point, seems to have been an error.
[5] The word, Priest, is left unaltered.
[6] regenerate, altered to, regenerated.   [7] *this Infant* with water and.
[8] *Godfathers and Godmothers*, altered to, *Sureties*.

Forasmuch as *this Child hath* promised by you *his* sureties to renounce the devil and all his works, to believe in God, and to serve him: Ye must remember that it is your parts and duties to see that *this Infant* be taught, so soon as *he* shall be able to learn, what a solemn vow, promise and profession *he hath* here made by you. And that *he* may know these things the better, ye call upon *him* to hear sermons; and chiefly ye shall provide that *he* may learn the Creed, the Lord's Prayer and the Ten Commandments in the vulgar tongue, and all other things which a Christian ought to know and believe to *his* soul's health; and that *this Child* may be virtuously brought up to lead a godly and a Christian life; remembering always, that Baptism doth represent unto us our profession; which is, to follow the example of our Saviour Christ, and to be made like unto him; that as he died and rose again for us, so should we, who are baptized, die from sin and rise again unto righteousness, continually mortifying all our evil and corrupt affections, and daily proceeding in all virtue and godliness of living.[1]

21 Then shall he add and say,

Ye are to take care that *this Child* be brought to the Bishop to be confirmed by him, so soon as *he* can say the Creed, the Lord's Prayer and the Ten Commandments in the vulgar tongue, and be further instructed in the Church Catechism set forth for that purpose.[2]

22 It is certain by God's Word, that children which are baptized, dying before they commit actual sin, are undoubtedly saved.[3]

23 To take away all scruple concerning the use of the sign of the Cross in Baptism; the true explication thereof, and the just reasons for the retaining of it, may be seen in the XXXth Canon, first published in the year MDCIV.[4]

---

[1] following this exhortation, the following rubric is inserted: *Then the Minister shall say to the Parents, if there, or to some of their near Relations. You have heard now what is your duty, do you promise conscientiously to perform It?*

[2] set forth for that purpose, these words struck out, and the following words added: and be otherwise duly prepared according to the Charge in the Exhortation to be made before Confirmation.

[3] Note on the interleaf: This rubric is either to be omitted, or to be proved by particular places of Scripture to be set in the margin.

[4] This rubric was struck out, and the following Declaration and Provisions added: *Whereas the Sign of the Cross is, by this Office, appointed to be used in Baptism according to the Ancient and laudable Custom of the Church, It is not thereby intended to add any new Rite to the Sacrament as a part of it, or as necessary to it; or that the Using that Sign is of any Virtue or Efficacy of itself; but only to remember all Christians of the Death and Cross of Christ, which is their Hope and their Glory; and to put them in Mind of their Obligation to bear the Cross in such manner as God shall think fit to lay it upon them, and to become comformable to Christ in his Suffering.*
The following was proposed but not agreed to, but left to further consideration: *Yet if there are any who, not satisfied with this Declaration, shall come some day before they offer their Children to be baptized, and declare to their Minister that they are persuaded in their*

1 THE ORDER OF CONFIRMATION,
OR LAYING ON OF HANDS UPON THOSE THAT ARE
BAPTIZED AND COME TO YEARS OF DISCRETION.

2 Upon the day appointed, all that are to be then confirmed, being placed, and
standing in order before the Bishop; he (or some other Minister appointed by him)
shall read this Preface following.

To the end that Confirmation may be ministered to the more edifying
of such as shall receive it, the Church hath thought good to order,
That none hereafter shall be confirmed, but such as can say the Creed,
the Lord's Prayer, and the Ten Commandments; and can also answer
to such other Questions, as in the short Catechism are contained:
which order is very convenient to be observed; to the end that children
being now come to the years of discretion, and having learned what
their Godfathers and Godmothers promised for them in Baptism, they
may themselves, with their own mouth and consent, openly before the
Church, ratify and confirm the same; and also promise, that by the
grace of God they will evermore endeavour themselves faithfully to
observe such things, as they by their own confession have assented
unto.[1]

3 Then shall the Bishop say,

Do ye here, in the presence of God, and of this Congregation, renew
the solemn promise and vow that was made in your name at your
Baptism; ratifying and confirming the same in your own persons, and
acknowledging yourselves bound to believe and to do all those things,
which your Godfathers and Godmothers then undertook for you?

4 And every one shall audibly answer,

I do.[2]

---

*Conscience, that they cannot without Sin offer their Child to be baptized according to the Form
here prescribed by admitting the Sign of the Cross, then it shall not be used.*

   *If any Minister at his Institution shall declare to his Bishop, that He cannot satisfy his conscience
in baptizing any with the Sign of the Cross; then the Bishop shall dispense with Him in that
particular, and shall name a Curate who shall baptize the children of Those in that Parish who
desire it may be done with the Sign of the Cross according to this Office.*

   [1] The whole of this Preface struck out, and the following new Preface inserted: You
have been lately informed for what end you ought to come hither. And I hope you are
come prepared according to the Exhortation then made to you; That is, with a serious
Desire and Resolution openly to ratify and confirm before the Church, with your own
Mouth and Consent, what your Sureties promised in your Names, when you were
baptized; and also to promise that, by the Grace of God, you will evermore endeavour
yourselves faithfully to observe such things, as You, by your own Confession have
assented unto.

   [2] The following Question added, without an Answer: Do you renounce, etc. as in
baptism.

5 The Bishop.

Our help is in the Name of the Lord;
Answer: Who hath made heaven and earth.
Bishop: Blessed be the name of the Lord;
Answer: Henceforth world without end.
Bishop: Lord, hear our prayers;
Answer: And let our cry come unto thee.

6 Bishop.

Let us pray.[1]

Almighty and everliving God, who hast vouchsafed to regenerate these thy servants by Water and the Holy Ghost, and hast given unto them forgiveness of all their sins: Strengthen them, we beseech thee, O Lord, with the Holy Ghost the Comforter, and daily increase in them thy manifold gift of grace; the spirit of wisdom and understanding; the spirit of counsel and ghostly strength; the spirit of knowledge and true godliness; and fill them, O Lord, with the spirit of thy holy fear, now and for ever. *Amen.*[2]

7 Then all of them in order kneeling before the Bishop, he shall lay his hand upon the head of everyone severally, saying,

Defend, O Lord, this thy Child (or *this thy Servant*) with thy heavenly grace, that *he* may continue thine for ever; and daily increase in thy Holy Spirit, more and more, until *he* come unto thy everlasting kingdom. Amen.

8 Then shall the Bishop say,

The Lord be with you.
Answer: And with thy spirit.

9 And (all kneeling down) the Bishop shall add,

Let us pray.

Our Father which art in heaven, Hallowed be thy Name, Thy kingdom

---

[1] Struck out.

[2] and hast given ... now and for ever. *Amen.* struck out, and the following passage inserted: for the forgiveness of Sin, Renew and strengthen Them, we beseech Thee O Lord, more and more, by the Holy Ghost the Comforter, and daily increase thy Graces in Them. Fill Them with the knowledge of thy will in all wisdom and spiritual understanding: and enable Them to walk worthy of their holy Calling with all lowliness and meekness. That they may be blameless and harmless the Sons of God without rebuke, shining as Lights in the world, to the praise and glory of thy name through Jesus Christ our Lord. Amen.

come, Thy will be done, in earth as it is in heaven. Give us this day our daily bread; And forgive us our trespasses, As we forgive them that trespass against us; And lead us not into temptation, But deliver us from evil. Amen.[1]

10   And this Collect.

Almighty and everliving God, who makest us both to will and to do those things that be good and acceptable unto thy divine Majesty; We make our humble supplications unto thee for these thy servants, upon whom (after the example of thy holy Apostles)[2] we have now laid our hands,[3] to certify them (by this sign) of thy favour and gracious goodness towards them.[4] Let thy fatherly hand, we beseech thee, ever be over them; let thy Holy Spirit ever be with them; and so lead them in the knowledge and obedience of thy Word, that in the end they may obtain everlasting life; through our Lord Jesus Christ, who with thee and the Holy Ghost liveth and reigneth, ever one God, world without end. *Amen.*

11   O almighty Lord, and everlasting God, vouchsafe, we beseech thee, to direct, sanctify and govern both our hearts and bodies, in the ways of thy laws, and in the works of thy commandments; that through thy most mighty protection, both here and ever, we may be preserved in body and soul; through our Lord and Saviour Jesus Christ. *Amen.*[5]

[1] Amen. struck out, and, for thine, etc. Amen., added.
[2] (after the example of thy holy Apostles) struck out.
[3] our hands, *comma* changed to a *full stop*.
[4] to certify them, . . . towards them. struck out.
[5] Between this prayer and the final Blessing the following additions were made: Accept good Lord of the dedication which these thy Servants have made of Themselves unto Thee by the Solemn Renewal of their baptismal Vow and Covenant. And as They have now given up Themselves unto Thee and consented to be governed in all Things by thy will: so do Thou vouchsafe to receive Them into thy special favour and Grace, to fulfil in Them all the good pleasure of thy Goodness and the work of Faith with power. Possess their minds perpetually with a serious and lively remembrance of what They have now promised. Confirm and settle the godly Resolutions They have now made. Sanctify Them throughout that They may become the Temples of the Holy Ghost, and in the End be presented faultless before the presence of thy glory, with exceeding Joy, through Jesus Christ our Lord. Amen.
   Then shall follow this Exhortation to the confirmed who are to be required to stay and hear it: Dearly Beloved you have now dedicated yourselves in your own persons to the fear and service of God, and have professed your Faith in our Lord Jesus Christ. I do therefore require and charge you, as you will answer It in the great day of the Lord, that you observe religiously the Vows which you have now made, and walk worthy of your holy Calling. That so your conversation may be in all things such as becomes the Gospel of Christ. Mortify all your unruly Appetites and inordinate Affections. Abstain from Adultery, Fornication, Uncleanness and Covetousness which is Idolatry for which Things sake the wrath of God cometh upon the children of disobedience: put away likewise all Anger, wrath, malice, evil speaking, lying, swearing, and filthy communication out of your

12 Then the Bishop shall bless them, saying thus,

The Blessing of God Almighty, the Father, the Son, and the Holy Ghost, be upon you, and remain with you, for ever. *Amen.*

13 And there shall none be admitted to the holy Communion, until such time as he be confirmed, or ready and desirous to be confirmed.[1]

---

mouths; and put on, as the Elect of God, Holy and beloved, bowels of mercies, kindness, humbleness of mind, meekness and Long suffering. Be ye followers of Christ. Take his yoke and learn of Him, who was meek and lowly in heart, and be ye holy, as he who has called you was holy, in all manner of Conversation. Be obedient to your Parents and Masters, diligent in your Callings, always building up yourselves in the Love of God, looking for the mercy of our Lord Jesus Christ unto eternal Life. He who establisheth us with you in Christ Jesus, and hath anointed us, is God, who hath also sealed us, and given us the earnest of his Spirit in our hearts. And if you continue faithful to the death, He will give you the Crown of Life. But if any man draws back, his soul shall have no Pleasure in Him, since he hath grieved the holy Spirit of Grace, for, if after you have escaped the Pollutions of the world through the knowledge of our Lord and Saviour Jesus Christ, you are again entangled therein, and overcome; your latter end will be worse than your beginning, watch ye therefore and pray that ye enter not into Temptation, for the Spirit indeed is willing, but the flesh is weak. And seeing ye are compassed about with such a cloud of witnesses, lay aside every weight, and run with patience the race that is set before you. Be ye stedfast, unmoveable, always abounding in the work of the Lord, forasmuch as your Labour is not in vain in the Lord. And I pray God to sanctify you wholly, that your whole spirit and soul and body may be preserved blameless unto the coming of our Lord Jesus Christ.

[1] This rubric altered as follows: *And there shall none be admitted to Confirmation, but such as shall be judged fit to receive the Communion upon the next Occasion.*

3. The Canadian Rites 1918

The Preface to the Canadian Revision of 1918 clearly states the purpose and the limits of this revision. "The Book of Common Prayer is a priceless possession of our Church. . . . But through the lapse of some three hundred years many changes have taken place in the life of the Church and in its outlook upon the world. The present life and larger outlook of the Church are seeking more adequate expression than the Book of Common Prayer has hitherto afforded, and seem to require judicious adaptation and enrichment of the Book in order that it may more fully meet the needs of the Church in this age and in this Dominion.

Therefore the General Synod of the Church of England in Canada determined to make such adaptations and enrichments in the body of the Book as would serve this purpose. But to avoid the risk of changes that might impair the character of the Book, the General Synod clearly ordained the limits within which such adaptations and enrichments might be made, forbidding any change in text or rubric which would involve or imply a change of doctrine or principle of the Church of England as set forth in the Book of Common Prayer, . . ."

The revisions carried out were very limited and were chiefly in the adaptation of rubrics to customs generally accepted at that time. The texts and alterations noted are from THE BOOK OF COMMON PRAYER *and Administration of the Sacraments and other Rites and Ceremonies of the Church according to the Use of* THE CHURCH OF ENGLAND IN THE DOMINION OF CANADA: *issued by the Authority of the General Synod of the Church of England in the Dominion of Canada, 1918.*

I THE MINISTRATION OF PUBLIC BAPTISM OF INFANTS
TO BE USED IN THE CHURCH

2 The Minister of the parish shall often admonish the people that they bring their children to baptism as soon as possible after birth, not later than the fourth or at the furthest the fifth Sunday, unless upon a great and reasonable cause.

3 The people are also to be admonished, that it is most fitting that Baptism should be administered upon Sundays, . . .

Continue as 1662 B2.

4 And note, That there shall be for every child to be baptized three sponsors: for every male, two Godfathers and one Godmother; and for every female, one Godfather and two Godmothers. Nevertheless, when three sponsors cannot be had, one Godfather and one Godmother shall suffice. Parents may be sponsors for their own children, if necessity so require.

5 When there are children to be baptized, the parents shall give timely notice thereof to the Minister. He shall thereupon appoint the time for baptism, which shall be either immediately after the last Lesson, or after the third Collect, at Morning or Evening Prayer; or at such other time as he by his discretion shall appoint.

6 The sponsors and the people, with the children, being ready at the Font, the Priest coming to the Font (which is then to be filled with pure Water), and standing there, shall say,

With the following alterations, the text reproduces the 1662 rite *The Ministration of Publick Baptism of Infants, to be used in the Church.*

5 Dearly beloved, . . .
But a living member ⟨lively members⟩

9 Almighty and everlasting God, . . .
Before this prayer the following rubric is included:
A Thanksgiving to be said of the whole congregation after the Minister.

11 Wilt thou then obediently keep God's holy will and commandments, and walk in the same all the days of thy life?
Answer. I will, God being my helper.

18 Our Father which art in heaven, . . .
Doxology included,

19 We yield thee hearty thanks, . . .
But ending:
So that finally, with all thy holy Church, *he* may be *an inheritor* of thine everlasting Kingdom; through Christ our Lord. *Amen.*

20 *Omit* in the vulgar tongue.

21 *Omit* in the vulgar tongue.

Between 21 and 22 insert:
Here may follow:
The grace of our Lord Jesus Christ, and the love of God and the fellowship of the Holy Ghost, be with us all evermore. *Amen.*

After 23 a further rubric is added:
When Baptism is administered at Morning or Evening Prayer, then all the prayers after the Third Collect may be omitted, except the Prayer of St Chrysostom and *The grace of our Lord* etc.

I THE ORDER OF CONFIRMATION
OR LAYING ON OF HANDS UPON THOSE THAT ARE
BAPTIZED AND COME TO YEARS OF DISCRETION

2 Upon the day appointed, all that are to be then confirmed, being placed and standing in order before the Bishop, the Minister shall present them unto the Bishop, and say,

Reverend Father in God, I present unto you these persons to receive the laying on of hands.

Bishop: Take heed that the persons whom ye present be duly prepared and meet to receive the laying on of hands

Minister: I have instructed them and enquired of them and believe them so to be.

3 Then the Bishop, or some other Minister appointed by him, shall read this Preface following.

Dearly beloved, To the end that Confirmation may be ministered to the more edifying of such as shall receive it, the Church hath thought good to order that none hereafter shall be confirmed, but such as can say the Creed, the Lord's Prayer, and the Ten Commandments, and can also answer to such other questions as in the Catechism are contained: and forasmuch as these persons present, being by baptism members of Christ's Church, are instructed and prepared as aforesaid, we are assembled together here to pray for them and to bless them by the laying on of hands. This order is very convenient to be observed for divers reasons.

First. Because it is evident from sundry places in holy Scripture that the Apostles prayed for and laid their hands upon those who were baptized; and the same is agreeable with the usage of the Church since the Apostles' time.

Secondly. In order that by prayer and laying on of hands they that are confirmed may be strengthened by the Holy Spirit.

Third. In order that persons, having now come to the years of discretion, and being mindful of their bounden duty to acknowledge openly the vows made by them, or by their Godfathers and Godmothers for them, in baptism, they may themselves, with their own mouth and consent, openly before the Church ratify and confirm the same; and also promise that by the grace of God they will evermore endeavour faithfully to observe such things as they by their own confession have assented unto.

4   Then the Bishop, or some Minister appointed by him, shall say,

Hear the words of holy Scripture written in the eighth chapter of the Acts of the Apostles, beginning at the fifth verse.
And Philip went down to the city of Samaria . . . (Acts 8.5-8, 12, 14-18, RV)

Hear also the words of holy Scripture written in the nineteenth chapter of the Acts of the Apostles, beginning at the first verse.
And it came to pass, that . . . (Acts 19.1-7, RV)

Hear also the words of holy Scripture written in the fifth chapter of the Epistle to the Hebrews, beginning at the twelfth verse, and in the sixth chapter beginning at the first verse.
For when by reason . . . (Heb. 5.12 and 6.1-3, RV)

5   Then the Bishop shall say,

Do you here, in the presence of God, and of this Congregation, renew the solemn promise and vow that you made, or that was made in your name, at your Baptism; ratifying and confirming the same in your own persons, and acknowledging yourselves bound to believe and to do all those things which you then undertook, or which your God-fathers and Godmothers then undertook for you?

6   And every one shall audibly answer,

I do.

7   Or else the Bishop shall say,

Do you here, in the presence of God and of this Congregation, renounce the devil and all his works, the pomps and vanity of this wicked world, and all the sinful lusts of the flesh?
Answer: I do.
Bishop: Do you believe all the Articles of the Christian faith as contained in the Apostles' Creed?
Answer: I do.
Bishop: Will you endeavour to keep God's holy will and commandments, and to walk in the same all the days of your life?
Answer: I will, God being my helper.

8   The Bishop
Our help is in the Name of the Lord; (CF14)

9 *Bishop.* Let us pray.
   Almighty and everliving God, . . . (CF15)

10 Then all of them in order kneeling before the Bishop, he shall lay his hand upon
    the head of every one severally, saying,

    Defend, O Lord, . . . (CF16)

11 Then shall the Bishop say,
    The Lord be with you.
    Answer: And with thy spirit.

12 And (all kneeling down) the Bishop shall add,

    Let us pray.
    Our Father who art in heaven, . . . (CF9)

13 And this Collect.

    Almighty and everliving God, . . . (CF17)

14 O almighty Lord, . . . (CF18)

15 Then the Bishop shall bless them, saying thus,

    The Blessing of God Almighty, . . . (CF19)

16 And there shall none be admitted to the holy Communion until such time as he
    be confirmed, or be ready and desirous to be confirmed.

4. *The Irish Rites 1926*

In 1878 the Church of Ireland authorized the use of a revised edition of the 1662 *Book of Common Prayer*. As this revision was somewhat limited, the need for further revision was soon felt. This need found expression, at the 1909 General Synod of the Church of Ireland, when the Bishops were requested to confer with a Committee of Synod Representatives, on the matter of Prayer Book Revision, "... and to report upon the best manner in which, without making any modification in doctrine or in the ritual Canons, the Rubrics and Services of the Church might be adapted to the requirements of the present time".[1] Under the direction of the General Synod, work on the revised Book ensued over the next sixteen years, in which time the Synod carefully considered a large number of proposals. The result of this labour was the authorization of the 1926 BOOK OF COMMON PRAYER *and Administration of the Sacraments and Other Rites and Ceremonies of the Church according to the Use of* THE CHURCH OF IRELAND, from which the following texts are taken.

I THE MINISTRATION OF PUBLICK BAPTISM OF INFANTS
TO BE USED IN THE CHURCH

2 The Curates of every Parish shall often admonish the people that they defer not the Baptism of their children longer than the fourth or fifth week next after their birth, unless upon a great and reasonable cause.

3 The people are to be admonished that it is most convenient that Baptism should be administered at some Publick Service of the Church: as well for that the Congregation there present may testify the receiving of them that be newly baptized into the number of Christ's Church; as also because in the Baptism of Infants every man present may be put in remembrance of his own profession made to God in his Baptism. For which cause also it is expedient that Baptism be ministered in the vulgar tongue.

4 And note, that there shall be for every Male Child to be baptized two Godfathers and one Godmother; and for every Female, one Godfather and two Godmothers.

5 Parents may be sponsors for their own children. When three sponsors cannot be found, two shall suffice; and if two cannot be found, one shall suffice. Sponsors must be persons of discreet age, and members of the Church of Ireland, or of a Church in communion therewith.

6 When there are children to be baptized, the Parents should give due notice to the Curate. And the Godfathers and Godmothers, and the people with the Children, must be ready at the Font, at Morning or Evening Prayer, immediately after the Third Collect, or at such other times as the Ordinary shall approve; provided that no parent shall be precluded from having his child baptized in the Publick Service, if he so desire.

7 When Baptism is administered at Morning or Evening Prayer, then all the Prayers after the Third Collect may be omitted.

[1] From The Preface, Prefixed at the Revision of 1926.

8 The Priest coming to the Font and standing there, shall say,

Hath this Child been already baptized, or no?

9 If they answer, No; then shall the Priest proceed as followeth:

Dearly beloved, forasmuch as all men are conceived and born in sin,
and that our Saviour Christ saith, Except a man be born again, he
cannot see the kingdom of God, and also saith, Except a man be born
of water and of the Spirit he cannot enter into the kingdom of God;
I beseech you to call upon God the Father, through our Lord Jesus
Christ, that of his bounteous mercy he will grant to *this Child* that
thing which by nature *he* cannot have; that *he* may be baptized with
water and the Holy Ghost, and received into Christ's holy Church,
and be made *a lively member* of the same.

10 Then, the people standing, the Priest shall say,

Almighty and immortal God, . . . (CF2)

11 Or this:

Almighty and everlasting God, . . . (1662 B6)

12 Then shall the Priest say,

Hear the words of the Gospel, written by Saint Mark, in the tenth
chapter, at the thirteenth verse.

They brought young children to Christ, . . . (CF3)

13 After the Gospel is read, the Minister shall make this brief Exhortation upon the
words of the Gospel:

Beloved, ye hear in this Gospel, . . . (1662 B9)

14 Then shall the Minister and the people say,

Almighty and everlasting God, . . . (CF4)

15 Then shall the Priest speak unto the Godfathers and Godmothers on this wise:

Dearly beloved, ye . . .

1662 B10, *but ending* I demand therefore.

16 Dost thou, . . .

1662 B11, *but* sinful ⟨carnal⟩ desires.

17 Minister.

Dost thou believe in God the Father Almighty, . . .

1662 B11, *but* descended ⟨went down⟩—and the third day rose again from the dead ⟨and also did rise again the third day⟩—shall come to judge ⟨shall come again at the end of the world, to judge⟩—the Forgiveness of sins ⟨the Remission of sins⟩—the Resurrection of the body ⟨the Resurrection of the flesh⟩—the life everlasting ⟨everlasting life after death⟩

Answer: All this I stedfastly believe.

18 Minister.

Wilt thou be baptized in this faith?
Answer: That is my desire.

19 Minister.

Wilt thou then obediently keep God's holy will and Commandments, and walk in the same all the days of thy life?
Answer: I will, God being my helper.

20 Then shall the Priest say,

O merciful God, . . . (CF5 abcd)

21 Almighty, everliving God, . . . (CF6)

22 Then the Priest shall take the Child into his hands, and shall say to the Godfathers and Godmothers,

Name this Child.

23 And then, naming it after them, he shall dip it in the water discreetly and warily, if they shall desire it, and he shall be certified that the Child may well endure it; otherwise it shall suffice to pour water upon it, saying always,

N. I baptize thee In the Name of the Father, and of the Son, and of the Holy Ghost. Amen.

24 Then shall the Priest say,

We receive this Child . . . (CF7)

25 Then shall the Priest say,

Seeing now, . . . (CF8)

26 Then shall be said, all kneeling:

Our Father, which art in heaven, . . . (CF11)

27 Then shall the Priest say,

We yield thee hearty thanks, most merciful Father, that it hath pleased thee to regenerate *this Infant* with thy Holy Spirit, to receive *him* for thine own *Child* by adoption, and to incorporate *him* into thy holy

Church. And humbly we beseech thee to grant, that *he*, being dead unto sin, may live unto righteousness, and being buried with Christ in his death, may also be *partaker* of his resurrection; so that finally, with the residue of thy holy Church, *he* may inherit thine everlasting kingdom; through Christ our Lord. *Amen.*

28 Then, all standing up, the Priest shall say to the Godfathers and Godmothers this Exhortation following:

Forasmuch as *this Child* . . .

1662 B20, *but omit,* may know these things . . . health; and *that this* child may. *With ending,* die to sin, and rise again unto righteousness; continually overcoming all our evil passions, and daily increasing in all virtues and godliness of living.

29 Ye are to take care . . .

1662 B21, *but omit* in the vulgar tongue

30 If Baptism be administered apart from the Publick Service, the Priest shall then say,

The grace of our Lord Jesus Christ, and the love of God, and the fellowship of the Holy Ghost, be with us all evermore. *Amen.*

31 It is certain by God's Word, that children which are baptized, dying before they commit actual sin, are undoubtedly saved. Whereas the sign of the Cross is by this Office appointed to be used in Baptism according to the ancient and laudable custom of the Church, it is not thereby intended to add any new rite to the Sacrament as a part of it, or necessary to it; or that the using that sign is of any virtue or efficacy of itself; but only to remind all Christians of the Death and Cross in such manner as God shall think fit to lay it upon them, and to become comformable to Christ in his sufferings; as more largely is expressed in the thirtieth Canon of the Church of England, which Canon is printed by direction of the General Synod at the end of the Canons of the Church of Ireland.

I THE ORDER FOR CONFIRMATION
OR LAYING ON OF HANDS UPON THOSE THAT ARE
BAPTIZED AND COME TO YEARS OF DISCRETION

2 Upon the day appointed, all that are to be then confirmed, being placed, and standing in order, before the Bishop; he (or some other Minister appointed by him) shall read this Preface following:

3 To the end that Confirmation . . .

1662 C3, *but* and have been further instructed in the Church Catechism set forth for that purpose: Which order is very fitting to be observed; ⟨and can also answer . . . convenient to be observed⟩

4 The Bishop may then, if he think fit, address the candidates.

5 Then shall the Bishop say,

Do you here, in the presence of God and of this Congregation, renew
and confirm the solemn promise and vow of your Baptism?
Answer: I do.

6 The Bishop.

Do you renounce the devil and all his works, the vain pomp and glory
of the world, with all covetous desires of the same, and the sinful
desires of the flesh, so that you will not follow nor be led by them?
Answer: I renounce them all.

7 The Bishop.

Do you believe in God the Father Almighty, Maker of heaven and
earth?
   And in Jesus Christ his only Son our Lord? And that he was conceived by the Holy Ghost, born of the Virgin Mary; that he suffered
under Pontius Pilate, was crucified, dead, and buried; that he descended
into hell, and the third day rose again from the dead; that he ascended
into heaven, and sitteth at the right hand of God the Father Almighty;
and from thence shall come to judge the quick and the dead?
   And do you believe in the Holy Ghost; the holy Catholick Church;
the Communion of Saints; the Forgiveness of sins; the Resurrection
of the body; and the life everlasting?
Answer: All this I stedfastly believe.

8 The Bishop.

Will you the obediently keep God's holy will and Commandments,
and walk in the same all the days of your life?
Answer: I will, by God's help.

9 Then shall the Congregation stand, and the Bishop shall say,

Our help is in the Name of the Lord; (CF14)

10 Then shall the Congregation kneel, as also those about to be confirmed, and the
Bishop, still standing, shall say,

Let us pray.
Almighty and everliving God, . . . (CF15)

11 Then, all of them in order kneeling before the Bishop, he shall lay his hand upon
the head of every one severally, saying,

Defend, O Lord, . . . (CF16)

12 Here may follow a Hymn, and the Bishop may address the newly confirmed, if he see fit.

13 Then shall the Bishop say,

The Lord be with you;
Answer. And with thy spirit.

14 And (all kneeling down) the Bishop shall add,

Let us pray.
Our Father, which art in heaven, . . . (CF9)

15 And this Collect.

Almighty and everliving God, who makest us . . .

CF17, *but* to assure them ⟨to certify them⟩

16 And also this, or some other Collect out of this Book, at his discretion.

O God, whose blessed Son was manifested that he might destroy the works of the devil, and make us the sons of God, and heirs of eternal life; Grant us, we beseech thee, that, having this hope, we may purify ourselves, even as he is pure; that when he shall appear again with power and great glory, we may be made like unto him in his eternal and glorious kingdom; where with thee, O Father, and thee, O Holy Ghost, he liveth and reigneth, ever one God, world without end. *Amen.*

17 Here may follow a Hymn.

18 Then the Bishop shall bless them, saying thus:

The blessing of God Almighty, . . . (CF19)

19 When Confirmation is ministered only to those baptized in riper years, the Preface shall be omitted.

20 Every person ought to present himself for Confirmation (unless prevented by some urgent reason) before he partakes of the Lord's Supper.

5. The Church of England Proposed Rites 1928

The first step towards twentieth-century revision of the Anglican Initiatory Rite took place in 1923 with the introduction of the *Revised Prayer Book (Permissive Use) Measure*; these proposals were set out in the document N.A.84. Work on the revision of the whole Prayer Book continued until 1927. On 7 February 1927 a Draft Book, a *Book Proposed to be Annexed to the Prayer Book Measure 192–*, was presented to the Convocations. This was a composite book containing the services of 1662, and new matter described as *"Permissive Additions and Deviations"*. At the Convocations a large number of amendments were introduced. The Draft Book was submitted, on 22 February 1927, to the Lower House, where further amendments were proposed. Further revision was carried out in the House of Bishops, which presented the final form to the Convocations on 29 March. Convocations commended the book to the National Assembly, which gave its final approval in July 1927. Receiving the support of the Assembly, the Measure came before Parliament later that year; where it was passed by the House of Lords, but rejected in the House of Commons.

After this rejection the Bishops decided on a new Measure in which a number of misunderstandings were removed. Once again the Measure was submitted to Parliament. In June 1928 it was rejected by the House of Commons by an increased majority, and thus failed to achieve legal authority.

Towards the end of 1928 *The Prayer Book as Proposed in 1928* was published as an ordinary book. In the impasse, created by the House of Commons when it rejected the Book, it was agreed by the Bishops that they could not "regard as inconsistent with loyalty to the principles of the Church of England the use of such additions or deviations as fall within the limits" of the 1928 Prayer Book. Use of matter from the 1928 Book depended on the permission of each Bishop in his own diocese, and on "the good will of the people as represented in the Parochial Church Council", and, as regards the Occasional Offices, on the consent of the parties concerned.

Many of the liturgies which follow reflect a number of the revisions which were suggested and yet rejected in 1928.

I GENERAL RUBRICKS OF THE MINISTRATION OF PUBLICK BAPTISM OF INFANTS

2 The Ministers of every Parish shall often admonish the people that they bring their children to Baptism as soon as possible after birth, and that they defer not the Baptism longer than the fourth, or, at furthest the fifth, Sunday unless upon a great and reasonable cause.

3 It is desirable where possible that Baptism should be administered upon Sundays and other Holy-days, when the most number of people come together; as well for that the congregation there present may testify the receiving of them that be newly baptized into the number of Christ's Church; as also because in the Baptism of infants every man present may be put in remembrance of his own profession made to God in his Baptism: for which cause it is expedient that Baptism be ministered in the vulgar tongue. Nevertheless (for sufficient cause), children may be baptized upon any other day.

4 And note, that there shall be for every male-child to be baptized two Godfathers and one Godmother; and for every female, one Godfather and two Godmothers. Nevertheless, when three sponsors cannot conveniently be had, one Godfather and one Godmother shall suffice. Parents, if need so require, may be sponsors for their own child provided that the child have one other sponsor. No person shall be admitted to be a sponsor who hath not been baptized.

5 In the absence of the Priest it is lawful that a Deacon baptize infants.

6 When there are children to be baptized, the Parents shall give due notice thereof to the Minister of the Parish. He shall thereupon appoint the time for the Baptism. Then the Godfathers and Godmothers, and the people with the children, must be ready at the Font either immediately after the last Lesson, or after the Third Collect at Morning or Evening Prayer; or at such other time as he in his discretion shall think fit.

7 It is certain by God's Word, that children which are baptized, dying before they commit actual sin, are undoubtedly saved.

8 To take away all scruple concerning the use of the sign of the Cross in Baptism; the true explication thereof, and the just reasons for the retaining of it, may be seen in the XXXth Canon, first published in the Year MDCIV.

9 AN ALTERNATIVE ORDER OF THE MINISTRATION OF PUBLICK BAPTISM OF INFANTS

10 Which may be used at the discretion of the Minister unless the parents require the use of the Form of 1662.

11 The Priest, coming to the Font (which is then to be filled with pure water), and standing there, shall say,

Hath this child been already baptized or no?

12 If they answer, No: then shall the Priest proceed as followeth:

Beloved in Christ Jesus, seeing that all men are from their birth prone to sin, but that God willeth all men to be saved, for God is love: and that our Saviour Christ saith, None can enter into the kingdom of God, except he be born anew of water and of the Holy Ghost; I beseech you to call upon God the Father, through our Lord Jesus Christ, that of his bounteous mercy he will grant to *this child*, that thing which by nature *he* cannot have, that *he* may be baptized with water and the Holy Ghost, and received into Christ's holy Church, and be made a *living member* of the same.

13   Then shall the Priest say, all standing,

Almighty and everlasting God, who by the Baptism of thy well-
beloved Son Jesus Christ, in the river Jordan, didst sanctify water to the
mystical washing away of sin: Mercifully look upon *this child*; wash
him and sanctify *him* with the Holy Spirit, that *he* may be received into
the ark of Christ's Church; and being stedfast in faith, joyful through
hope, and rooted in charity, may so pass the waves of this troublesome
world, that finally *he* may come to the land of everlasting life, there to
reign with thee world without end; through Jesus Christ our Lord.
Amen.

14   Or this

Almighty and immortal God . . .

CF2, *but* remission of sin ⟨remission of his sins⟩—that *this infant*, being washed
from sin, may enjoy thy heavenly benediction ⟨that *this infant* may enjoy the
everlasting benediction of thy heavenly washing⟩

15   Then shall the Priest say:

Hear the words of the Gospel, written by Saint Mark, in the tenth
chapter, at the thirteenth verse.
Answer: Glory be to thee, O Lord.
They brought young children to Christ . . . (CF3)
Answer: Praise be to thee, O Christ.

16   Then shall the Priest read this brief Exhortation upon the words of the Gospel.

You hear in this Gospel the words of our Saviour Christ, when he
commanded the children to be brought unto him. You perceive how
he took them in his arms, and blessed them. Jesus Christ is the same
yesterday, and to day, and for ever. Doubt not therefore, but earnestly
believe, that he loveth *this child*, that he approveth this work of ours
in bringing *him* to Holy Baptism, that he is ready to receive *him*, to
embrace *him* with the arms of his mercy, and to give *him* the blessing
of eternal life. Wherefore, we being thus persuaded of the good will
of our heavenly Father towards *this infant*, declared by his Son Jesus
Christ, let us faithfully and devoutly give thanks unto him, and say,

17   Then shall the Priest and people, still standing, say,

Almighty and everlasting God . . .

CF4, *but* called us ⟨vouchsafed to call us⟩—and to faith in thee ⟨and faith in
thee⟩

THE PROMISES

18   Then shall the Priest speak unto the Godfathers and Godmothers on this wise,

Dearly beloved, you have brought *this child* here to be baptized, you have prayed that our Lord Jesus Christ would be pleased to receive *him*, to cleanse *him*, and to sanctify *him*. Our Lord hath promised in his Gospel to grant all these things that you have prayed for; which promise he, for his part, will most surely keep and perform.

You, on your part, must undertake on behalf of *this infant* three things: first, that *he* will renounce the devil and all his works; secondly, that *he* will constantly believe God's holy Word; and thirdly, that *he* will obediently keep his commandments.

I demand therefore,

Dost thou, in the name of this child, renounce the devil and all his works, the vain pomp and glory of the world, with all covetous desires of the same, and the sinful desires of the flesh, so that thou will not follow nor be led by them?
Answer: I do.
Dost thou in the name of this child profess the Christian Faith?
Answer: I do.

19   Then shall be said by the Priest and the Godparents the Apostles' Creed as followeth:

I believe in God the Father Almighty, . . . (CF12)

20   Then shall the Priest say,

O merciful God . . .

CF5abcd, *but in b* evil desires of the flesh ⟨carnal affections⟩

THE BLESSING OF THE WATER

21   After which the Priest shall proceed, saying,

The Lord be with you;
Answer: And with thy spirit.
Priest: Lift up your hearts;
Answer: We lift them up unto the Lord.
Priest: Let us give thanks unto our Lord God;
Answer: It is meet and right so to do.
Priest: It is very meet, right, and our bounden duty, that we should give thanks unto thee, O Lord, Holy Father, Almighty, Everlasting

God, for that thy most dearly beloved Son Jesus Christ, for the forgiveness of our sins, did shed out of his most precious side both water
and blood; and gave commandment to his disciples, that they should
go teach all nations, and baptize them In the name of the Father, and
of the Son, and of the Holy Ghost. Hear, we beseech thee, the prayer
of thy people; sanctify this water to the mystical washing away of sin;
and grant, that *this child*, now to be baptized therein, may receive the
fulness of thy grace, and ever remain in the number of thy faithful and
elect children; through Jesus Christ our Lord, to whom with thee in
the unity of the Holy Spirit, be all honour and glory, now and evermore. *Amen.*

THE BAPTISM

22 Then shall the Priest take the child into his arms, or by the hand, and shall say to
the Godfathers and Godmothers,

Name this child.

23 And then naming it after them, he shall dip it in the water, or pour water upon it,
saying,

N. I baptize thee In the name of the Father, and of the Son, and of the
Holy Ghost. Amen.

24 Then shall the Priest say,

We receive this child . . . (CF7)

THE THANKSGIVING

25 Then shall the Priest say,

CF8, *but* born again, and received into the family ⟨regenerate, and grafted into
the body⟩

26 Then shall be said by all, standing,

Our Father, which art in heaven, . . . (CF11)

27 Then shall the Priest say,

We yield thee hearty thanks, most merciful Father, that it hath pleased
thee to regenerate *this infant* with thy Holy Spirit, to receive *him* for
thine own *child* by adoption, and to make *him* a member of thy holy
Church. *Amen.*

Grant, O Lord, that, being buried with Christ by baptism into his
death, *he* may also be made partaker of his resurrection; so that, serving
thee here in newness of life, *he* may finally, with the rest of thy holy

Church, be *an inheritor* of thine everlasting kingdom; through Jesus Christ our Lord. *Amen.*

28   Then may follow this Prayer for the Home.

Almighty God, our heavenly Father, whose blessed Son did share at Nazareth the life of an earthly home: Bless, we beseech thee, the home of *this child*, and grant wisdom and understanding to all who have the care of *him*: that *he* may grow up in thy constant fear and love; through the same thy Son Jesus Christ our Lord. *Amen.*

THE DUTIES OF THE GODFATHERS AND GODMOTHERS

29   Then the Priest shall say to the Godfathers and Godmothers and Parents this Exhortation following,

You who have brought *this child* to be baptized into the family of Christ's Church, must see that *he* be taught the Creed, the Lord's Prayer, and the Ten Commandments, as set forth in the Church Catechism, and all other things which a Christian ought to know and believe to his soul's health.

See also that *he* be virtuously brought up to lead a godly and Christian life.

See also that *he* be brought to the Bishop to be confirmed by him; so that, strengthened with the gift of the Holy Spirit, *he* may come with due preparation to receive the Holy Communion of the Body and Blood of Christ, and go forth into the world to serve God faithfully in the fellowship of his Church.

Will you help *him* to learn and to do all these things?
Answer: I will, the Lord being my helper.

Remember always that Baptism doth represent unto us our Christian profession, which is to follow the example of our Saviour Christ, and to be made like unto him; that as he died and rose again for us, so should we, who are baptized, die unto sin and rise again unto righteousness, continually mortifying all evil desires, and daily advancing in all virtue and godliness of living.

30   If the Baptism be administered otherwise than at Morning or Evening Prayer, the Priest shall dismiss those that are gathered together with this Blessing:

The Lord bless you, and keep you: the Lord make his face to shine upon you, and be gracious unto you: the Lord lift up the light of his countenance upon you, and give you peace, now and for evermore. *Amen.*

1 GENERAL RUBRICKS OF
THE ORDER OF CONFIRMATION
OR LAYING ON OF HANDS UPON THOSE THAT ARE
BAPTIZED AND COME TO YEARS OF DISCRETION

2 To the end that Confirmation may be ministered to the more edifying of such as shall receive it, the Church hath thought good to order, That none hereafter shall be confirmed, but such as can say the Creed, the Lord's Prayer, and the Ten Commandments; and can also answer to such other questions, as in the short Catechism are contained: which order is very convenient to be observed; to the end that children being now come to the years of discretion, and having learned what their Godfathers and Godmothers promised for them in Baptism, they may themselves, with their own mouth and consent, openly before the Church, ratify and confess the same; and also promise, that by the grace of God they will evermore endeavour themselves faithfully to observe such things, as they by their own confession have assented unto.

3 So soon as children are come to a competent age, and can say, in their mother tongue, the Creed, the Lord's Prayer, and the Ten Commandments; and also can answer to such other questions as in the short Catechism are contained, they shall be brought to the Bishop.

4 The Minister shall from time to time make diligent enquiry whether there be any in his Parish who, having been baptized, were not confirmed in their youth; and, if he find any such, and think them meet to be confirmed, he shall earnestly move them to prepare themselves to seek God's grace in Confirmation.

5 And whensoever the Bishop shall give knowledge for children or others to be brought unto him for their Confirmation, the Curate of every Parish shall either bring, or send in writing, with his hand subscribed thereto, the names and ages of all such persons within his Parish as he shall think fit to be presented to the Bishop to be confirmed. And, if the Bishop approve of them, he shall confirm them in the manner following.

6 It is convenient that every one shall have a Godfather or a Godmother as a witness of their Confirmation.

7 And there shall none be admitted to the Holy Communion, until such time as he be confirmed, or be found in the judgement of the Bishop to be ready and desirous to be confirmed.

8 AN ALTERNATIVE
ORDER OF CONFIRMATION

9 Upon the time appointed, all that are then to be confirmed, being placed, and standing in order, before the Bishop; he (or some other Minister appointed by him) shall read this Preface following, unless he shall otherwise determine.

10 Dearly beloved in the Lord, . . . (CF20)

THE RENEWAL OF BAPTISMAL VOWS

11 Then shall the Bishop say,

Do ye here, in the presence of God . . . (CF13)

12   Or else the Bishop shall say,

Do ye here, in the presence of God, and of this congregation, renounce the devil and all his works, the pomps and vanity of this wicked world, and all the sinful lusts of the flesh, so that ye will not follow nor be led by them?
Answer: I do.
Do ye believe all the Articles of the Christian Faith as contained in the Apostles' Creed?
Answer: I do.
Will ye endeavour to keep God's holy will and commandments, and walk in the same all the days of your life?
Answer: I will.

THE CONFIRMATION

13   Then shall the Bishop begin the Confirmation; and no Hymn or Address shall be introduced into this part of the Service, except that a Hymn may be sung, if needed, in the course of the laying on of hands.

The Bishop: Our help is in the name of the Lord; (CF14)

14   *The Bishop:* Let us pray.
Almighty and everliving God, . . . (CF15)

15   Then all of them in order kneeling before the Bishop, he shall lay his hands upon the head of every one severally, saying,

Defend, O Lord, . . . (CF16)

16   Then shall the Bishop say,

The Lord be with you;
Answer: And with thy spirit.

17   Let us pray.
Our Father, which art in heaven, . . . (CF11)

18   Then shall the Bishop add these Prayers.

Almighty and everliving God, who makest us . . . (CF17)

THE CONCLUSION

19   O almighty Lord, . . . (CF18)

20   Then the Bishop shall bless them, saying thus,

Go forth into the world in peace; be of good courage; hold fast that which is good; render to no man evil for evil; strengthen the faint-

hearted; support the weak; help the afflicted; honour all men; love
and serve the Lord, rejoicing in the power of the Holy Spirit.

And the blessing of God Almighty, the Father, the Son, and the
Holy Ghost, be upon you and remain with you for ever. *Amen.*

6. *The American Rites 1928*

The texts which follow are those in use at the present time and are from THE BOOK OF COMMON PRAYER *and Administration of the Sacraments and Other Rites and Ceremonies of the Church, according to the use of the Protestant Episcopal Church in the United States of America*, as conforming to the Standard Book of 1928 and amended by subsequent actions of General Conventions. The Baptismal Rite is used for both Infants and Adults.

In 1950, the Standing Liturgical Commission published *Prayer Book Studies*. 1 (New York, The Church Pension Fund, 1950) which contained proposed revisions for the rites of Baptism and Confirmation. As proposed revisions these rites received very little support, and were never authorized or used. The Liturgical Commission now has no intention of asking for their permissive use.

The General Convention, meeting in Seattle, in September 1967, agreed to carry out a complete revision of *The American Prayer Book*. The first report on this revision is to be made to the General Convention of 1970. When this report is submitted, revised rites of Baptism and Confirmation will probably be presented for experimental use.

1 THE MINISTRATION OF HOLY BAPTISM

2 The Minister of every Parish shall often admonish the People, that they defer not the Baptism of their Children, and that it is most convenient that Baptism should be administered upon Sundays and other Holy Days. Nevertheless, if necessity so require, Baptism may be administered upon any other day. And also he shall warn them that, except for urgent cause, they seek not to have their Children baptized in their houses.

3 There shall be for every Male-child to be baptized, when they can be had, two Godfathers and one Godmother; and for every Female, one Godfather and two Godmothers; and Parents shall be admitted as Sponsors, if it be desired.

4 When there are Children to be baptized, the Parents or Sponsors shall give knowledge thereof to the Minister. And then the Godfathers and Godmothers, and the People with the Children, must be ready at the Font, either immediately after the Second Lesson at Morning or Evening Prayer, or at such other time as the Minister shall appoint.

5 When any such Persons as are of riper years are to be baptized, timely notice shall be given to the Minister; that so due care may be taken for their examination, whether they be sufficiently instructed in the Principles of the Christian Religion; and that they may be exhorted to prepare themselves, with Prayers and Fasting for the receiving of this holy Sacrament. And NOTE, That at the time of the Baptism of an Adult, there shall be present with him at the Font at least two Witnesses.

6 The Minister, having come to the Font, which is then to be filled with pure Water, shall say as followeth, the People all standing,

Hath this Child (Person) been already baptized, or no?

7   If they answer, No: then shall the Minister proceed as followeth.

Dearly beloved, forasmuch as our Saviour Christ saith, None can
enter into the kingdom of God, except he be regenerate and born anew
of Water and of the Holy Ghost; I beseech you to call upon God the
Father, through our Lord Jesus Christ, that of his bounteous mercy he
will grant to *this Child* (*this Person*) that which by nature *he* cannot have;
that *he* may be baptized with Water and the Holy Ghost, and received
into Christ's holy Church and be made *a* living *member* of the same.

8   Then shall the Minister say,

Let us pray.

Almighty and immortal God, . . .

CF2, *but this Child* (*this thy Servant*) ⟨*this Infant*⟩

9   Then the Minister shall say as followeth.

Hear the words of the Gospel, written by Saint Mark, in the tenth
Chapter, at the thirteenth Verse.
They brought young children to Christ, . . . (CF3)

10 Or this.

Hear the words of the Gospel, written by Saint John, in the third
Chapter, at the first Verse.

There was a man of the Pharisees, named Nicodemus, a ruler of the
Jews: . . . (John 3. 1–8, AV)

11 Or this.

Hear the words of the Gospel, written by Saint Matthew, in the
twenty-eighth Chapter, at the eighteenth Verse.

Jesus came and spake unto them, . . . (Matt. 28. 18–20, AV)

12 Then shall the Minister say,

And now, being persuaded of the good will of our heavenly Father
toward *this Child* (*this Person*), declared by his Son Jesus Christ; let us
faithfully and devoutly give thanks unto him, and say,

Almighty and everlasting God, . . .

CF4, *but said by Minister and People—this Child* (*this thy servant*) ⟨*this Infant*⟩

13 When the Office is used for Children, the Minister shall speak unto the Godfathers and Godmothers on this wise.

Dearly beloved, ye have brought *this Child* here to be baptized; ye have prayed that our Lord Jesus Christ would vouchsafe to receive *him*, to release *him* from sin, to sanctify *him* with the Holy Ghost, to give *him* the kingdom of heaven, and everlasting life.

Dost thou, therefore, in the name of this Child, renounce the devil and all his works, the vain pomp and glory of the world, with all covetous desires of the same, and the sinful desires of the flesh, so that thou wilt not follow, nor be led by them?

Answer: I renounce them all; and, by God's help, will endeavour not to follow, nor be led by them.

Minister: Dost thou believe all the Articles of the Christian Faith, as contained in the Apostles' Creed?

Answer: I do.

Minister: Wilt thou be baptized in this Faith?

Answer: That is my desire.

Minister: Wilt thou then obediently keep God's holy will and commandments, and walk in the same all the days of thy life?

Answer: I will, by God's help.

Minister: Having now, in the name of this Child, made these promises, wilt thou also on thy part take heed that this Child learn the Creed, the Lord's Prayer, and the Ten Commandments, and all other things which a Christian ought to know and believe to his soul's health?

Answer: I will, by God's help.

Minister: Wilt thou take heed that this Child, so soon as sufficiently instructed, be brought to the Bishop to be confirmed by him?

Answer: I will, God being my helper.

14 When the Office is used for Adults, the Minister shall address them on this wise, the Persons to be baptized answering the questions for themselves.

Well-beloved, you have come hither desiring to receive holy Baptism. We have prayed that our Lord Jesus Christ would vouchsafe to receive you, to release you from sin, to sanctify you with the Holy Ghost, to give you the kingdom of heaven, and everlasting life.

Dost thou renounce the devil and all his works, the vain pomp and glory of the world, with all covetous desires of the same, and the sinful desires of the flesh, so that thou wilt not follow, nor be led by them?

Answer: I renounce them all; and, by God's help, will endeavour not to follow, nor be led by them.

Minister: Dost thou believe in Jesus the Christ, the Son of the Living God?

Answer: I do.

Minister: Dost thou accept him, and desire to follow him as thy Saviour and Lord?

Answer: I do.

Minister: Dost thou believe all the Articles of the Christian Faith, as contained in the Apostles' Creed?

Answer: I do.

Minister: Wilt thou be baptized in this Faith?

Answer: That is my desire.

Minister: Wilt thou then obediently keep God's holy will and commandments, and walk in the same all the days of thy life?

Answer: I will, by God's help.

15 Then shall the Minister say,

O merciful God, grant that like as Christ died and rose again, so *this Child* (*this* thy *Servant*) may die to sin and rise to newness of life. *Amen.*

CF5bcd, *but in b* sinful affections ⟨carnal affections⟩

Minister: The Lord be with you.

Answer: And with thy spirit.

Minister: Lift up your hearts.

Answer: We lift them up unto the Lord.

Minister: Let us give thanks unto our Lord God.

Answer: It is meet and right so to do.

16 Then the Minister shall say,

It is very meet, right, and our bounden duty, that we should give thanks unto thee, O Lord, Holy Father Almighty, Everlasting God, for that thy dearly beloved Son Jesus Christ, for the forgiveness of our sins, did shed out of his most precious side both water and blood; and gave commandment to his disciples, that they should go teach all nations, and baptize them In the Name of the Father, and of the Son, and of the Holy Ghost. Regard, we beseech thee, the supplications of thy congregation; sanctify this Water to the mystical washing away of sin; and grant that *this Child* (*this* thy *Servant*) now to be baptized therein, may receive the fulness of thy grace, and ever remain in the number of thy faithful children; through the same Jesus Christ our Lord, to whom, with thee, in the unity of the Holy Spirit, be all honour and glory, now and evermore. *Amen.*

17   Then the Minister shall take the Child into his arms, and shall say to the Godfathers and Godmothers,

Name this Child.

18   And then, naming the Child after them, he shall dip him in the Water discreetly or shall pour Water upon him, saying,

N. I baptize thee In the Name of the Father, and of the Son, and of the Holy Ghost. Amen.

19   But NOTE, That if the Person to be baptized be an Adult, the Minister shall take him by the hand, and shall ask the Witnesses the Name; and then shall dip him in the Water, or pour Water upon him, using the same form of words.

20   We receive . . .

CF7, *but Child (Person)* ⟨*Child*⟩

21   Seeing now . . .

CF8, *but Child (Person)* ⟨*Child*⟩

22   Our father, who art in heaven, . . . (CF11)

23   Then shall the Minister say,

We yield thee hearty thanks, most merciful Father, that it hath pleased thee to regenerate *this Child* (*this* thy *Servant*) with thy Holy Spirit, to receive *him* for thine own *Child*, and to incorporate *him* into thy holy Church. And humbly we beseech thee to grant, that *he*, being dead unto sin, may live unto righteousness, and being buried with Christ in his death, may also be *partaker* of his resurrection; so that finally, with the residue of thy holy Church, *he* may be *an inheritor* of thine everlasting kingdom; through Christ our Lord. *Amen.*

24   Then the Minister shall add,

The Almighty God, the Father of our Lord Jesus Christ, of whom the whole family in heaven and earth is named; Grant you to be strengthened with might by his Spirit in the inner man; that, Christ dwelling in your hearts by faith, ye may be filled with all the fulness of God. *Amen.*

25   It is expedient that every Adult, thus baptized, should be confirmed by the Bishop, so soon after his Baptism as conveniently may be; that so he may be admitted to the Holy Communion.

1 THE ORDER OF CONFIRMATION
OR LAYING ON OF HANDS UPON THOSE THAT ARE
BAPTIZED AND COME TO YEARS OF DISCRETION

2 Upon the day appointed, all that are to be confirmed, shall stand in order before the Bishop, sitting in his chair near to the Holy Table, the People standing until the Lord's Prayer; and the Minister shall say,

Reverend Father in God, I present unto you these persons to receive the Laying on of Hands.

3 Then the Bishop, or some Minister appointed by him, may say,

Hear the words of the Evangelist Saint Luke, in the eighth Chapter of the Acts of the Apostles:
When the apostles which were at Jerusalem heard that Samaria had received ... (Acts 8.14–17, AV)

4 Then shall the Bishop say,

Do ye here, in the presence of God, and of this congregation, renew the solemn promise and vow that ye made, or that was made in your name at your Baptism; ratifying and confessing the same; and acknowledging yourselves bound to believe and to do all those things which ye then undertook, or your Sponsors then undertook for you?

5 And every one shall audibly answer,

I do.

6 Then shall the Bishop say,

Do ye promise to follow Jesus Christ as your Lord and Saviour?

7 And every one shall anwer,

I do.

8 *Bishop:* Our help is in the name of the Lord;

CF14, *but* prayer ⟨prayers⟩

9 *Bishop:* Let us pray.
Almighty and everliving God, ... (CF15)

10 Then all of them in order kneeling before the Bishop, he shall lay his hand upon the head of every one severally, saying,

Defend, O Lord, ...

CF16, *but omit* (or *this thy Servant*)

11   Then shall the Bishop say,

The Lord be with you,
Answer: **And with thy spirit.**

12   *Bishop:* **Let us pray.**

13   Then shall the Bishop say the Lord's Prayer, the People kneeling and repeating it with him.

Our Father, who art in heaven, . . . (CF11)

14   Then shall the Bishop say,

Almighty and everliving God, who makest us both to will and to do those things which are good . . .

CF17, *but omit* brackets—the same Holy Spirit ⟨Holy Ghost⟩

15   **O almighty Lord, . . . (CF18)**

16   Then the Bishop shall bless them, saying, thus,

The Blessing of God Almighty, . . . (CF19)

17   The Minister shall not omit earnestly to move the Persons confirmed to come, without delay, to the Lord's Supper.

18   And there shall none be admitted to the Holy Communion, until such time as he be confirmed, or ready and desirous to be confirmed.

7. *The Scottish Episcopal Rites 1929*

The official rites of Public Baptism of Infants and the Order of Confirmation in the Episcopal Church of Scotland are contained in *The Scottish Book of Common Prayer*, as approved in September 1929. With a small number of alterations these Rites reproduce those contained in the English PRAYER BOOK *as Proposed in 1928*.

1 THE MINISTRATION OF
PUBLIC BAPTISM OF INFANTS
TO BE USED IN THE CHURCH

2 CANON XXVII OF THE ADMINISTRATION OF HOLY
BAPTISM

In the administration of the Sacrament of Baptism the sponsors must have been themselves baptized, and shall, if possible, be communicants.

In default of others, the parents of the child may be admitted as sponsors, and in case of necessity, of which the Clergyman shall be judge, one sponsor shall be deemed sufficient.

3 Ministers shall often admonish their people that they defer not the Baptism of their children longer than the fourth or fifth Sunday next after their birth, unless upon a great and reasonable cause.

4 It is desirable that Baptism should be administered . . .

1928 IB3, *but* everyone ⟨every man⟩—*omit* for which cause . . . vulgar tongue

5 And note, that there shall be for every male child to be baptized two Godfathers and one Godmother; and for every female, one Godfather and two Godmothers.

6 In the absence of the Priest it is lawful that a Deacon baptize infants. When a Deacon baptizeth instead of the Blessing, where that is provided, he shall say *The Grace*.

7 When there are children to be baptized, the parents shall give due notice to the Priest. He shall thereupon appoint the time for the Baptism, which shall be either immediately after the Second Lesson or after the Third Collect at the Morning or Evening Prayer; or at such other time as he in his discretion shall think fit. And the Minister coming to the Font, (which is then to be filled with pure water,) and standing there shall say,

Hath this child been already baptized or no?

8 If they answer, No: then shall the Minister proceed as followeth.

Beloved in Christ Jesus, we are taught in Holy Scripture that all men from their birth are prone to sin, but that God willeth all men to be saved, for God is love. Seeing therefore that our Saviour Christ saith, None can . . . (1928 IB12)

9 Then shall the Minister say,

Let us pray.

Almighty and everlasting God, . . . (1928 IB13)

10 Or this,

Almighty and immortal God, . . .

CF2, *but* remission of sin ⟨remission of *his* sins⟩

11 Then the Minister shall say,

Hear the Words of the Gospel, written by Saint Mark in the tenth chapter at the thirteenth verse.
Answer: Glory be to thee, O Lord.
They brought young children to Christ, that he should touch them; and his disciples rebuked them. . . . (CF3)
Answer: Thanks be to thee, O Lord, for this thy glorious Gospel.

12 After the Gospel is read, the Minister may make this brief Exhortation upon the words of the Gospel, but if it be omitted he shall say *Let us pray.*

You hear in this Gospel . . . (1928 IB16)

13 Almighty and everlasting God, . . .

CF4, *but* thanks that thou ⟨thanks, for that thou⟩—and faith in thee ⟨and to faith in thee⟩

THE PROMISE

14 Then shall the Minister speak unto the Godfathers and Godmothers on this wise.

Dearly beloved, . . .

1928 IB18, *but* promise ⟨undertake⟩—*for first Answer read* I renounce them all.

15 Then shall be said by the Minister and the Godparents the Apostles' Creed, as followeth:

I believe in God the Father Almighty, . . . (CF12)

16 Minister.

Dost thou, in the name of this child, promise obedience to God's holy will and commandments?
Answer: I do.
Dost thou, in the name of this child, ask for baptism?
Answer: I do.

17 Then shall the Minister say,

O merciful God, . . .

CF5abcd, *but in b* evil desires of the flesh ⟨carnal affections⟩

THE BLESSING OF THE WATER

18 After which the Minister shall proceed, saying,

The Lord be with you;
Answer: And with thy spirit.
Minister: Lift up your hearts;

1928 IB21, *but Minister* ⟨*Priest*⟩—Regard . . . the supplication of thy Congregation ⟨Hear . . . the prayer of thy people⟩

THE BAPTISM

19 Then the Minister shall take the child into his hands, and shall say to the Godfathers and Godmothers,

Name this child.

20 And then naming it after them, he shall dip it in the water, or pour water upon it, saying,

N. I baptize thee in the Name of the Father, and of the Son, and of the Holy Ghost. Amen.

21 Then the Minister shall say,

We receive this child . . . (CF7)

THE THANKSGIVING

22 Then shall the Minister say,

Seeing now, . . .

CF8, *but* born again, and received into the family ⟨regenerate, and grafted into the body⟩

23 Then shall be said by all,

Our Father which art in heaven, . . . (CF11)

24 Then shall the Minister say,

We yield thee hearty thanks, . . .

1928 IB27, *but* incorporate *him* into ⟨make *him* a member of⟩

25 Then may follow this prayer for the Home.

Almighty God, ... (1928 IB28)

THE DUTIES OF THE GODFATHERS AND GODMOTHERS

26 Then the Minister shall say to the Godfathers and Godmothers this Exhortation following.

You who have brought *this child* ...

1928 IB29, *but* blessed Sacrament 〈Holy Communion〉—pray for *this Child* and help *him* 〈help *him*〉

27 When Baptism is administered at Morning or Evening Prayer, then all the prayer after the Third Collect may be omitted.

28 The ministration of Baptism, if used as a separate Service or at the end of Mattins or Evensong, shall be concluded by the Priest with this Blessing:

The blessing of God Almighty, ... (CF19)

29 It is certain by God's word, that children which are baptized, dying before they commit actual sin, are undoubtedly saved.

I THE ORDER OF CONFIRMATION
OR LAYING ON OF HANDS UPON THOSE THAT ARE BAPTIZED
AND COME TO YEARS OF DISCRETION

2 To the end that Confirmation ...

1928 C2, *but* none shall 〈none hereafter shall〉

3 So soon as children ...

1928 C3, *but end* to be confirmed by him.

4 FROM CANON XXIX
OF THE ADMINISTRATION OF CONFIRMATION
OR LAYING ON OF HANDS

2. The Bishop shall give due notice to every Clergyman of the time and place at which Confirmation is to be administered for members of his Congregation, and the Clergyman shall earnestly endeavour to prepare those of his Congregation who are desirous of receiving this Holy Ordinance.
3. Before presenting any candidate for Confirmation, the Clergyman shall satisfy himself that the candidate has been baptized.
4. Not less than seven days before the Confirmation, unless the Bishop dispense with notice, the Clergyman shall give to the Bishop a list of the persons to be presented for Confirmation, and he shall answer any question that may be put to him by the Bishop respecting their ages and qualifications.
5. Each candidate for Confirmation shall, whenever possible, have a Witness present as his Godparent at Confirmation.

THE INTRODUCTION

5 Upon the day appointed the Bishop (or some other Minister appointed by him) shall read this Preface following, unless he shall otherwise determine.

Dearly beloved in the Lord, ... (CF20)

THE RENEWAL OF BAPTISMAL VOWS

6 Then shall the Bishop say,

Dost thou renounce the devil and all his works, the vain pomp and glory of the world, with all covetous desires of the same, and the sinful desires of the flesh, so that thou wilt not follow nor be led by them?
Answer: I do.
Dost thou believe the Christian Faith as contained in the Apostles' Creed?
Answer: I do.

7 Then shall be said by the Candidates, with the Bishop, as followeth;

I believe in God the Father Almighty, . . . (CF12)

8 The Bishop.

Dost thou promise that thou wilt endeavour to keep God's holy will and commandments, and to walk in the same all the days of thy life?
Answer: I do.

THE CONFIRMATION

9 No Instruction or Hymn shall intervene between *Our help, etc.* and the Laying on of hands, but a Hymn may be sung in the course of the Laying on of hands.

10 The Bishop.

Our help is in the Name of the Lord; (CF14)

11 The Bishop.

Let us pray.

Almighty and Everliving God, . . . (CF15)

12 Sign them, O Lord, and mark them to be thine for ever by the virtue of the holy cross; mercifully confirm them with the inward unction of the Holy Ghost, that they may attain unto everlasting life. *Amen.*

13 Then all of them in order kneeling before the Bishop, he shall lay his hand upon the head of every one severally, saying,

N. I sign thee with the sign of the cross★ and I lay my hands (*or* hand) upon thee, In the Name of the Father, and of the Son, and of the Holy Ghost.

★ Here the Bishop shall sign the person with the sign of the cross on the forehead.

14 Defend, O Lord, . . .

CF16, *but omit* (or *this thy Servant*)

15   Then shall the Bishop say,

The Lord be with you:
Answer: And with thy spirit.

16   And (the people kneeling down) the Bishop shall add,

Let us pray.

Bishop and people

Our Father which art in heaven, . . . (CF9)

17   And this Collect.

Almighty and Everliving God, . . . (CF17)

THE DISMISSAL

18   O almighty Lord, . . . (CF18)

19   Then the Bishop shall bless them saying thus,

The blessing of God Almighty, . . . (CF19)

20   And there shall none be admitted to the Holy Communion, until such time as he be confirmed, or be ready and desirous to be confirmed.

21   When Confirmation is administered at Morning or Evening Prayer, then all the prayers after the Third Collect may be omitted.

8. The Church of India, Pakistan, Burma, and Ceylon Rites 1951

Liturgical revision in the Church of India, Pakistan, Burma, and Ceylon, began soon after it became an autonomous Province of the Anglican Communion in 1930. At the first meeting of the Provincial Synod the 1928 English Prayer Book was authorized for general use. In 1945 the Episcopal Synod of the Province instructed the Liturgical Committee to begin work on a completely new Prayer Book. The work of this Committee was examined, and partially revised, by the Episcopal Synod at Calcutta in 1951. The Synod then authorized the publication and experimental use of the new book, which was issued under the title: A PROPOSED PRAYER BOOK, *Containing Forms of Worship, Supplementary and Alternative to the Book of Common Prayer, authorized by the Episcopal Synod of the Church of India, Pakistan, Burma, and Ceylon in 1951.*

1 THE MINISTRATION OF HOLY BAPTISM
GENERAL RUBRICS

2 It is desirable where possible that Baptism should be administered upon Sundays and other Feast Days, when the most number of people come together; as well for that the congregation there present may testify the receiving of them that be newly baptized into the number of Christ's Church; as also that in the ministration of Baptism every man present may be put in remembrance of his own profession made to God in his Baptism; for which cause it is expedient that Baptism be ministered in the vulgar tongue. Nevertheless (for sufficient cause) Baptism may be ministered upon any other day.

3 The ordinary rule of the Church of the Province of India, Pakistan, Burma, and Ceylon with regard to the qualifications of Godparents is that they must be communicant members of this Church, as laid down in Canon 29 of 1603:

"No person shall be admitted Godfather or Godmother to any child at Christening or Confirmation, before the said person so undertaking hath received the Holy Communion."

It is the duty of the Parish Priest to impress on all intending Godparents the solemnity of the obligation which they will take on themselves; and it is within the competence of the Parish Priest not to accept as sponsors those whose fitness to undertake the responsibilities he has serious reason to doubt (Resolution 15 of the Episcopal Synod of 1942).

4 When any persons of riper years are to be baptized, timely notice shall be given by the Parish Priest to the Bishop, or whom he shall appoint for that purpose, so that after due inquiry his permission may be given. Due care shall be taken for their examination, whether they be sufficiently instructed in the principles of the Christian religion, and they shall be exhorted to prepare themselves with prayers and fasting for the receiving of this Holy Sacrament.

5 And note, that for every person of riper years, who is found fit, there shall be three

Godfathers or Godmothers; and for every male child to be baptized there shall be two Godfathers and one Godmother; and for every female, one Godfather and two Godmothers. Parents, if need so require, may be sponsors for their own child, provided that the child have at least one other sponsor.

6   The Parish Priest shall often admonish the people that they bring their children to Baptism as soon as possible after birth, and that they defer not the Baptism longer than the fourth, or at furthest the fifth, Sunday unless upon a great and reasonable cause.

7   When there are children to be baptized, the Parents shall give due notice thereof to the Parish Priest. He shall thereupon appoint the time for the Baptism. Then the Godfathers and Godmothers, and the people with the children, must be ready at the Font either immediately after the last Lesson, or after the Collects at Morning or Evening Prayer; or at such other time as he in his discretion shall think fit. And in the same way he shall appoint a time for the Baptism of such as be of riper years.

8   In the absence of the Priest it is lawful that a Deacon baptize infants.

9   THE MINISTRATION OF HOLY BAPTISM

10   All stand throughout, unless otherwise directed.

11   When the people are gathered at the Font (which is to be filled with pure water), the Priest shall ask the Godparents and Parents,

12   Has this person (child) been already baptized, or no?

13   If they answer, No: then the Priest shall speak to them of the meaning and purpose of Baptism, saying

Dearly beloved, forasmuch as our Saviour Christ saith, . . . (CF1)

14   Then shall the Priest say one or both of these prayers following,

Let us pray.

Almighty and immortal God, . . .

CF2, *but this person (child) ⟨this Infant⟩ throughout the service*—remission of sin ⟨remission of *his* sins⟩—*omit* Receive him . . . that knock; that *this Infant*—*continue* Grant that he may enjoy . . .

15   Almighty and everlasting God, . . . (1662 IB6)

16   Then shall the Priest read one of the Gospels appointed below. Before the Gospel he shall say,

Hear the words of the Gospel, written by Saint *N.*, in the . . . chapter, at the . . . verse.
Answer: Glory be to thee, O Lord.
For Adults: St John 3.1.
There was a man of the Pharisees, . . . (John 3.1–8, AV)
Or, St Matthew 28.18.
Jesus came and spake unto them, . . . (Matt. 28.18–20, AV)

For Children: St Mark 10.13.
They brought young children to Christ, . . . (CF3)

17 The Gospel being ended, the people shall say,

Praise be to thee, O Christ.

18 *Priest:* Beloved, being persuaded of the good will of our heavenly
Father towards *this person* (*child*), declared by his Son Jesus Christ, let
us faithfully and devoutly give thanks unto him, and say together,
Priest and people: Almighty and everlasting God, . . . (CF4)

THE PROMISES

19 Here, when the Office is used for *Adults,* or *Children able to answer for themselves*,
the Priest shall speak to the persons to be baptized on this wise:

Well-beloved, who are come hither desiring to receive Holy Baptism,
you have heard how the congregation has prayed, that our Lord Jesus
Christ would vouchsafe to receive you and bless you, to release you of
your sins, to give you the kingdom of heaven, and everlasting life.
Our Lord Jesus Christ has promised to grant all these things; which
promise he, for his part, will most surely keep and perform.

I ask therefore in the presence of these your witnesses and this whole
congregation,

20 When the Office is used for *Children who are not able to answer for themselves*, the
Priest shall speak to the Parents and Godparents on this wise:

Dearly beloved, you have brought *this child* here to be baptized, you
have prayed that our Lord Jesus Christ would vouchsafe to receive
him, to release *him* of *his sins*, to sanctify *him* with the Holy Ghost, to
give *him* the kingdom of heaven, and everlasting life. Our Lord Jesus
Christ has promised to grant all these things; which promise he, for his
part, will most surely keep and perform.

Answer therefore on behalf of *this child*,

21 Do you renounce the devil and all his works?
Answer: I renounce them.
Do you renounce the vain pomp and glory of the world, with all
covetous desires of the same?
Answer: I renounce them.
Do you renounce the sinful desires of the flesh, so that you will not
follow nor be led by them?
Answer: I renounce them.

Do you believe in God the Father Almighty, Maker of heaven and earth?

Answer: I believe.

Do you believe in Jesus Christ his only-begotten Son our Lord? And that he was conceived by the Holy Ghost; born of the Virgin Mary; that he suffered under Pontius Pilate, was crucified, dead, and buried; that he went down into hell, and also did rise again the third day; that he ascended into heaven, and sitteth at the right hand of God the Father Almighty; and from thence shall come again at the end of the world, to judge the quick and the dead? Do you believe this?

Answer: I believe.

Do you believe in the Holy Ghost; the holy Catholic Church; the Communion of Saints; the Remission of sins; the Resurrection of the body; and everlasting life after death?

Answer: I believe.

Will you be baptized in this faith?

Answer: That is my desire.

Will you then obediently keep God's holy will and commandments, and walk in the same all the days of your life?

Answer: I will.

22   Then shall the Priest say unto the Parents and Godparents,

Having now in the name of *this child* made these promises, will you also for your part take heed that *this child* learn the Creed, the Lord's Prayer, and the Ten Commandments, and all other things which a Christian ought to know and believe to his soul's health?

Answer: I will, by God's help.

Will you take heed that *this child*, so soon as *he* is sufficiently instructed, be brought to the Bishop to be confirmed by him?

Answer: I will, God being my helper.

THE BLESSING OF THE WATER

23   Then shall the Priest say,

O merciful God, grant that the old Adam in *him* who shall be baptized in this water may be so buried, that the new man may be raised up in *him. Amen.*

Grant that . . .

CF5bcd, *but in b* evil desires of the flesh ⟨carnal affections⟩

24 After which the Priest shall proceed, saying,

The Lord be with you;

1928 IB21, *but* through the same Jesus Christ ⟨through Jesus Christ⟩

THE BAPTISM

25 If an infant is to be baptized, the Priest shall take it into his arms: otherwise he shall take the person to be baptized by the right hand: and shall then say to the God-parents,

Name this person (child).

26 And then naming him after them, he shall dip him in the water, or pour water upon him, saying,

N. I baptize thee In the name of the Father, and of the Son, and of the Holy Ghost, Amen.

27 Then shall the Priest say,

We receive this person (child) into the congregation of Christ's flock, ✠ and do sign *him* with the sign of the Cross, ✠ Here the Priest shall make a Cross upon the person's (child's) forehead.
*in token that hereafter *he* shall not be ashamed to confess the faith of Christ crucified, and manfully to fight under his banner, against sin, the world, and the devil; and to continue Christ's faithful soldier and servant unto *his* life's end, Amen.*

(* . . . * Where there are several persons or children baptized these words may be omitted, and after the baptism of the last the Priest shall say for all of them:

We have received these *persons* (*children*) into the congregation of Christ's flock, and have signed them with the sign of the Cross, in token that hereafter they shall not be ashamed to confess the faith of Christ crucified, and manfully to fight under his banner, against sin, the world, and the devil; and to continue Christ's faithful soldiers and servants unto their lives' end. Amen.)

28 Then (or immediately after the Baptism) the Godparents may put upon each candidate a white vesture, and when the candidate or candidates be so vested, the Priest shall say,

Take this white vesture for a token of innocency, which by God's grace in this holy Sacrament of Baptism is given unto you: and for a sign whereby you are admonished to give yourself henceforth to innocency of living, that after this transitory life you may be *partaker* of the life everlasting. *Amen.*

29   Then the Priest may deliver to each candidate a lighted taper, saying,

Receive this burning light, in token that you have been made *the child* of God and of the light by faith in Jesus Christ. Preserve the grace of your Baptism without reproach; keep the commandments, that you may walk worthy of your Christian calling; remembering always that Baptism represents unto us our profession, which is, to follow the example of our Saviour Christ, and to be made like unto him. *Amen.*

THE THANKSGIVING

30   Then shall the Priest say,

Seeing now, . . . (CF8)

31   Then shall be said by Priest and people together,

Our Father, which art in heaven, . . . (CF11)

32   Then shall the Priest say,

We yield thee hearty thanks, . . .

CF10, *but omit* he being dead . . . death of thy Son *and end* through the same Jesus Christ our lord. *Amen.*

33   Here, when a child is baptized may follow this Prayer for the Home:

Almighty God, . . . (1928 IB28)

34   If a husband and wife are baptized together, this Prayer may be said:

O God, who hast taught us that it should never be lawful to put asunder those whom thou by Matrimony hadst made one, and hast consecrated the state of Matrimony to such an excellent mystery, that in it is signified and represented the spiritual marriage and unity betwixt Christ and his Church: Look mercifully upon these thy servants, that both *this man* may love *his wife*, according to thy Word, (as Christ did love his spouse the Church, who gave himself for it, loving and cherishing it even as his own flesh,) and also that *this woman* may be loving and amiable, and faithful to *her husband*; and in all quietness, sobriety, and peace, be a *follower* of holy and godly matrons. O Lord, bless them (both), and grant them to inherit thy everlasting kingdom; through the same Jesus Christ our Lord. *Amen.*

35   Then, if the Baptism be administered otherwise than at Morning or Evening Prayer, the Priest shall dismiss those that are gathered together with this Blessing:

May God Almighty, the Father of our Lord Jesus Christ, from whom every family in heaven and on earth is named, grant you to be strengthened with might by his Spirit in the inner man; that Christ may dwell in your hearts through faith, and ye may be filled unto all the fulness of God. *Amen.*

36 It is expedient that every Adult thus baptized should be confirmed by the Bishop, so soon after his Baptism as conveniently may be, that so he may be admitted to the Holy Communion: save in circumstance where further instruction in preparation for Confirmation is deemed desirable.

37 It is certain by God's Word, that children which are baptized, dying before they commit actual sin, are undoubtedly saved.

38 If a child that has been privately baptized be brought to the church at the same time with a child that is to be baptized, the Priest, having certified the sufficiency of the Private Baptism, shall begin the Ministration of Holy Baptism; and in due course shall put the appointed questions to the sponsors of the children; save that the question *Will you be baptized in this faith?* be not asked of the sponsors of the child already baptized. Then having baptized and received the child that had not been baptized, he shall receive the child that had been privately baptized. Which done, he shall proceed with the rest of the Ministration of Holy Baptism.

THE ORDER OF CONFIRMATION
OR LAYING ON OF HANDS UPON THOSE THAT ARE
BAPTIZED AND COME TO YEARS OF DISCRETION

GENERAL RUBRICS

2 To the end that Confirmation ...

1928 C2, *but has* ⟨*hath*⟩

3 So soon as children ... (1928 C3)

4 The Minister shall ... (1928 C4)

5 And whensoever the Bishop shall give notice for children or others to be brought unto him for their Confirmation, every Parish Priest shall either bring, or send in writing, with his hand subscribed thereto, the names and ages of all such persons within his parish, of whose baptism he is well assured, whom he shall think fit to be presented to the Bishop to be confirmed. And, if the Bishop approve of them, he shall confirm them in the manner following. When there is any doubt concerning the Baptism of any such person, he shall be conditionally baptized, as enjoined in the rubric at the end of the Form for the Public Receiving of such as have been Privately Baptized.

6 It is convenient ... (1928 C6)

7 And there shall none ... (1928 C7)

8 When Unction is used, the Bishop may make the sign of the Cross with the Holy Chrism on the foreheads of the candidates after the words, *Defend, O Lord,* The alternative Form for the Laying on of Hands appended to this Service may also be used with or without the Holy Chrism.

9   THE ORDER OF CONFIRMATION

10   At the time of the Confirmation, when the Bishop is seated in his chair, the Priests in order shall cause their candidates to stand and present them before the Bishop, saying,

Reverend Father in God, I present unto you these persons to receive the laying on of hands.

The Bishop: Take heed that the persons whom you present be duly prepared, and meet to receive the laying on of hands.

Priest: I have instructed them, and enquired of them, and believe them so to be.

11   Then the Bishop, or some Minister appointed by him, shall say,

Dearly beloved in the Lord, . . .

CF20, *but ending at* . . . received the Holy Ghost.

THE RENEWAL OF BAPTISMAL VOWS

12   Then shall the Bishop ask the following questions:

Do you here in the presence of God, and of this congregation, renounce the devil and all his works, the pomps and vanity of this wicked world, and all the sinful lusts of the flesh, so that you will not follow nor be led by them?
Answer: I do
Do you believe all the Articles of the Christian Faith as contained in the Apostles' Creed?
Answer: I do.
Will you endeavour to keep God's holy will and commandments, and to walk in the same all the days of your life?
Answer: I will.
Do you acknowledge yourselves bound to confess the faith of Christ crucified, to fight manfully under his banner, and to continue his faithful soldiers and servants unto your life's end, bearing witness to him both in word and deed?
Answer: I do.

13   Or else the Bishop shall say,

Do you here, in the presence of God, and of this congregation, renew the solemn promise and vow that was made at your Baptism; acknowledging yourselves bound to confess the faith of Christ crucified, to fight manfully under his banner, and to continue his faithful soldiers and servants unto your life's end, bearing witness to him both in word and in deed?

14 And every one shall audibly answer,

I do.

THE CONFIRMATION

15 Then shall the Bishop begin the Confirmation; and no Hymn or Address shall be introduced into this part of the Service, except that a Hymn may be sung, if needed, in the course of the laying on of hands.

16 *The Bishop.* Our help is in the name of the Lord;

CF14, *but throughout read The Bishop*

17 The Bishop.
Let us pray.

Almighty and everliving God, . . . (CF15)

18 Then all of them in order kneeling before the Bishop, he shall lay his hand upon the head of everyone severally, saying,

Defend, O Lord, . . .

CF16, *but omit* (or *this thy Servant*)

19 Then shall the Bishop say,

The peace of the Lord abide with you;
Answer: And with thy spirit.

20 Let us pray.
Our Father, which art in heaven, . . . (CF11)

21 Then shall the Bishop add these Prayers,

Almighty and everliving God, . . . (CF17)

THE CONCLUSION

22 O almighty Lord, . . . (CF18)

23 Then the Bishop may deliver the following charge,

Go forth into the world in peace; . . .

1928 C20, *but ending at* . . . power of the Holy Spirit.

24 After which he shall bless them, saying,

The blessing of God Almighty, . . . (CF19)

1 ALTERNATIVE FORM FOR
   THE LAYING ON OF HANDS

2 After the *Amen* following the prayer for the sevenfold gift of the Holy Spirit, the
   Bishop shall say,

Sign them, O Lord, and mark them to be thine for ever by the virtue
of Christ's holy Cross and Passion; mercifully seal them with the
inward unction of the Holy Ghost, that they may attain unto everlasting life. *Amen.*

3 Then the Bishop shall make the sign of the Cross on their foreheads, with or without the Holy Chrism, at his discretion, and lay his hand on their heads, saying,

N. I sign thee ✠ with the sign of the Cross, and lay my hand upon
thee; In the name of the Father, and of the Son, and of the Holy Ghost.
Amen.

4 When he has laid his hand on every candidate, the Bishop shall say,

Defend, O Lord, these thy children with thy heavenly grace, that they
may continue thine for ever; and daily increase in thy Holy Spirit
more and more, until they come unto thy everlasting kingdom. Amen.

9. *The South African Rites 1954*

While the 1662 BCP is still the official Prayer Book in South Africa, this Book is hardly ever used. Its place has been taken by the present South African Prayer Book, which is a revision of the 1662 BCP, undertaken between 1918–1950. Originally the revised South African Rites came out in separate booklets, and were bound in a single volume by O.U.P. in 1954. The Rites of Infant Baptism and Confirmation contained in this book are those in general use at the present time. The Baptismal Rite follows that found in *Revised Prayer Book (Permissive Use) Measure* (N.A.84); where it differs from N.A.84, it follows the proposals made by the Alcuin Club "Orange Book".[1] The main features taken from the "Orange Book" are: a eucharistic form for blessing the font, the giving of the chrysom, and the lighted taper.

When these texts, which are to be regarded as alternatives to those in the 1662 BCP are used, they must be used in their entirety, and not adapted. They are reproduced from A BOOK OF COMMON PRAYER . . . , *set forth by authority for use in the Church of the Province of South Africa, 1954.*

1 THE MINISTRATION OF
PUBLICK BAPTISM OF INFANTS
TO BE USED IN THE CHURCH

2 The Curate . . .

1928 IB2, *but Curate* ⟨*Minister*⟩

3 It is desirable . . . (1928 IB3)

4 And note, . . .

1928 IB4 *but ending*
provided that there be one other sponsor. In no case shall any person be admitted to be a sponsor who is unbaptized; and it is plainly the intention of the Church that all sponsors should be communicant members of the Church.

5 If the Priest be absent it is lawful that a Deacon baptize infants.

6 When there are children to be baptized, the Parents shall give due notice thereof to the Priest. He shall thereupon appoint the time for the Baptism, which shall be immediately after the last lesson at Morning or Evening Prayer; or at such other time as he in his discretion shall think fit.

7 And the Priest, coming to the Font, (which is then to be filled with pure water,) and standing there shall say to the Sponsors,

8 Has this child been already baptized or no?

[1] *A Survey of the Proposals for the Alternative Prayer Book. Part II. Occasional Offices.* Alcuin Pamphlet, XIII.

9   If they answer, *No*:

Will you take care, to the best of your ability, that this child be brought up as a faithful member of Christ's holy Church?
Answer: I will.

10   Then shall the Priest proceed as follows:

Seeing that all men are born with a sinful nature; and that our Saviour Christ saith, None can enter into the kingdom of God, except he be born anew of water and of the Holy Ghost; I beseech you to call upon God the Father, through our Lord Jesus Christ, that of his bounteous mercy he will grant unto *this child* that which by nature *he* cannot have; that *he* may be baptized with Water and the Holy Ghost, and received into Christ's holy Church, and be made *a living member* of the same.

11   While all continue standing, the Priest shall say one or both of the prayers following.

Almighty and everlasting God, . . .

1928 IB13, *but* Holy Ghost ⟨Holy Spirit⟩—rooted in love ⟨rooted in charity⟩

Almighty and immortal God, . . .

CF2, *but* everlasting grace ⟨remission of his sins⟩—that *this Infant,* being cleansed and hallowed by the heavenly washing may come ⟨that *this Infant* may enjoy the everlasting benediction of thy heavenly washing, and may come⟩

12   Then the Priest shall say,

Hear the words of the Gospel, written by Saint Mark, in the tenth chapter, at the thirteenth verse.
Answer. Glory be to thee, O Lord.
They brought young children to Christ, . . . (CF3)

13   Then shall the people say,

Thanks be to thee, O Lord.

14   After the Gospel is read, the Priest shall make this brief Exhortation upon the words of the Gospel.

You hear in this Gospel the words of our Saviour Christ, when he commanded the children to be brought unto him. You perceive how he took them in his arms, and blessed them. He is the same yesterday, to day, and for ever. Doubt you not therefore, but earnestly believe, that he loves *this child,* that he approves this work of ours in bringing *him* to Holy Baptism, that he is ready to receive *him,* to embrace *him* with the arms of his mercy, and to give *him* the blessing of eternal life. Wherefore let us faithfully and devoutly give thanks unto him, and say,

15 Then shall the Priest and people, still standing, repeat together,

Almighty and everlasting God, ...

CF4, *but* thanks that thou hast called us ⟨for that thanks that thou hast vouchsafed to call us⟩—and to faith in thee ⟨and faith in thee⟩

THE PROMISES

16 Then shall the Priest speak to the Godfathers and Godmothers on this wise,

Dearly beloved, you have brought *this child* here to be baptized, you have prayed that our Lord Jesus Christ would vouchsafe to receive *him*, to cleanse *him*, and to sanctify *him*. Our Lord has promised in his Gospel to grant all these things that you have prayed for; which promise he, for his part, will most surely keep and perform.

You, on your part, must promise in the name of *this infant*, three things: first, that *he* will renounce the devil and all his works; secondly, that *he* will constantly believe God's holy Word; and thirdly, that *he* will obediently keep his commandments.

I demand therefore,

Dost thou, in the name of this child, renounce the devil and all his works, the vain pomp and glory of the world, with the covetous desires of the same, and the carnal desires of the flesh, so that thou wilt not follow, nor be led by them?
Answer: I renounce them all.
Dost thou believe in God the Father Almighty, Maker of heaven and earth?
Answer: I do.
Dost thou believe in Jesus Christ his only Son our Lord; and that he was conceived by the Holy Ghost, born of the Virgin Mary; that he suffered under Pontius Pilate, was crucified, dead, and buried; that he descended into hell, and also did rise again the third day from the dead; that he ascended into heaven, and sitteth at the right hand of God the Father Almighty; and from thence shall come again at the end of the world to judge the quick and the dead?
Answer: I do.
Dost thou believe in the Holy Ghost; The holy Catholick Church;

The Communion of Saints; The Forgiveness of sins; The Resurrection of the Body; And the Life everlasting?
Answer: I do.
Dost thou in the name of this child profess this faith?
Answer: I do.
Dost thou promise in *his* name obedience to God's holy will and commandments?
Answer: I do.
Dost thou in *his* name ask for baptism?
Answer: I do.

17 Then the Priest shall say,

O merciful God, ...

CF5abcd, *but in b* evil desires of the flesh ⟨carnal affections⟩—*in d* Grant that *he* being dedicated ⟨Grant that whosoever is here dedicated⟩

THE BLESSING OF THE WATER

18 *Priest.* The Lord be with you; ...

1928 IB21, *but* Regard ... the supplications of thy congregation ⟨Hear ... the prayer of thy people⟩

THE BAPTISM

19 Then shall the Priest take the child into his arms, or by the hand, and shall say to the Godfathers and Godmothers,

Name this child.

20 And then naming it after them he shall dip it in the water, or pour water upon it, saying,

N. I baptize thee In the name of the Father, and of the Son, and of the Holy Ghost. Amen.

21 Then shall the Priest say,

We receive this child ... (CF7)

22 (If it is so desired, the Priest shall put upon the child the white vesture commonly called the Chrysom, saying,

We give this white vesture, a token of the innocency bestowed upon thee, and for a sign whereby thou art admonished to give thyself to pureness of living, that after this transitory life thou mayest be partaker of the life everlasting.

23 And shall give to him, or to the Godfather, a lighted candle, saying,

Receive the light of Christ, that when the Bridegroom cometh thou mayest go forth with all the saints to meet him; and see that thou keep the grace of thy baptism.)

THE THANKSGIVING

24 Then shall the Priest say,

Seeing how, dearly beloved brethren, that *this child* is born again, . . . (CF8)

25 Then shall be said by all, standing,

Our Father who art in heaven, . . . (CF11)

26 Then shall the Priest say,

We yield thee hearty thanks, . . .

1928 IB27, *but omit Amen and continue:*

Grant, O Lord, that *he*, being buried with Christ by baptism and made *partaker* of his death, may also be *partaker* of his resurrection; that, serving thee here in newness of life, *he* may finally, with the rest of thy holy Church, come to thine everlasting kingdom; through Jesus Christ our Lord. *Amen.*

27 After which the Priest may add,

Let us pray for *this child's home.*
O heavenly Father, after whom all fatherhood in heaven and earth is named, bless, we beseech thee, the parents of *this child* and give to them and to all in whose charge *he* may be, the spirit of wisdom and love, that *his home* may be to *him* an image of thy kingdom, and the care of *his* parents a likeness of thy love; through Jesus Christ our Lord. *Amen.*

28 Then the Priest shall say to the Godfathers, Godmothers, and Parents this Exhortation following.

You who have brought *this child* to be baptized into the family of Christ's Church, must see that *he* be taught the meaning of the promises which have been made in *his* name, that *he* learn the things which a Christian ought to know, to believe, and to do, for the sake of *his* soul's welfare.

See especially that *he* be taught the Creed, the Lord's Prayer, and the Ten Commandments, as set forth in the Church Catechism, and that *he* be virtuously brought up to lead a godly and a Christian life. Take care that *he* be brought to the Bishop in due time to be confirmed by him; so that, strengthened with the gift of the Holy Spirit, *he* may come with due preparation to receive the most comfortable sacrament of the Body and Blood of Christ.

Remember always that Baptism represents unto us our Christian profession, which is to follow the example of our Saviour Christ, and to be made like unto him; that as he died and rose again for us, so should we, who are baptized, die unto sin and rise again unto righteousness, continually mortifying all evil desires, and daily advancing in all virtue and godliness of living.

29 If the Baptism be not joined to another service, the Minister shall pronounce the Blessing, the people kneeling:

The Lord bless you,... (1928 IB30)

30 It is certain by God's Word, that children who are baptized, dying before they commit actual sin, are undoubtedly saved.

31 When Baptism is administered at Morning or Evening Prayer, then all the prayers after the Third Collect may be omitted, except the Prayer of St Chrysostom and the Grace of our Lord Jesus Christ, etc.

32 If a child that has been privately baptized be brought to the church at the same time with a child that is to be baptized, the Priest, having certified the sufficiency of Private Baptism, shall begin the Order of the Ministration of Publick Baptism of Infants; putting the appointed questions to the sponsors of both the children; save that the question, "Do you in his name ask for baptism?" be not asked of the sponsors of the child already baptized. Then, having baptized and received the child that has not been baptized, he shall demand the name of the child that has been privately baptized and receive him. Which done, he shall proceed with the rest of the Order of Publick Baptism.

I THE ORDER OF CONFIRMATION
OR LAYING ON OF HANDS UPON THOSE THAT ARE
BAPTIZED AND COME TO YEARS OF DISCRETION

2 To the end that Confirmation may be ministered to the more edifying of such as shall receive it, the Church has thought good to order, that those who come to be confirmed by the Bishop shall have been instructed in the Creed, the Lord's Prayer, and the Ten Commandments, as well as the law of Christian life, and the two Sacraments of the Gospel; and can also answer to such questions, as in the short Catechism are contained: which order is very convenient to be observed; to the end that when children have reached years of understanding, and have learned what their Godfathers and Godmothers promised for them in Baptism, they may themselves, with their own mouth, and consent, openly before the Church, ratify and renew the same; and also promise, that by the grace of God they will evermore endeavour themselves faithfully to observe such things, as they by their own confession have assented unto.

3 The Curate...

1928 C4, *but Curate* ⟨Minister⟩

4 It is desirable... (1928 C6)

5 And whensoever the Bishop shall give notice that he will minister Confirmation, the Curate of every Parish shall either bring, or send in writing, with his hand subscribed thereunto, the names of all such persons within his Parish as he shall think fit to be presented to the Bishop to be confirmed. And, if the Bishop approve of them, he shall confirm them in the manner following.

6 The service shall be said from the words *Our help is*, etc., down to the Laying on of Hands by the Bishop, without any interruption by preaching or other instruction, or by the singing of any hymn or anthem.

7 Upon the day appointed, all that are then to be confirmed, being placed, and standing in order, before the Bishop, he (or some other Minister appointed by him) shall read the following Introduction, unless he shall otherwise determine.

THE INTRODUCTION

8 Dearly beloved in the Lord, in ministering Confirmation the Church follows the example of the Apostles of Christ, For in the eighth chapter of the Acts of the Apostles we thus read: . . .

CF20, *but for* The Scripture . . . hath pledged you. *read,*

Holy Scripture here teaches us that in Confirmation there is both an outward sign, which is the laying on of hands with prayer, and an inward grace, which is the strengthening gift of the Holy Spirit. And, forasmuch as this gift comes from God alone, let us make our supplications to Almighty God, as the Apostles did, that he will pour forth his Spirit upon these persons who in Baptism were made his children by adoption and grace.

Furthermore, in order that this congregation may be assured that you who are to be confirmed stedfastly purpose to confess the faith of Christ crucified and to serve loyally under his banner; and that you yourselves may ever have printed in your remembrance what is your calling and how greatly you need the continual help of the Holy Spirit, the Church has thought good to order that, before you receive the laying on of hands, you shall openly acknowledge yourselves bound to fulfil the Christian duties to which Holy Baptism has pledged you.

THE QUESTION

9 Then shall the Bishop say,

Do you here, in the presence of God, and of this congregation, renounce the devil, the world, and the flesh, so that you will not follow nor be led by them?
Answer: I do.

Do you believe the Christian Faith as contained in the Apostles' Creed?

Answer: I do.

Do you purpose as a loyal member of Christ's holy Church, to keep God's will and commandments, and to walk in the same all the days of your life?

Answer: I do.

10   These three questions may be put together with one answer *I do.* Or else the Bishop shall say,

Do you here, in the presence of God, and of this congregation, renew the solemn promise and vow that was made in your name at your Baptism; ratifying the same in your own persons, and acknowledging yourselves bound to believe, and to do, all those things, which your Godfathers and Godmothers then undertook for you?

11   And every one shall answer audibly,

I do.

12   Here may be sung *Veni Creator Spiritus,* or some other hymn to the Holy Spirit, all kneeling.

THE CONFIRMATION

13   Then shall the Bishop confirm on this wise:

The Bishop: Our help is in the name of the Lord; . . .

CF14, *but* prayer ⟨prayers⟩

14   The Bishop:
                              Let us pray.

Almighty and everliving God, . . . (CF15)

15   Then all of them kneeling in order before the Bishop, he (may sign them upon the forehead, using at this discretion the Holy Chrism, and saying, *N.* I sign thee with the sign of the Cross, and I lay my hand upon thee, and) shall lay his hand upon their heads, saying,

Defend, O Lord, . . .

CF16, *but omit* (or *this thy Servant*)

16   And when all have been confirmed, then the Bishop may make the following declaration, all standing:

Beloved, you have now, in the presence of God, who knows and sees all, ratified the promises of your Baptism, and have received of God the gift of his Holy Spirit.

Wherefore I pronounce that you be admitted to receive the Communion of the Body and Blood of Christ: In the name of the Father, and of the Son, and of the Holy Ghost. The Lord grant you his grace to consecrate your whole life and all your powers to his will and service in Christ Jesus.

17 Then the Bishop shall say,

The Lord be with you.
Answer: And with thy spirit.

18 And the people kneeling, the Bishop shall add,

Let us pray.
Our Father who art in heaven, . . . (CF11)

19 And this Collect,

Almighty and everliving God, . . .

CF17, *but omit* to certify . . . goodness towards them.

20 O almighty and most merciful God, of thy bountiful goodness, keep us, we beseech thee, from all things that may hurt us; that we, being ready both in body and soul, may cheerfully accomplish those things that thou wouldest have done; through Jesus Christ our Lord. *Amen.*

21 Or,

O Almighty Lord, . . . (CF18)

22 Then the Bishop shall bless them, saying,

Go forth into the world in peace; be of good courage; fight the good fight of faith; that you may finish your course with joy.
And the blessing of God Almighty, the Father, the Son, and the Holy Ghost, be upon you, and remain with you for ever. *Amen.*

23 And there shall none be admitted to Holy Communion, until such time as he be confirmed, or be ready and desirous to be confirmed.

10. *The Canadian Rites 1959*

These texts are from THE BOOK OF COMMON PRAYER and *Administration of The Sacraments and Other Rites and Ceremonies of The Church, according to the use of The Anglican Church of Canada*, as revised in 1959.

While further revision of the Canadian Prayer Book is being carried out, it is thought that it will be some time before a new Prayer Book is produced.

1 THE MINISTRATION OF HOLY BAPTISM TO CHILDREN
TO BE USED IN THE CHURCH

2 The Minister of the Parish shall often admonish the people that they bring their children to the Church for Baptism as soon as possible after birth; and that except for urgent cause and necessity they seek not to have their children baptized in their houses.

3 It is fitting that Baptism should be administered upon Sundays and other Holy-days at a public Service, so that the Congregation may witness the receiving of the newly baptized into the number of Christ's Church, and also may be reminded of the benefits which they themselves received and the profession which they made in holy Baptism.

4 There shall be for every male child to be baptized two Godfathers and one Godmother; and for every female, one Godfather and two Godmothers. Nevertheless, when three Sponsors cannot be had, one Godfather and one Godmother shall suffice. Parents, if necessity so require, may be Sponsors for their own child. The Sponsors shall be baptized persons and able to make the promises required.

5 In the absence of a Priest, it is lawful for a Deacon to baptize children.

6 When there are children to be baptized, the Parents shall give due notice thereof to the Minister of the Parish. He shall thereupon appoint the time for Baptism, which shall be either immediately after the last Lesson at Morning or Evening Prayer, or at such other time as he shall appoint.

7 Before proceeding with the Service, the Priest shall require assurance that the child brought to him for Baptism has not already received this Sacrament.

8 The Priest and the people may remain standing throughout the Baptismal Service.

9 The Priest shall meet the Parents, Sponsors, and the Candidates for Baptism at the Font, which is to be filled with pure water in the presence of the people.

10 A Psalm or Hymn may be said or sung at the Font, or while the Priest comes to the Font.

11 Standing at the Font, the Priest shall say:

Dearly beloved in Christ, seeing that God willeth all men to be saved from the fault and corruption of the nature which they inherit, as well as from the actual sins which they commit, and that our Saviour Christ saith, None can enter into the kingdom of God, except he be born anew of Water and of the Holy Spirit, I beseech you to call upon God the Father, through our Lord Jesus Christ, that he will grant to *this Child* that which by nature *he* cannot have; that *he* may be baptized with Water and the Holy Spirit, and received into Christ's holy Church, and be made *a* living *member* of the same.

12   Then he shall say one or both of the following prayers:

Almighty and everlasting God, who through thy well-beloved Son Jesus Christ didst sanctify Water to the mystical washing away of sin: We beseech thee mercifully to look upon *this Child*; wash *him* and sanctify *him* with the Holy Spirit; that *he* may be received into thy holy Church; and being stedfast in faith, joyful through hope, and rooted in charity, may so pass through the dangers of this troublesome world, that finally *he* may come to the land of everlasting life, there to reign with thee world without end; through Jesus Christ our Lord. *Amen.*

Almighty and immortal God, the aid of all that need, the helper of all that flee to thee for succour: We call upon thee for *this Child*, that *he*, coming to thy holy Baptism, may receive remission of sin by spiritual regeneration. Receive *him*, O Lord, as thou hast promised by thy well-beloved Son, saying, Ask, and ye shall have; seek, and ye shall find; knock, and it shall be opened unto you: So give now unto us that ask; let us that seek find; open the gate unto us that knock; that *this Child* may enjoy the everlasting benediction of thy heavenly washing, and may come to the eternal kingdom which thou hast promised by him who is the Resurrection and the Life, Jesus Christ our Lord. *Amen.*

13   Then, the people standing, one of the Ministers shall say:

Hear the words of the Gospel, written by Saint Mark, in the tenth chapter, beginning at the thirteenth verse.
People: Glory be to thee, O Lord.
They brought young children to Christ, . . . (CF3)
People: Praise be to thee, O Christ.

14   Then the Minister shall say:

Beloved, you hear in this Gospel the words of our Saviour Christ, that he commanded the children to be brought unto him; how he blamed those that would have kept them from him; how he exhorteth all men to follow their innocency. You perceive how by his own outward gesture and deed he declared his good will toward them; for he embraced them in his arms, he laid his hands upon them, and blessed them. Be ye, therefore, assured that he will likewise favourably receive *this* present *Child*; that he will embrace *him* with the arms of his mercy; that he will give unto *him* the blessing of eternal life, and make *him* *partaker* of his everlasting kingdom. Wherefore we being thus persuaded of the good will of our heavenly Father toward *this Child*, declared by his Son Jesus Christ; let us faithfully and devoutly give thanks unto him, and say together:

15   Almighty and everlasting God, . . .

CF4, *but* called ⟨vouchsafed to call⟩—*this Child* ⟨*this Infant*⟩ *throughout the service.*

THE PROMISES

16   Then shall the Priest say to the Sponsors:

Dearly beloved, you have prayed that our Lord Jesus Christ may be pleased to receive, cleanse, and sanctify *this Child*, and grant unto *him* the blessing of eternal life, which thing Christ, for his part, will most surely perform. And now *this Child*, on *his* part, must through you, *his* Sponsors, promise and vow that *he* will renounce the devil and all his works, believe in Christ, and obediently keep God's commandments.

I demand therefore:

Do you, in the name of this Child, renounce the devil and all his works, the vain pomp and glory of the world, with all covetous desires of the same, and the sinful desires of the flesh, so that you will not follow nor be led by them?
Answer: I do.
Priest: Let us recite the Articles of our Belief.

17   Then shall be said by the Priest and the Godparents, and the whole Congregation, the Apostles' Creed.

I believe in God the Father Almighty, . . . (CF12)

18   Note that the words in the Creed *He descended into hell* are considered as the same meaning as *He went into the place of departed spirits.*

19   Then shall the Priest say to the Sponsors:

Do you, in the name of this Child, profess this faith?
Answer: I do.

Do you, in the name of this Child, seek Baptism into this faith?
Answer: I do.
Do you, in the name of this Child, acknowledge the duty to keep God's holy will and commandments, walking stedfastly in the Way of Christ?
Answer: I do.
Will you pray for this Child, and take care that *he* may learn and do all these things?
Answer: I will.

20 Then shall the Priest make the following supplications, and after each of them the Congregation shall answer *Amen.*

O merciful God, grant that all sinful desires may die in *this Child,* and that all things belonging to the Spirit may live and grow in *him. Amen.*
Grant that *he* . . . (CF5c)
Grant that whosoever here shall begin to be of thy flock may evermore continue in the same. *Amen.*
Grant that . . . (CF5d)

THE BAPTISM

21 *Priest:* The Lord be with you;
People: And with thy spirit.
Priest: Lift up your hearts;
People: We lift them up unto the Lord.
Priest: Let us give thanks unto our Lord God;
People: It is meet and right so to do.

22 Then shall the Priest say:

It is very meet, right, and our bounden duty, that we should at all times, and in all places, give thanks unto thee, O Lord, Holy Father, Almighty, Everlasting God, for that thy most dearly beloved Son Jesus Christ upon the Cross, for the forgiveness of our sins, did shed out of his most precious side both water and blood; and after his glorious Resurrection gave commandment to his disciples, saying, All power is given unto me in heaven and in earth. Go ye therefore, and make disciples of all nations, baptizing them in the Name of the Father, and of the Son, and of the Holy Ghost.

Regard, we beseech thee, the prayers of thy Church. Sanctify this Water to the mystical washing away of sin; and grant that *this Child,* now to be baptized therein, may receive the fulness of thy grace and ever remain in the number of thy faithful and elect children; through Jesus Christ our Lord, to whom with thee, in the unity of the Holy Spirit, be all honour and glory, throughout all ages, world without end. *Amen.*

23 The Priest, taking the Child into his arms, or by the right hand, shall say to the Sponsors:

Name this Child.

24 And then, naming him after them, he shall dip him in the Water or pour Water upon him, saying:

N. I baptize thee In the Name of the Father, and of the Son, and of the Holy Ghost. Amen.

25 Then shall the Priest say:

We receive this child . . . (CF7)

26 Then shall the Priest say:

Seeing now, . . . (CF8)

27 Then shall be said by all:

Our Father who art in heaven, . . . (CF11)

28 Then shall the Priest say:

We yield thee hearty thanks, most merciful Father, that it hath pleased thee to regenerate *this Child* with thy Holy Spirit, to receive *him* for thine own *Child* by adoption, and to make *him a member* of thy holy Church. Grant, O Lord, that being baptized into the death of Christ, *he* may also be made *partaker* of his resurrection, so that serving thee here in newness of life, *he* may finally, with all thy holy Church, inherit thine everlasting kingdom; through Jesus Christ our Lord. *Amen.*

THE DUTIES

29 The Priest shall say to the Sponsors and Parents:

Dearly beloved, forasmuch as you have brought *this Child* to be baptized into the family of Christ's Church, and have promised that *he* shall renounce the devil and all his works, and shall believe in God, and serve him: you must remember that it is your part and duty to see that *he* be taught what a solemn vow, promise and profession *he has* here made by you, and be instructed in all other things which a Christian ought to know and believe to his soul's health.

Use all diligence therefore to see that *he* be virtuously brought up to lead a godly and a Christian life; and to that end you should teach *him* to pray, and bring *him* to take *his* part in public worship.

Take care that *he* be taught the Creed, the Ten Commandments and the Lord's Prayer, and be further instructed in the Church Catechism; and then that *he* be brought to the Bishop to be confirmed by him; so that *he* may be strengthened by the Holy Spirit, and may come to receive the holy Communion of the Body and Blood of Christ, and go forth into the world to serve God faithfully in the fellowship of his Church.

Remember always that Baptism represents unto us our profession; which is, to follow our Saviour Christ, and to be made like unto him; that as he died and rose again for us, so should we, who are baptized, die from sin, and rise again unto righteousness, continually mortifying all evil desires, and daily increasing in all virtue and godliness of living.

Will you be faithful in the fulfilment of these duties?
Answer: I will, the Lord being my helper.

30 Then the Priest may say one or both of the following prayers:

Almighty God, our heavenly Father, whose beloved Son did share in Nazareth the life of an earthly home: Bless, we beseech thee, the *home* of *this Child*, and grant wisdom and understanding to all who shall have care of *him*, that *he* may grow up in stedfast love and reverence of thy holy Name; through the same thy Son Jesus Christ our Lord. *Amen.*

Grant, O Lord, that *this Child* may by thy mercy grow in health of body and mind, and serve thee faithfully according to thy will all the days of *his* life; through Jesus Christ our Lord. *Amen.*

31 Then shall follow Benedictus or Nunc Dimittis, if the Office has been used at Morning or Evening Prayer. In that case the Canticle shall be followed by the Mutual Salutation, after which the Priest shall say, *Let us pray*, and proceed to the Collect of the day and the other prayers, and so end Morning or Evening Prayer.

32 When this Office is used as a separate Service, the Priest may say:

The grace of our Lord Jesus Christ, and the love of God, and the fellowship of the Holy Ghost, be with us all evermore. *Amen.*

1 THE ORDER OF CONFIRMATION
OR LAYING ON OF HANDS WITH PRAYER UPON THOSE
THAT ARE BAPTIZED AND COME TO YEARS OF DISCRETION

2 This Service may be taken by itself, or in combination with other Services in this Book, the arrangements for the Service, including the place of the Sermon, and the place and choice of Hymns, being subject to the direction of the Bishop. The Apostles' Creed may be recited if the Bishop so determine, and Collects and other devotions from this Book may be used.

3 Upon the day appointed, all that are to be then confirmed, being placed and standing in order before the Bishop, the Minister shall present them unto the Bishop, and say:

4 Reverend Father in God, I present unto you these persons to receive the laying on of hands.

Bishop: Take heed that the persons whom ye present be duly prepared and meet to receive the laying on of hands.

Minister: I have instructed them and inquired of them and believe them so to be.

5 Then the Bishop shall read the Preface following:

Brethren, these are they to whom we purpose, God willing, to administer the Apostolic rite of the laying on of hands.

The Church has thought good to order that none shall be confirmed, but such as can say the Creed, the Lord's Prayer, and the Ten Commandments, and are further instructed in the Church Catechism, set forth for that purpose.

We are assured that these persons present, being by baptism members of Christ's Church, are prepared as aforesaid, and we are assembled here to bless them by the laying on of hands with prayer.

This order is very convenient to be observed.

First. Because it is evident from sundry places in holy Scripture that the Apostles prayed for and laid their hands upon those who were baptized; and the same is agreeable with the usage of the Church since the Apostles' time. This holy rite is reckoned in the Epistle to the Hebrews to be one of the first principles of Christ.

Secondly. In order that persons, having come to the years of discretion, may acknowledge openly the vows made at their Baptism and dedicate their lives to the will of God.

Thirdly. In order that by prayer and laying on of hands they may be strengthened by the Holy Spirit, manfully to fight under the banner of Christ crucified, against sin, the world, and the devil, and to continue Christ's faithful soldiers and servants unto their life's end.

6 Then the Bishop, or some Minister appointed by him, shall read the following Lessons from holy Scripture.

Here the words of holy Scripture written in the eighth chapter of the Acts of the Apostles, begininng at the fourth verse.

Therefore they that were scattered abroad... (Acts 8.4–8, 12, 14–17, RV)

7 Here also the words of holy Scripture written in the nineteenth chapter of the Acts of the Apostles, beginning at the first verse.

And it came to pass, ... (Acts 19.1–7, RV)

8 The Bishop shall then require THE RENEWAL OF BAPTISMAL VOWS, saying:

Do you here, in the presence of God and of this Congregation, renew the solemn promises and vows which were made at your Baptism?

9 And every one shall audibly answer:

I do.

10 Or else the Bishop shall say:

Do you here, in the presence of God and of this Congregation, renounce the devil and all his works, the pomps and vanity of this wicked world, and all the sinful lusts of the flesh?
Answer: I do.
Bishop: Do you believe the Christian Faith as it is set forth in the Apostles' Creed?
Answer: I do.
Bishop: Will you endeavour to keep God's holy will and commandments, and to walk in the same all the days of your life?
Answer: I will, God being my helper.

11 Then shall the Bishop proceed with THE CONFIRMATION, commending those who are to be confirmed to the prayers of the Congregation, and saying:

Our help is in the Name of the Lord; ... (CF14)

12 Bishop.

Let us pray

Almighty and everliving God,...

CF15, but Holy Spirit ⟨Holy Ghost⟩—Confirm and strengthen ⟨strengthen⟩ —might ⟨ghostly strength⟩

13 Then all of them in order kneeling before the Bishop, he shall lay his hand upon the head of every one severally, saying:

Defend, O Lord, this thy Servant with . . . (CF15)

14 Then shall the Bishop say:
The Lord be with you;
Answer: And with thy spirit.

15 *Bishop:* Let us pray.

Then shall be said by all:

Our Father who art in heaven, . . . (CF11)

16 Then the Bishop shall say:
Almighty and everliving God, who makest us both to will and to do such things . . . (CF17)

17 O almighty Lord, . . . (CF18)

18 Then the Bishop shall bless them, saying thus:
The blessing of God Almighty, . . . (CF19)

19 It is desirable that everyone shall have a Godfather or Godmother as witness at the Confirmation.
20 When the Confirmation follows immediately after holy Baptism, the shortened form on page 538[1] may be used.
21 And there shall none be admitted to the holy Communion, until such time as he be confirmed, or be ready and desirous to be confirmed.

[1] Of *The Book of Common Prayer of Canada, 1959.*

11. The Church of India, Pakistan, Burma, and Ceylon Rites 1960

THE PROPOSED PRAYER BOOK of 1951 was not universally accepted and further revision began soon after its publication. In 1960 a new Prayer Book was finally approved, which was found acceptable to all schools of thought. The texts which follow are from this book; THE BOOK OF COMMON PRAYER *and Administration of the Sacraments and other Rites and Ceremonies of the Church according to the use of the Church of India, Pakistan, Burma, and Ceylon*, as presented by the Episcopal Synod of the General Council of the Church of India, Pakistan, Burma, and Ceylon for concurrence on 13 January 1960, and published in 1961.

While the texts here reproduced represent those in use at present throughout the Province, there are certain *Permissive Ceremonies* which can be used at the services of Baptism and Confirmation. These *Permissive Ceremonies* are contained in THE SUPPLEMENT *to the Book of Common Prayer*. The forms contained in this *Supplement* were authorized for use in churches by the Episcopal Synod in January 1960.

I THE MINISTRATION OF HOLY BAPTISM
GENERAL RUBRICS

2 It is desirable . . .

IPBC 51 B2, *but Festivals ⟨Feast Days⟩—in order that ⟨as well for that⟩—and also ⟨as also⟩—omit for which cause . . . vulgar tongue.*

3 The rule of the Church . . .

IPBC 51 B3, *but omit as laid down* . . . Communion—*omit* (*Resolution 15 of the Episcopal Synod of 1942*)

4 When any person . . . (IPBC 51 B4)

5 And note, . . .

IPBC 51 B5, *but add*
two Godmothers. Nevertheless, when three Godparents cannot conveniently be had, one Godfather and one Godmother shall suffice.

6 The Parish Priest . . . (IPBC 51 B6)

7 When there are . . . (IPBC 51 B7)

8 In the absence . . . (IPBC 51 B8)

9 THE BAPTISM OF INFANTS

10 All stand throughout the Service, unless otherwise directed.

11 When the people are gathered at the Font (which is to be filled with pure water), the Priest shall ask the Godparents and Parents,

12 Has this child been already baptized, or no?

13 If they answer, *No*: then the Priest shall speak to them of the meaning and purpose of Baptism, saying,

Dearly beloved in Christ, seeing that God willeth all men to be saved from the fault and corruption of the nature which they inherit, as well as from the actual sins which they commit, and that our Saviour Christ . . .

Continue as CF1, *but* Holy Spirit ⟨Holy Ghost⟩

14 Then shall the Priest say,

Let us pray.

Almighty and everlasting God, . . . (1662 B6)

15 After which he may also say this prayer:

Almighty and immortal God, . . .

CF2, *but this child* ⟨*this Infant*⟩ *throughout the service—omit* Receive . . . us that knock *and continue* Grant that *he* . . .

16 Then shall the Priest read the Gospel appointed below. Before the Gospel he shall say,

Hear the words of the Gospel, written by Saint Mark, in the tenth chapter, at the thirteenth verse.
Answer: Glory be to thee, O Lord.
They brought young children to Christ, . . . (CF3)

17 The Gospel being ended, the people shall say,

Praise be to thee, O Christ.

18 *Priest.* Beloved, being persuaded of the good will of our heavenly Father towards *this child*, declared by his Son Jesus Christ, let us faithfully and devoutly give thanks unto him, and say together,

19 *Priest and People:* Almighty and everlasting God, . . . (CF4)

THE PROMISES

20 Then shall the Priest speak to the Parents and Godparents on this wise:

Dearly beloved, . . . (IPBC 51 B20)

21 Do you renounce the devil and all his works?

IPBC 51 B21, *but for second Answer read* I renounce them all.—Holy Spirit ⟨Holy Ghost⟩

22 Then shall the Priest say unto the Parents and Godparents,

Having now . . . (IPBC 51 B22)

THE BLESSING OF THE WATER

23 The Priest shall bless the water in this form:

The Lord be with you:
Answer: And with thy spirit.

1928 IB21, *but* Holy Spirit ⟨Holy Ghost⟩—through the same Jesus Christ ⟨through Jesus Christ⟩

24 Then shall the Priest say,

O merciful God, . . . (IPBC 51 B23)

25 The Blessing of the Water may take place at the beginning of the service instead of at this place.

THE BAPTISM

26 Then the Priest shall take the child into his arms, and shall say to the Godparents:

Name this child.

27 And then naming him after them, he shall dip him in the water, or pour water upon him, saying,

N. I baptize thee In the name of the Father, and of the Son, and of the Holy Spirit. Amen.

28 Then shall the Priest say,

We receive this child . . . (CF7)

29 Then may the Priest say to them that have been baptized:

God preserve in you the grace of your Baptism without reproach, that you may obediently keep his commandments and walk worthily of your Christian calling; remembering always that Baptism represents unto us our profession, which is, to follow the example of our Saviour Christ, and to be made like unto him; to whom be all glory, now and in eternity. *Amen.*

THE THANKSGIVING

30 Then shall the Priest say,

Seeing now, . . . (CF8)

31 Then shall be said by Priest and people together,

Our Father, who art in heaven, . . . (CF11)

32 Then shall the Priest say,

We yield thee hearty thanks, . . .

IPBC 51 B32, *but* with all thy holy Church *he* may inherit ⟨with the residue of thy holy Church *he* may be *an inheritor* of⟩

33 Here may follow this Prayer for the Home:

Almighty God, . . . (1928 IB28)

34 Then, if the Baptism be administered . . . (IPBC 51 B35)

35 The blessing of God Almighty, the Father, the Son, and the Holy Spirit, be amongst you and remain with you always. *Amen.*

36 It is certain by God's Word, . . . (IPBC 51 B37)

37 If a child . . . (IPBC 51 B38)

38 Seeing that the gifts and calling of God are without repentance, a person who has once been baptized cannot be baptized again.

I THE MINISTRATION OF HOLY BAPTISM
THE PERMISSIVE CEREMONIES

2 The ceremony of the white vesture and the ceremony of the burning light may be introduced after the Baptism in the manner following.

THE BAPTISM

3 Then the Priest shall take each person to be baptized by the right hand, and shall say to the Godparents,

Name this person (child).

4 And then naming him after them, he shall dip him in the water, or pour water upon him, saying,

N. I baptize thee In the name of the Father, and of the Son, and of the Holy Spirit. Amen.

5 Then shall the Priest say,

We receive this person (child) . . . (CF7)

6 Then (or immediately after the Baptism) each candidate may be clothed with a white vesture. And after the candidates have been received and are so vested, the Priest shall say,

This white vesture is a token of innocency, which by God's grace in this holy Sacrament of Baptism is given unto you; and is a sign whereby you are admonished to give *yourself* henceforth to innocency of living, that after this transitory life you may be *partaker* of the life everlasting. *Amen.*

7 Then the Priest may deliver to each candidate a burning light, saying,

Receive this burning light, and walk in the light by faith in Jesus Christ. *Amen.*

8 Then may the Priest say to those who have been baptized:

God preserve in you the grace of your Baptism without reproach, that you may obediently keep his commandments and walk worthy of your Christian calling. Walk by the Spirit, and you shall not fulfil the lust of the flesh; for the fruit of the Spirit is love, joy, peace, longsuffering, kindness, goodness, faithfulness, meekness, self-control. Remember always that Baptism represents unto us our profession, which is, to follow the example of our Saviour Christ, and to be made like unto him; to whom be all glory, now and in eternity. *Amen.*

I THE ORDER OF CONFIRMATION
OR LAYING ON OF HANDS WITH PRAYER UPON THOSE
THAT ARE BAPTIZED AND COME TO YEARS OF DISCRETION

GENERAL RUBRICS

2 To the end that Confirmation . . .

1928 C2, *but read*
the Ten Commandments; and have been sufficiently instructed in the teaching contained in the Catechism: which order is very desirable to be observed; to the end that children . . .

3 So soon as children . . .

1928 C2, *but read*
the Ten Commandments; and have been sufficiently instructed in the teaching contained in the Catechism, they shall be brought to the Bishop.

4 The Minister shall from time to time . . . (1928 C4)

5 And whensoever the Bishop . . . (IPBC 51 C5)

6 It is desirable . . . (1928 C6)

7 And there shall none . . . (1928 C7)

8   When Confirmation is administered to candidates immediately after they have
     been baptized, the Introduction and Renewal of Baptismal Vows shall be omitted,
     and the Bishop shall begin the Confirmation with the versicle *Our help is in the
     name of the Lord.*

9   THE ORDER OF CONFIRMATION

10   At the time of the Confirmation, . . . (IPBC 51 C10)

11   Then the Bishop, or some Minister appointed by him, shall say,

You that are to be confirmed shall remember that the Lord Jesus Christ,
before he ascended up into heaven, promised to his first disciples the
gift of the Holy Spirit, saying, Ye shall receive power, when the Holy
Spirit is come upon you: and ye shall be my witnesses both in Jerusalem
and in all Judaea and in Samaria, and unto the uttermost part of the
earth.

At our Baptism we were signed with the Cross on our foreheads, in
token that we too should not be ashamed to confess before all the
world the faith of Christ crucified, and manfully continue his faithful
soldiers and servants unto our lives' end.

We trust you are come here with an understanding of the obligations
you are now publicly to acknowledge, and with an humble and
stedfast belief that the power of the Holy Spirit will enable you to be
faithful witnesses to Christ, wherever you may be: and therefore we
call upon you in the presence of God and of this congregation to
pledge yourselves to his service by the renewal of your Baptismal vows.

THE RENEWAL OF BAPTISMAL VOWS

12   Then shall the Bishop ask the following questions:

Do you here, in the presence of God and of this congregation renounce
the devil, and all his works, the vain pomp and glory of the world,
with all covetous desires of the same, and the sinful desires of the flesh,
so that you will not follow, nor be led by them?
Answer: I renounce them all.
Do you believe all the Articles of the Christian Faith as contained in
the Apostle's Creed?
Answer: I believe.
Will you obediently keep God's holy will and commandments, and
walk in the same all the days of your life?
Answer: I will, by God's help.
At your Baptism you were signed with the cross on your foreheads.
Do you acknowledge yourselves bound by this token to confess the

faith of Christ crucified, to fight manfully under his banner, and to continue his faithful soldiers and servants unto your lives' end, bearing witness to him both in word and in deed?

Answer: I acknowledge myself bound so to do.

13 Or else the Bishop shall say,

Do you here, in the presence of God, . . . (IPBC 51 C13)

14 And every one shall audibly answer,

I do.

THE LAYING ON OF HANDS

15 Then, the people kneeling, the Bishop shall say,

Our help is in the name of the Lord; (CF14)

16 Then shall the Bishop say this prayer; and while reciting it, he may stretch out his hands over the candidates.

Let us pray.

Almighty and everliving God, . . .

CF15, *but* Holy Spirit ⟨Holy Ghost⟩

17 Then all of them in order kneeling before the Bishop, he shall lay his hand upon the head of every one severally, saying,

Defend, O Lord . . .

CF16 *but omit* (or *this thy Servant*)

18 Then shall the Bishop say,

The Peace of the Lord abide with you.

Answer. And with thy spirit.

19 Let us pray,

Our Father, who art in heaven, . . . (CF11)

20 Then shall the Bishop add these Prayers.

Almighty and everlasting God, . . .

CF17, *but* and the same Spirit ⟨and the Holy Ghost⟩

THE CONCLUSION

21 O Almighty Lord, . . . (CF18)

22 Then the Bishop may deliver the following charge,

Go forth into the world in peace; . . .

1928 C20, *but ending at* . . . power of the Holy Spirit.

23 After which he shall bless them saying,
The Blessing of God Almighty, . . . (CF19)

THE ORDER OF CONFIRMATION
AN ALTERNATIVE FORM FOR THE LAYING ON OF HANDS

This Alternative Form reproduces that of IPBC 51, Alternative Form . . . ,
but Holy Spirit ⟨Holy Ghost⟩ and add:

5. The holy Chrism may be used with the Form appointed in *The Book of Common Prayer* at the words, *Defend, O Lord.*

12. *The West Indian Rites 1964*

These texts are from *The Order for Baptism and Confirmation*, published by S.P.C.K. 1963; and are issued by the Authority of Provincial Synod for permissive use as directed in each Diocese by the Bishop.

The Order for Baptism is to be used for both Infants and Adults.

I THE ORDER FOR THE ADMINISTRATION OF HOLY BAPTISM

GENERAL RUBRICS

2 It is desirable that Baptism be administered on Sundays and other Holy-Days when the greatest number of people come together, so that the congregation may witness the reception of the new members into Christ's Church and may also be reminded of the benefits which they themselves received in their Baptism and of the vows which they renewed in their Confirmation. Nevertheless, for sufficient cause Baptism may be administered on any other day.

3 It is the duty of Christian parents to be present at the Baptism of their children which should be not later than the fourth week after birth unless there is reasonable cause for delay.

4 When children are to be baptized timely notice shall be given to the Parish Priest that he may arrange for the instruction of the Parents and Godparents in the duties they are to fulfil.

5 There shall be for every Male-child to be baptized two Godfathers and one God-mother; and for every Female, one Godfather and two Godmothers. For sufficient cause one Godparent only shall suffice.

6 When adults are to be baptized the Parish Priest shall make sure that they are duly instructed in the Christian Faith and in the vows they shall make. He shall exhort them to prepare themselves by prayer, repentance, and fasting for this Holy Sacrament.

7 The Bishop shall be given timely notice of the Baptism of an adult. The newly baptized adult shall be confirmed without delay.

8 At the Baptism of an adult there shall be present with him at the Font two witnesses, or at least one.

9 No person shall be admitted as a Godparent or a Witness who is not a regular communicant of the Church.

10 When a Priest cannot be present it is lawful for a Deacon to baptize and, when extreme urgency compels and neither Priest nor Deacon is at hand, it is lawful for any baptized person to baptize in the form prescribed for Private Baptism.

11 The Parish Priest must make sure that a candidate for Baptism, whether an adult or child, has not already been baptized (christened).

12 The Font shall be filled with pure water, either before the Service or immediately before the Blessing of the Water.

13 The Priest and people remain standing throughout the Service.

14 THE ORDER FOR THE
ADMINISTRATION OF HOLY BAPTISM
TO BE USED IN THE CHURCH

THE INTRODUCTION

15 At the time appointed the Priest shall meet the Witnesses at the Baptism of Adults and the Godparents at the Baptism of Children, together with those to be baptized, near the Church Door or at the Font, as he shall appoint. He shall then say,

Beloved in Christ Jesus, it is the will of God that all men should be saved from the fault and corruption of the nature which they inherit and from the actual sins which they commit. Also, our Saviour Christ saith, None can enter the kingdom of God except he be born again of water and the Holy Ghost; Let us therefore beseech him of his great mercy to grant to *this person* (*child*) that which by nature *he* cannot have, that through holy Baptism *he* may be born again and received into Christ's Church, and be made *a* lively *member* of the same.

16 Then shall he say the following prayer.

Almighty and immortal God, the helper and defender of all who turn to thee for succour, the life and peace of those who believe: We call upon thee for *this person* (*child*) that *he* coming to thy holy Baptism may receive remission of sin and thine eternal grace by spiritual re-generation. Receive *him*, O Lord, as thou hast promised by thy well-beloved Son, saying, Ask, and ye shall have; seek, and ye shall find; knock, and it shall be opened unto you: So give now unto us who ask; Let us who seek find; open the gate unto us who knock; that *this person* (*child*) may enjoy the everlasting benediction of thy heavenly washing, and may come to the eternal kingdom which thou hast promised by him who is the Resurrection and the Life, Jesus Christ our Lord. R. Amen.

17 He may add,

O Lord God of hosts, before the terrors of whose presence the armies of Hell are put to flight: Deliver *this* thy *servant* from the might of Satan; cast out from *him* every evil and unclean spirit that lurketh in the heart and make *him* ready to receive the Holy Spirit of grace; through Jesus Christ our Lord. R. Amen.

18 Then shall the Priest or one of the Ministers say,

V. The Lord be with you;
R. And with thy spirit.

Hear the words of the Gospel according to Saint John.
R. Glory be to thee, O Lord.
There was a man of the Pharisees, named Nicodemus, a ruler of the
Jews: ... (John 3.1–8, AV)
R. Praise be to thee, O Christ.

9   At the Baptism of Children the following Lesson may be read instead of the above.

V. The Lord be with you;
R. And with thy spirit.
Hear the words of the Gospel according to Saint Mark.
R. Glory be to thee, O Lord.
They brought young children to Christ, ... (CF3)
R. Praise be to thee, O Christ.

0   Then shall the Priest say,

Beloved, let us now faithfully and devoutly give thanks unto God our
heavenly Father and say together,

Almighty and everlasting God, heavenly Father, We give thee humble
thanks That thou hast called us to the knowledge of thy grace And to
faith in thee: Increase this knowledge and confirm this faith in us evermore. Give thy Holy Spirit to *this person* (*child*) That *he* may be born
again And be made *an heir* of everlasting salvation; through Jesus
Christ, thy Son, our Lord, Who liveth and reigneth with thee in the
unity of the same Holy Spirit, Now and ever. Amen.

1   The Priest shall lead them to the Font. Meanwhile one of the following Psalms
may be sung or said.

Like as the hart desireth the water-brooks: so longeth my soul after
thee, O God. (Ps. 42.1–7, BCP)

or

The Lord is my shepherd: therefore can I lack nothing. (Ps. 23, BCP)

THE BAPTISM
THE BLESSING OF THE WATER

2   Then shall the Priest (or the Bishop, if he be present) bless the water, saying,

V. The Lord be with you;
R. And with thy spirit.
V. Lift up your hearts;
R. We lift them up unto the Lord.

V. Let us give thanks unto our Lord God;
R. It is meet and right so to do.

23 Then shall he continue,

It is very meet, right and our bounden duty, that we should at all times and in all places give thanks unto thee, O Lord, Holy Father, Almighty, Everlasting God.

But now are we chiefly bound to praise thee because thou hast appointed the water of Baptism for the regeneration of mankind through thy beloved Son; Upon whom, when he was baptized in the river Jordan, the Holy Spirit came down in the likeness of a dove; and who, for the forgiveness of our sins, did shed out of his most precious side both water and blood, and after his mighty Resurrection gave commandment to his Apostles to go and teach all nations, baptizing them in the name of the Father, and of the Son, and of the Holy Ghost:

Hear, we beseech thee, the prayers of thy Church; Sanctify this water, by the same Holy Spirit to the mystical washing away of sin, and grant that all who are to be baptized herein, being buried with Christ into his death, may be raised with him unto newness of life and, serving thee faithfully with all thy Saints, may attain to the kingdom of thy Glory;

Through the same Jesus Christ, thy Son, our Lord, to whom with thee and the same Holy Spirit, be all honour and glory, throughout all ages, world without end. R. Amen.

24 The Priest shall then make these supplications,

O merciful God, . . .

CF5ac, *but in a, this person (child)* ⟨*this child*⟩—*then continue*:

Grant that *he* being steadfast in faith, joyful through hope, and rooted in charity, may at last come to thy heavenly kingdom through thy mercy, O blessed Lord God, who dost live and govern all things, world without end. R. Amen.

25 The Priest shall ask all who are to be baptized the following questions.

26 When Children are to be baptized the questions shall be answered by the God-parents, to whom the Priest shall first say,

You, Godparents, who have brought *this child* to be baptized and stand in the presence of God and his people, must now make on *his* behalf the promises which *he* will renew in *his* own *person* when *he* *comes* in due time to be confirmed.

THE PROMISES

27 Do you renounce the Devil and all his works, the covetous desires of the world, and all the sinful lusts of the flesh?

Answer: I renounce them all.

Do you believe in God the Father Almighty, maker of Heaven and Earth?

Answer: I believe.

Do you believe in Jesus Christ, his only Son our Lord? that he was conceived by the Holy Ghost, born of the Virgin Mary; that he suffered under Pontius Pilate, was crucified, dead and buried; that he descended into hell, and the third day rose again from the dead; that he ascended into heaven, and sitteth at the right hand of God the Father Almighty; and from thence shall come to judge the quick and the dead?

Answer: I believe.

Do you believe in the Holy Ghost; the holy Catholic Church, the Communion of Saints, the Forgiveness of sins, the Resurrection of the body, and the Life everlasting?

Answer: I believe.

Do you desire to be baptized into this faith?

Answer: That is my desire.

Will you obediently keep God's holy will and commandments and walk in the way of Christ all the days of your life?

Answer: I will with the help of God.

28 Then shall the Priest take each person to be baptized by the hand or each child into his arms and say to the Witnesses or Godparents,

Name this *person (child)*.

29 Then naming the person or child after them, he shall dip him into the water or pour water upon him, three times, once at the mention of each Person of the Trinity, saying,

N. I baptize thee in the Name of the Father, and of the Son, and of the Holy Ghost. Amen.

30 The Priest shall make a cross upon the forehead of each person (child) baptized, saying,

Seeing that this *person (child)* has now by Baptism been made a member of Christ's Church I sign *him* with the sign of the Cross in token that hereafter *he* shall not be ashamed to confess the faith of Christ crucified, and manfully to fight under his banner against sin, the world, and the devil, and to continue Christ's faithful soldier and servant unto *his* life's end. Amen.

31 He may give to each person, or for a child to one of the Godparents, a lighted candle, after which he shall say,

Receive the Light of Christ and walk as a child of light, that when the Lord cometh you may appear before him in the company of the Saints.

32 At the Baptism of Adults the Priest shall say,

Beloved, you have been born again through the power of the Holy Spirit and made God's own child. Wherefore I now bid you call upon God as Father in the prayer which Christ his only-begotten Son has taught us, saying

(and the newly baptized shall say the Lord's Prayer, the people saying it with him (them))

Our Father, which art in heaven, . . . (CF9)

33 At the Baptism of Children the Priest shall say,

Beloved, *this child has* been born again through the power of the Holy Spirit and made God's own *child*. Wherefore I bid you on *his* behalf to call upon God *his* Father in the prayer which Christ his only-begotten Son has taught us, saying,

(and the Godparents shall say together the Lord's Prayer, the people saying it with them)

Our Father (as above)

34 Then shall the Priest say,

Almighty God we most heartily thank thee that it hath pleased thee to regenerate *this child* with thy Holy Spirit, to receive *him* as thine own *child* by adoption, and to make *him* a *member* of thy holy Church and *an inheritor* of thine everlasting kingdom; through Jesus Christ thy Son, our Lord, to whom with thee in the unity of the same Holy Spirit, be all honour and glory, world without end. R. Amen.

35 When Adults only are baptized and Baptism is administered as a separate Service the Priest shall say,

Depart in peace, and the Lord be with you. R. Amen.

36 At the Baptism of Children the following prayer is said.

Almighty God, our heavenly Father, whose dearly beloved Son Jesus Christ shared with the Blessed Virgin Mary and Saint Joseph the life of an earthly home at Nazareth: Bless, we beseech thee, the *home of this child*; and give such grace and wisdom to all who have the care of *him*, that by their word and good example *he* may learn truly to know and love thee, and so come to thy eternal home in heaven; through the same thy Son Jesus Christ our Saviour. *R*. Amen.

37 The Priest shall say to the Godparents and Parents,

You who have brought *this child* to be baptized into the family of Christ's Church must see that *he is* instructed in the Creed, the Lord's Prayer, and the Ten Commandments as set forth in the Church Catechism, and all other things which a Christian ought to know and believe to his soul's health.

See also that *he is* brought up to worship with the Church, to hear sermons, and to be regular in private prayer.

Help *him* by your prayers and example to walk worthily of *his* Christian calling, remembering always that by Baptism we are pledged to follow the example of our Saviour Christ and to be made like unto him.

See also that *this child is* brought to the Bishop to be confirmed so that, strengthened by the Holy Spirit, *he* may devoutly and regularly receive the Body and Blood of Christ in the Holy Communion, and may go forth into the world to serve God faithfully in the fellowship of his Church.

Will you do these duties faithfully?
Godparents and parents: I will.

38 When Baptism is administered as a separate Service the Priest shall say,

Depart in peace, and the Lord be with you. *R*. Amen.

I THE ORDER FOR CONFIRMATION
OR LAYING ON OF HANDS WITH PRAYER
UPON THOSE WHO ARE BAPTIZED AND
COME TO YEARS OF DISCRETION

2 The Parish Priest shall make sure that those whom he presents for Confirmation have already been baptized.

3 It is desirable that everyone shall have a Witness of his Confirmation who is a regular communicant.

4 When the only candidates present are those whose Confirmation follows immediately on their Baptism the Renewal of Baptismal Vows shall be omitted.

5 The arrangements of the Service, including the place of the Sermon and the choice of Hymns, are subject to the direction of the Bishop.

6 There shall be no Sermon or Hymn between *Our help, etc.* and the Laying on of hands.

5—C.I.

7   No one shall be admitted to the Holy Communion until he has been confirmed, or is ready and desirous to be confirmed.

THE INTRODUCTION

8   At the entry of the Bishop and his Assistants the following Psalm may be sung or else a suitable Hymn:

The Lord is my light, and my salvation; . . . (Ps. 27.1–7 BCP)

9   All who are to be confirmed shall stand before the Bishop, and a Priest appointed by him shall present them, saying,

Reverend Father in God, I present unto you these persons who have been duly baptized, to be confirmed.

10   Then shall the Bishop say,

Have you examined them and found them ready and desirous to be confirmed?

11   And the Priest shall answer,

I have examined them and found them so to be.

12   Then the Bishop (or some other Minister appointed by him) may read the following Preface.

Dearly Beloved in the Lord, . . .

CF20 *as far as* . . . received the Holy Ghost. *Then continue:*

In this passage of Holy Scripture we read of an outward sign which is the laying on of hands with prayer and of an inward grace which is the gift of the Holy Spirit. And because this gift comes from God alone, we shall ask him, as the Apostles did, that he will pour forth his Spirit in Confirmation upon these persons who in Baptism were made his children.

THE RENEWAL OF BAPTISMAL VOWS

13   Then shall the Bishop say,

You who have come to be confirmed and stand in the presence of God and of this congregation must now renew your Baptismal Vows.

Do you renounce the devil and all his works, the covetous desires of the world, and the sinful lusts of the flesh?
Answer: I renounce them all.

Do you believe the Christian Faith as it is set forth in the Apostles' Creed?

Answer: I believe.

Will you obediently keep God's Holy Will and Commandments and walk in the way of Christ all the days of your life?

Answer: I will with the help of God.

14 Here may be sung kneeling the Hymn *Veni Creator Spiritus*, or some other hymn to the Holy Spirit.

THE CONFIRMATION

15 The people still kneeling, the Bishop shall stand and say,

V. Our help is in the Name of the Lord; . . .

CF14, *but* From this time forth for evermore ⟨Henceforth, world without end⟩

16 Stretching forth his hands towards those who are to be confirmed, the Bishop shall say,

Almighty God, the Father of our Lord Jesus Christ, who hast been pleased to regenerate these thy servants by water and the Holy Spirit, and hast given unto them forgiveness of all their sins: Strengthen them, we beseech thee, O Lord, with the same Holy Spirit, the Comforter, and daily increase in them thy manifold gifts of grace; the spirit of wisdom and understanding; the spirit of counsel and might; the spirit of knowledge and true godliness; and fill them, O Lord, with the spirit of thy holy fear, in the Name of our Lord Jesus Christ, who liveth and reigneth with thee in the unity of the same Holy Spirit, God throughout all ages, world without end. *R.* Amen.

17 Then all of them in order, kneeling before the Bishop, he shall lay his right hand upon the head of each of them (and using at his discretion the Holy Chrism shall sign each one on the forehead) saying,

Confirm, O Lord, this thy child N. with thy heavenly grace, that *he* may continue thine for ever; and daily increase in thy Holy Spirit more and more until *he* come unto thy everlasting kingdom.

18 And each one shall answer, *Amen*.

19 When all have been confirmed the Bishop shall say,

V. The peace of the Lord be always with you;
R. And with thy spirit.

Let us pray.

20 Then shall be said by all,

Our Father, who art in heaven, . . . (CF9)

21 Then shall the Bishop say,

Almighty and everlasting God, we make our humble supplications unto thee for these thy servants upon whom, after the example of thy holy Apostles, we have now laid our hands. Let thy fatherly hand, we beseech thee, ever be over them; let thy Holy Spirit ever be with them; and make them so faithfully to receive the blessed Sacrament of the Body and Blood of thy Son that, nourished continually with the grace thereof and walking in the knowledge and obedience of thy Word, they may obtain in the end everlasting life; through the same Jesus Christ our Lord, who with thee and the same Holy Spirit liveth and reigneth, ever one God, world without end. *R.* Amen.

22 The Bishop shall then bless the newly confirmed saying,

The blessing of God . . . (CF19)

13. *The South African Rites 1967*

These texts are from *Proposals for the Revision of the Rites of Baptism and Confirmation*, which was published by the Liturgical Committee of the Synod of Bishops of the Church of the Province of South Africa, in 1967. The Rites have not been officially authorized, but have been put forward for experimental use, where permission is granted by the Bishop of the Diocese.

In the Introductory Notes it is stated that the service for the baptism of adults is placed first in the book, as this is the archetypal form. The service of infant baptism follows as being a necessary form. This change, in the order of the Rites, is to express more clearly the scriptural teaching on baptism, which implies the response of conscious faith, of which children are incapable.

1 THE ADMINISTRATION OF BAPTISM
TO CHILDREN AND OTHERS WHO ARE
UNABLE TO ANSWER FOR THEMSELVES

2 It is desirable where possible that baptism be administered during public worship, which should normally be the service of Holy Communion; not only that the whole congregation may be witness to the reception of the newly baptized into the Church, but also that every member may be reminded of his own profession made to God in his baptism.

3 If there is no Holy Communion, the whole service may take place at the font.

4 If the Priest is unavoidably absent, it is lawful that a Deacon baptize children who are unable to answer for themselves.

5 The service begins with these verses from Psalm 119, or a suitable hymn may be sung,

Let my cry come before thee, O Lord:
R. Give me understanding according to thy word.
Let my supplication come before thee:
R. Deliver me according to thy word.
My lips shall pour forth thy praise:
R. Because thou hast taught me thy statutes.
Yea, my tongue shall sing of thy word:
R. For all thy commandments are righteous.
Let thine hand be strong to help me:
R. For I have chosen thy precepts.
O let me live that I may praise thee:
R. And let thy judgements help me.
The earth, O Lord, is full of thy mercy:
R. O teach me thy statutes.

Let thy loving mercy come unto me, O Lord:
R. Even thy salvation according to thy word.

6   The following Collect, Lesson and Gospel are generally to be used,

7   THE COLLECT

Almighty God, our heavenly Father, who in baptism hast made us thy children, and called us to knowledge of thy grace and to faith in thee: Give thy Holy Spirit to these children, that they may be born again and made heirs of everlasting life; through Jesus Christ our Lord, who lives and reigns with thee and the same Spirit, one God, for ever and ever. *Amen.*

8   THE LESSON

See what love the Father has given us, . . . (1 John 3.1–2, RSV)

9   THE GOSPEL

And Jesus came and said to them, . . . (Matt. 28.18–20, RSV)

10   The Sermon may follow. Then the Priest reads this address to the parents and sponsors of the children, standing before him at the font,

We have come together here to administer the sacrament of Baptism, by which men become Christians. It is the belief of Christians that Baptism is a sign, by means of which God gives us the greatest gift that even he can give; he sets us free from the power of evil, and he makes us his own children, by giving us, through his Holy Spirit, a new birth to a new life, which is a sharing in the risen life of our Lord Jesus Christ, both now and through all eternity.

This is God's free gift, and he asks us simply to accept it. This we do by faith. Therefore, when we are baptized, we profess our faith in God the Father, who gives us this gift; in God the Son, whose death makes this gift possible, and whose life enables us to live; and in God the Holy Spirit, by whose presence in our hearts this gift is brought to us. But, in order that the Church may be assured of the sincerity of those who come to be baptized, we ask them also to declare that they truly intend, both to forsake the service of the devil, with all the evil that is in the world around them or in the desires of their own hearts, and also to live according to God's will.

By bringing these children here to be baptized, you are asking God to give them this gift; by making the act of faith and the promises in their name, you are asking the Church to accept your assurance that they will grow up with this faith and intention. This is the responsibility which you are now undertaking. This means that you must help them, by your example and teaching, to know God as their Father through prayer, and to learn what it means to be a member of his family by taking part in the worship and life of that family, the Church. You must help them to learn the meaning of the faith they have professed and the promises they have made. And finally, you must do all that is in your power to ensure that they come at the proper time to be confirmed. For what we are now beginning has still to be completed. They will themselves make the profession and promises which you are now making in their name, and the life of Christ which is now given to them, and which the Holy Spirit will then renew, will be continually strengthened and matured when they come to our Lord with their fellow-Christians in the Holy Communion.

Parents and sponsors of these children, do you accept this responsibility?
Answer: We do.

11 Then the Priest says,

God be with you;
Answer: And with you also.

Let us pray.

We give thanks to thee, Almighty Father, everlasting God, through thy beloved Son, Jesus Christ our Lord:

Through whom in the beginning thou didst create the world, and therein make man in thine own image;

Whom in the fullness of time thou didst send into the world to redeem mankind, fallen into sin through disobedience;

Who, though he was himself born without sin, received the baptism of repentance for man's sake, and for man's sake was anointed with the Holy Spirit;

Whom thou didst deliver up to suffer death, that he might purify unto himself a People for his own possession;

Whom thou didst raise from the dead, that he might be the first-born among many brethren;

Who, when he ascended up on high, poured forth the Spirit of promise on thine adopted sons, that, being born again of water and the Holy Spirit, they might be made in him a new creation.

Hear us, O merciful Father, we most humbly beseech thee; sanctify this water to the washing away of sin; and grant that all to be baptized herein may be made members of thy Church, which is the Body of thy Son our Lord; that so, being baptized into his death, and being made partakers of his resurrection, they may die to sin, and rise again to righteousness; and, serving thee faithfully with all thy saints, may inherit the kingdom of thy glory;

Through the same thy Son Jesus Christ our Lord, to whom with thee and the Holy Spirit be all might, majesty, dominion and power, to all generations, for ever and ever. *Amen.*

12 Then the Priest asks the children to be baptized the following questions, which the parents and sponsors answer on their behalf,

Do you renounce the devil and all his works, the wickedness that is in the world, and all your sinful desires?

13 And they answer audibly,

I renounce them all.

14 Those to be baptized are brought, one by one, to the font, and the Priest asks each in turn the three questions following; and after each answer of faith he dips him in the water, or pours water upon him.

The Priest: Do you believe in God the Father?
Answer: I believe.
Priest: Do you believe in Jesus Christ, his only Son our Lord?
Answer: I believe.
Priest: Do you believe in the Holy Spirit?
Answer: I believe.

15 And before he gives back the child, the Priest declares to the congregation,

N., the child of God, is baptized in the Name of the Father, and of the Son, and of the Holy Spirit.

16 And the people answer, *Amen.*

17 And, when all have been baptized, the Priest asks this last question,

Do you promise, as loyal members of Christ's holy Church, to seek to grow in God's grace, and to strive by your daily obedience to his will to proclaim his eternal kingdom?

18 And the parents and sponsors answer,

I promise.

9 The Nicene Creed is said by the Priest and all the people in the following form,

We believe in one God the Father Almighty, Maker of heaven and earth, And of all things visible and invisible:

And in one Lord Jesus Christ, the only-begotten Son of God, Begotten of his Father before all worlds, God of God, Light of Light, Very God of very God, Begotten, not made, Being of one substance with the Father, By whom all things were made: Who for us men, and for our salvation, came down from heaven, And was incarnate by the Holy Ghost of the Virgin Mary, And was made man, And was crucified also for us under Pontius Pilate. He suffered and was buried, And the third day he rose again according to the Scriptures, And ascended into heaven, And sitteth on the right hand of the Father. And he shall come again with glory to judge both the quick and the dead: Whose kingdom shall have no end.

And we believe in the Holy Ghost, the Lord, the Giver of Life, Who proceedeth from the Father and the Son, Who with the Father and the Son together is worshipped and glorified, Who spake by the prophets. And we believe One, Holy, Catholick and Apostolick Church. We acknowledge one Baptism for the remission of sins, And we look for the Resurrection of the dead, And the life of the world to come. Amen.

10 After which, the service of Holy Communion is continued.

I But, if there is no Holy Communion, the Priest says,

Let us pray.

Lord, have mercy.
Christ have mercy.
Lord, have mercy.
Our Father, who art in heaven, . . . (CF9)

We give thanks to thee, O merciful Father, because it has pleased thee by the power of thy Holy Spirit to give new birth to these children, to receive them for thine own children by adoption, and to make them members of thy Holy Church, which is the Body of thy Son Jesus Christ. And we humbly beseech thee to grant that, confessing the faith in which they have been baptized, and renewing the promises made in their name, they may be strengthened by thy holy and life-giving Spirit, and ever be nourished with the Body and Blood of thy Son, Who lives and reigns with thee and the Holy Spirit, one God, for ever and ever, *Amen.*

Let us pray for the whole Church.

Almighty and everlasting God, by whose Spirit the whole body of the Church is governed and sanctified: Receive our supplications and prayers, which we offer before thee for all estates of men in thy holy Church, that every member of the same, in his vocation and ministry, may truly and godly serve thee; through our Lord and Saviour Jesus Christ. *Amen.*

22   After which the Priest may add,

Let us pray for the homes of these children.

O heavenly Father, after whom all fatherhood in heaven and earth is named: Bless, we beseech thee, the parents of these children, and give to them and all in whose charge they may be, the spirit of wisdom and love, that their homes may be to them an image of thy kingdom, and the care of their parents a likeness of thy love; through Jesus Christ our Lord. *Amen.*

23   Then the Priest blesses those who have been newly baptized, saying,

May the God of peace himself sanctify you wholly; and may you be kept sound and blameless at the coming of our Lord Jesus Christ. *Amen.*

24   Adults are generally to be baptized by the Bishop, who will at the same time confirm them according to the form for the Administration of Baptism and Confirmation to those of an age to answer for themselves. Unless there is danger of death, such persons shall not receive baptism only, without the permission of the Bishop being first obtained. In such cases the service for the Administration of Baptism to Children is to be used, those to be baptized answering the questions for themselves. And the Priest may either instruct those to be baptized in his own words, or he may read the address given in that service, replacing the last paragraph thereof with the following words,

By coming here to be baptized, you are asking God for this gift; by making the act of faith you are, as it were, stretching out your hands to receive it from him. Yet, although your baptism will be a close personal meeting between you and Christ our Saviour, you must remember that God's gift is not given to you alone. As God's *son,* you will be a member of his family, the Church; as one in whom Christ lives, you will be one of many members of his Body. You must therefore be confirmed by the Bishop with the least possible delay, so that you may take your place in the worship and life of the Church, and that the life of Christ in you may be continually strengthened and renewed when you come to him, with your fellow-Christians, in the Holy Communion.

1 **THE ADMINISTRATION OF CONFIRMATION**
TO THOSE ALREADY BAPTIZED

2 The service of Holy Communion begins with these verses of Psalm 118, or a suitable hymn may be sung,

O give thanks to the Lord, for he is gracious:
R. For his mercy endures for ever.
Let them now that fear the Lord declare:
R. That his mercy endures for ever.
I called upon the Lord in trouble:
R. And the Lord heard me and set me free.
The Lord is on my side, I will not fear:
R. What can man do to me?
It is better to take refuge in the Lord:
R. Than to put any trust in man.
The Lord is my strength and my defence:
R. And is become my salvation.
Thou art my God and I will thank thee:
R. Thou art my God and I will exalt thee.
O give thanks to the Lord, for he is gracious:
R. And his mercy endures for ever.

3 The following Collect, Lessons and Gospel are generally to be used.

4 **THE COLLECT**
Grant, we beseech thee, Almighty God, that these thy servants may be strengthened by the gift of thy Holy Spirit; and, as thou has destined them in love to be thy children by adoption, make them to grow daily in the likeness of thy Son Jesus Christ, who lives and reigns with thee and the same Spirit, one God, for ever and ever. *Amen.*

5 **THE FIRST LESSON**
And it shall come to pass afterward, ... (Joel 2.28–9, RSV)

6 **THE SECOND LESSON**
Jesus presented himself alive... (Acts 1.3–9, RSV)

7 **THE GOSPEL**
Jesus said to his disciples,... (John 14.15–17, RSV)

8 The Sermon follows.

9 Then the Bishop says to those who are to be confirmed, as they stand before him,

Children of God, when you were baptized, a solemn renunciation of evil was made in your name. Do you now yourselves renounce the devil and all his works, the wickedness that is in the world, and all your sinful desires?

10 And they answer audibly,

I renounce them all.

11 *The Bishop:* Now that you come to be confirmed, and stand here in the presence of God and of his Church, you must also reaffirm in your own persons the great profession of faith which was then made on your behalf:

12 Do you believe in God the Father?... (SA IB14)

13 Then the Bishop stands and prays over the candidates, who kneel before him.

The Bishop: Our help is in the name of the Lord;
Answer: Who made heaven and earth.
Bishop: Blessed be the name of the Lord;
Answer: From this time forth, and for evermore.

14 *The Bishop:* Let us pray.

15 Stretching out his hands towards those to be confirmed, he continues,

Almighty God, the Father of our Lord Jesus Christ, by whose grace thy servants have been set free from sin, and born anew of water and the Holy Spirit: send down upon them, we beseech thee, thy Holy Spirit the Comforter, and daily increase in them the spirit of wisdom and understanding, the spirit of counsel and might, the spirit of knowledge and godliness, and the spirit of the fear of God, in the name of our Lord Jesus Christ, with whom thou livest and reignest in the unity of the same Spirit, one God, for ever and ever.

16 And all the people say, *Amen.*

17 Each candidate in turn now kneels before the Bishop, who lays his hand on *his* head in silence; after which the candidate stands, and the Bishop greets *him,* saying,

Peace be with you, *N.*;

18 And the newly confirmed person answers,

And with you also.

19 When all have returned to their places, the Bishop asks this last question,

Do you promise, as loyal members of Christ's holy Church, to seek to grow in God's grace, and to strive by your daily obedience to his will to proclaim his eternal kingdom?

20 And all those who have been confirmed reply,

I promise.

21 The Bishop, with the newly confirmed and the whole congregation, says the Nicene Creed in the following form, and then begins the Offertory; and the newly confirmed communicate with him.

We believe in one God, the Father Almighty,... (SA IB19)

22 But, if there is no Holy Communion, after the Nicene Creed the Bishop says the following prayers,

Let us pray.

Lord, have mercy.
Christ, have mercy,
Lord, have mercy.

Our Father who art in heaven,... (CF9)

Let us pray for those who have now been confirmed:

Almighty and everliving God, who makest us both to will and to do those things that be good and acceptable unto thy Divine Majesty: We make our humble supplication unto thee for these thy servants, upon whom (after the example of thy holy Apostles) we have now laid our hands. Let thy fatherly hand, we beseech thee, ever be over them; let thy Holy Spirit ever be with them; and so lead them in the knowledge and obedience of thy Word, that in the end they may obtain everlasting life; through our Lord Jesus Christ, who with thee and the Holy Ghost liveth and reigneth, ever one God, world without end. *Amen.*

Let us pray for the whole Church.

Almighty and everlasting God, by whose Spirit the whole body of the Church is governed and sanctified: Receive our supplications and prayers, which we offer before thee for all estates of men in thy holy Church, that every member of the same, in his vocation and ministry, may truly and godly serve thee; through our Lord and Saviour Jesus Christ. *Amen.*

23   Then the Bishop blesses those who have been newly confirmed saying,

May the God of peace himself sanctify you wholly; and may you be kept sound and blameless at the coming of our Lord Jesus Christ. *Amen.*

24   And no one is to be admitted to Holy Communion, until such time as he be confirmed, or be ready and desirous to be confirmed.

I   # THE ADMINISTRATION OF BAPTISM AND CONFIRMATION
TO THOSE OF AN AGE TO ANSWER FOR THEMSELVES

2   Those to be baptized and those already baptized who are now to be confirmed are placed together, preferably near the font. But if this is not convenient, they may be gathered in front of the congregation; in which case a moveable font may be made ready at the entrance to the chancel.

3   The Bishop will generally officiate throughout the whole service; but, when there is a large number to be baptized, he may find it more convenient to baptize only the first candidates to be brought forward.

4   The service of Holy Communion begins with these verses from Psalm 107, or a suitable hymn may be sung,

O give thanks to the Lord, for he is gracious:
R. And his mercy endures for ever.
This let them say whom the Lord has redeemed:
R. Whom he has redeemed from the hand of the enemy.
And gathered them out of the lands, from the east and from the west:
R. From the north and from the south.
O that men would therefore praise the Lord for his goodness:
R. And for his wonders that he does for the children of men.
They cried to the Lord in their trouble:
R. And he delivered them out of their distress.
He sent his word and healed them:
R. And saved them from destruction.
He led them by a straight path:
R. Until they came to a city where men dwelt.
He satisfies the thirsty soul:
R. And fills the hungry soul with good.
O give thanks to the Lord, for he is gracious:
R. And his mercy endures for ever.

5   The following Collect, Lessons and Gospel are generally to be used.

6   THE COLLECT

Almighty God, whose will it is that all men should be saved and brought to new birth as thy children: Look in mercy upon these persons, and receive them into thy Church, that cleansed from their sin and strengthened by thy Holy Spirit, they may worship and serve thee in newness of life; through Jesus Christ our Lord. *Amen.*

7 THE FIRST LESSON

Thus says the Lord: I will take you . . . (Ezek. 36.24–8, RSV)

8 SECOND LESSON

Paul passed through the upper country . . . (Acts 19.1–6, RSV)

9 THE GOSPEL

The beginning of the gospel of Jesus Christ, . . . (Mark 1.1–11, RSV)

10 The Sermon follows.

11 After the Sermon, the Bishop goes to the font, and all the people stand. Then the Bishop faces the people, so that the font is between him and them, and says,

God be with you;
Answer: And with you also.

Let us pray.

We give thanks to thee, Almighty Father, . . . (SA IB11)

12 Then the Bishop asks all those to be baptized and confirmed,

Do you renounce . . . (SA IB12)

13 And they answer audibly,

I renounce them all.

14 Those to be baptized are brought, one by one, to the font, and the Bishop asks each . . .

SA IB14, *but Bishop ⟨Priest⟩*

15 After which, with the newly baptized person still standing before him, the Bishop declares to the congregation,

N., the child of God, is baptized in the Name of the Father, and of the Son, and of the Holy Spirit.

16 And the people answer *Amen.*

17 When all have been baptized and returned to their places, the Bishop turns to those others who have come to be confirmed, and asks the same three questions, that they may renew the confession of faith made at their baptism; and they all answer,

I believe.

18 If the baptism has taken place at the chancel steps, the font is now removed. The Bishop stands and prays over the candidates, who kneel before him,

19 *The Bishop:* Our help is in the name of the Lord;
Answer: Who made heaven and earth.
Bishop: Blessed be the name of the Lord;
Answer: From this time forth, and for ever more.

20 *The Bishop:* Let us pray.

21 Stretching out his hands towards those to be confirmed he continues,

Almighty God... (SA C15)

22 And all the people say *Amen.*

23 Each candidate in turn ... (SA C17)

24 And the newly confirmed person answers (SA C18)

25 When all have returned ... (SA C19)

26 And all those who have been confirmed reply

I promise.

27 Then the Bishop leads the newly confirmed to their place in the body of the Church, if all has taken place at the font. The service of Holy Communion is continued at the Nicene Creed, which for this occasion is said by all the people in the following form,

We believe in one God the Father Almighty,... (SA IB19)

28 The newly confirmed with the witnesses and others receive Holy Communion with the Bishop.

14. *The Australian Rites 1967*

In 1966 the Church of England in Australia Liturgical Commission submitted to the General Synod revised rites of Baptism and Confirmation. These revised services were first published in 1967 under the authority of the Standing Committee of the General Synod of the Church of England in Australia, for experimental use. The Rites are now available for use in any parish which asks for them, provided the diocesan bishop gives his consent. Such permission is now possible under the "deviations proviso" of Section 4 of the recently adopted Constitution of the Church of England in Australia. However, it should be pointed out that the Rites are not widely used, and cannot be said to represent the mind of the majority in the Australian Church. Before they are accepted for general use they are likely to undergo considerable revision.

In Australia the 1928 Alternative Rites are those in general use in most dioceses, with the exception of a few which use those of 1662.

1 THE ADMINISTRATION OF BAPTISM
TO CHILDREN AND OTHERS WHO ARE
UNABLE TO ANSWER FOR THEMSELVES

2 The clergy, the sponsors and their candidates gather at the font.

3 The sponsors shall then present their candidate to the priest:

Reverend Sir, I present *N.*, a candidate for holy baptism in the threefold name of God.

4 The priest shall then say,

Let us pray.

Almighty God, our heavenly Father, who at the baptism of your Son, Jesus Christ, in the river Jordan declared him to be your only and most loved Son; grant that *those* who here *come* to holy baptism may be born again, and as *members* of your well-loved Son may become your *children* by adoption and grace; through our Lord Jesus Christ, who lives and reigns with you, in the unity of the Holy Spirit, one God for ever and ever. *Amen*

5 The Old Testament lesson, Joel 2.28,29,32, shall then be read by a minister or a layman.

6 Then a psalm or hymn may be sung. Suggested psalms are: 27, 42.1–7, 48, 97.

7 The Epistle, Galatians 4.4–7, shall be read by the priest or some one appointed by him.

8 Response at conclusion:

Thanks be to God.

9 The Gospel shall then be read by the priest or a deacon appointed by him:

The Holy Gospel is written in the . . . chapter of the Gospel according to St . . . , beginning at the . . . verse.

10 *Response:* Glory be to you, O Lord.

11 John 15.1–5, or Mark 10.13–16.

12 *Response:* Praise be to you, O Christ.

13 The priest shall then address the sponsors, and put to them clearly their solemn duties in the name of Christ and his church. This address will lead into the renunciations and affirmations, made by the sponsors on behalf of the candidates:

14 *Priest:* Do you renounce the devil and all his works?
Sponsors: I do renounce them.
Priest: Do you renounce all pride and worldliness?
Sponsors: I do renounce them.
Priest: Do you renounce the sins of the flesh?
Sponsors: I do renounce them.
Priest: Do you believe in God, the Father almighty, maker of heaven and earth?
Sponsors: I do believe in him.
Priest: Do you believe in Jesus Christ, his only Son, our Lord? who was conceived by the Holy Spirit, born of the Virgin Mary: who suffered under Pontius Pilate, was crucified, dead and buried; who went down to Hades, and also rose again the third day; who ascended into heaven, and is seated at the right hand of God the Father Almighty, and from thence shall come again to judge the living and the dead?
Sponsors: I do believe in him.
Priest: Do you believe in the Holy Spirit; the holy catholic church; the communion of saints; the forgiveness of sins; the resurrection of the body, and the life everlasting?
Sponsors: All this I firmly believe.
Priest: Will you keep the law of God, and serve him faithfully for the rest of your life?
Sponsors: With his help, I intend to do so.

THE PRAYERS AT THE FONT

15 Merciful God, grant that in the waters of baptism the old self in *these children* may be so buried that the new man may come to life in *them. Amen.*

16 Grant that all evil desires of the flesh may die in *them* and that all things belonging to the spirit may live and grow in *them. Amen.*

17 Grant that *they* may have power and strength to win the victory and to triumph against the devil, the world and the flesh. *Amen.*

18 Grant that as *they are* here dedicated to you, by this ministry of ours, *they* may also be endowed with heavenly virtues and rewarded with everlasting life, through your kindly mercy, blessed Lord God, who live and govern all things, world without end. *Amen.*

19 *Priest:* The Lord be with you.
R. And with your spirit.
Lift up your hearts.
R. We lift them up to the Lord.
Let us give thanks to our Lord God.
R. It is right and just that we should do so.
It is indeed right and just, and for our lasting good, that we should always and everywhere give thanks to you, almighty Father, eternal God, through your most dearly loved Son, Jesus Christ our Lord, through whom in the beginning you created the world, and made men in your own likeness.

20 Minister (clerical or lay):
Let us bless the Lord.
R. Thanks be to God.

Then, when the time was fulfilled, you sent your Son into the world, to redeem mankind fallen into sin through disobedience.

He, being conceived by the Holy Spirit without any taint of sin, received for man's sake the baptism of repentance and was anointed by the Holy Spirit.

Let us bless the Lord.
R. Thanks be to God.

He by your holy will became obedient to death, even the death of the cross, that he might secure forgiveness for us, and make for himself a chosen race, a royal priesthood for his own people.

Let us bless the Lord.
R. Thanks be to God.

He, when he had ascended up on high, poured forth the spirit of promise upon those who are declared to be sons, that being born of water and Holy Spirit they might become in him a new creation.

Let us bless the Lord.
R. Thanks be to God.

Wherefore, hear us, merciful Father, we most humbly pray you, and sanctify this water for the sacramental washing away of sin, that your *servants* to be baptized here may be made *members* of your church, which is the body of your Son, our Lord.

Lord, hear our prayer,
R. and let our cry come to you.

Grant that as *they are* buried by baptism into the death of your Son and *are* made *partakers* of his resurrection, *they* may die daily to sin, and rise again to righteousness, that serving you faithfully, in the fellowship of all your saints, *they* may inherit your glorious kingdom; all this we pray, through Jesus Christ, your Son, our Lord; to whom, with you and the Holy Spirit, belong all might, majesty, dominion and power, through all the ages, world without end. *Amen.*

THE NAMING AND THE BAPTISM

21 The sponsors shall bring their candidates to the font, one by one. The presenting sponsor shall give the candidate's name. The priest appointed shall then immerse the candidate or pour water on his head, and say:

N., I baptize you in the name of the Father, and of the Son, and of the Holy Spirit. *Amen.*

22 We receive this child into the congregation of Christ's flock. From this time on, may *he* never be ashamed to confess the faith of Christ crucified, and manfully to fight under his banner against sin, the world and the devil, and to continue as Christ's faithful soldier and servant to *his* life's end. *Amen.*

23 O Lord God, we thank you that this child is born again, incorporated in the mystical body of your Son. Let the light of your countenance shine upon your servant, and let the cross of your only and most loved Son be marked in *his* heart and *his* thoughts,

(Here let the priest make the sign of the cross upon him)

that *he* may continue your faithful soldier and servant to the end of *his* life. Grant, O Lord, that *he* may always confess your holy name, and in due time be strengthened with the gift of the Holy Spirit in confirmation and come with due preparation to receive the holy communion of the body and blood of your Son, and go forth into the world to serve you faithfully in the fellowship of your Church. *Amen.*

24 The Lord's Prayer

25 The priest shall add the following prayer for the home:

Almighty God, our heavenly Father, whose blessed Son shared at Nazareth the life of an earthly home; bless the home of *this child* and grant wisdom and understanding to all who have care of *him* that *he* may grow up in the knowledge of your love: through the same your Son, Jesus Christ our Lord. *Amen.*

26 and a blessing, if the baptism is not within the context of another public service:

The Lord bless you and keep you; the Lord make his face to shine upon you and be gracious unto you; the Lord lift up his countenance upon you and give you peace, now and for evermore. *Amen.*

1 A SERVICE OF CONFIRMATION
FOR THOSE PREVIOUSLY BAPTIZED

2 A hymn or psalm (e.g. Psalm 27.1–7) may be sung.

3 The priest and sponsors will then present their candidates to the Bishop:

Reverend Father in God, I present *N.*, who has already been baptized, as a candidate for confirmation.

4 The bishop shall then address the people, at his discretion, using some such form as this:

We are gathered together in God's sight to confirm the candidates now presented. These persons have been baptized and they have been instructed in the christian faith and in the practice of christian living. They come in penitence and faith now to receive in confirmation the power of the Holy Spirit, who will consecrate them to the service of almighty God, and bestow upon them his sevenfold gifts.

Our Lord promised that he would pray the Father to give his apostles the Spirit who would remain with them forever. On the day of Pentecost this promise was fulfilled in the outpouring of the Spirit upon the church, as had been foretold by the prophet Joel; enabling the disciples to be Christ's witnesses to the furthest part of the earth.

We now pray that this same Spirit who was given to the apostles at Pentecost may be given to these persons at the prayer of the church, when they receive the laying-on of hands, and that they may faithfully serve him all the days of their life, till they come to his everlasting kingdom.

5 *Bishop:* The Lord be with you;

   Response: and with your spirit

Let us pray.

Almighty God, our heavenly Father, you have called these your servants and made them your children in the waters of baptism; mercifully grant that they may ratify the promises made for them by their sponsors and witness to their faith in the lives they lead. Grant that the good work which you have begun in them may be strengthened by the outpouring of your holy Spirit; through Jesus Christ, your Son, our Lord, who lives and reigns with you in the unity of the same Spirit, one God, always, world without end. *Amen.*

6 The Old Testament lesson, Joel 2.28,29,32, shall then be read by a minister or a layman.

7 A hymn or psalm (e.g. Psalm 43, 48, or 97) may be sung.

8 The Lesson or Epistle shall then be read by the priest or someone appointed by him: Acts 10.36–43,   Romans 1.1–6,   I Corinthians 15.1–11

9 The Gospel shall then be read by the priest or by a deacon appointed by him.

The holy Gospel is written in the fourteenth chapter of the Gospel according to St John, beginning at the fifteenth verse.

Response: Glory be to you, O Lord.
John 14.15–17.
Response: Praise be to you, O Christ.

10 The Bishop then delivers a short charge to the candidates, leading into the renunciations and affirmations. The candidates reply individually.

Bishop: Do you renounce the devil and all his works?
Response: I do renounce them. (A IB14)

11 The bishop shall then mark the forehead of each candidate with the sign of the cross (or anoint him with the chrism if so allowed by the canons) and say,

The seal of the gift of the Holy Spirit.

12 And he shall add

Blessed be the Lord God Almighty; for he has turned to his people and has set them free; he has made the morning sun of heaven to rise upon them, and to shine upon those who live in darkness; according to his mercy he saves *these* his *servants* by the washing of regeneration and the renewing of the Holy Spirit, giving *them* forgiveness of all *their* sins. Strengthen in *them*, O God, we pray, your manifold gifts of grace, the spirit of wisdom and understanding, the spirit of counsel and might, the spirit of knowledge and true godliness, and fill *them* with the spirit of your holy fear now and forever. *Amen.*

13 Then the candidates shall kneel before him and the bishop shall lay his hand on each one of them saying,

Defend, O Lord, your child *N*. . . . with your heavenly grace, that *he* may continue yours forever, and daily increase in your holy Spirit more and more, until *he* comes to your everlasting kingdom. *Amen.*

The Lord be with you.
R. And with your spirit.

14 The Lord's Prayer.

15 This prayer may be added

Almighty and everlasting God, we offer our prayers for your *servants* upon whom, after the example of your apostles, we have now laid our hands. Let your fatherly hand, we pray, always be over *them*, let your holy Spirit always be with *them*. Strengthen *them* evermore with the body and blood of your Son, and lead *them* to know and obey your word, that finally *they* may attain everlasting life; through Jesus Christ our Lord. *Amen.*

Our help is in the name of the Lord.
R. Who has made heaven and earth.
Blessed be the name of the Lord
R. Now and for ever, world without end.

16 The bishop shall add one of the following sentences if the service is not followed by the Holy Communion:

May the God of peace himself sanctify you wholly, . . . (1 Thess. 5.23, RSV)
Now may the God of peace who brought again . . . (Heb. 13.20, RSV)
May the God of all grace . . . (1 Pet. 5.10–11, RSV)

17 Then may follow Te Deum Laudamus or a similar hymn of praise, as the service of Holy Communion commences and the candidates take their places with the assembled Christians

18   The bishop may mark the forehead of each candidate with the sign of the cross: or anoint him with the chrism, if so allowed by the canons, saying *The seal of the gift of the Holy Spirit*: before he lays hands on the candidate

19   When the service is followed by the Communion, the first two sections may be omitted.

20   If there is no Communion, the bishop will give a customary blessing at the end of the service.

1 A RITE OF
BAPTISM AND CONFIRMATION
OF ADULT CANDIDATES

2   The procession of bishop and other clergy, with the candidates and their sponsors proceeds directly to the font, and the congregation gathers conveniently. Psalm 51 is said or sung.

3   The sponsors present their candidates to the bishop, saying,

Reverend Father in God, I present *N*., a candidate for membership in the family of God and in the body of Christ.

4   The bishop reads the invocatory prayer:

Almighty God, our heavenly Father, . . .

A IB4, *but* become ⟨may become⟩

5   If the service does not take place within the framework of the Holy Communion, the priest shall here read the lessons: Ezekiel 36.24–28; Romans 6.1–11; Mark 1.1–11, or John 3.3–15.

6   The Gospel at least, with its appropriate responses, shall be read.

7   The bishop then delivers a short charge to the candidates, leading into the renunciations and affirmations. The candidates reply individually.

8   *Bishop:* Do you renounce the devil and all his works?
Reply: I do renounce . . . (A IB14)

9   The prayers at the font are said by the officiating priests as appointed by the bishop:

10–13   Merciful God, . . . (A IB15, 16, 17, 18)

14   *Priest:* The Lord be with you,
R. and with you. (A IB19)

15   Minister (clerical or lay):

Let us bless the Lord.
R. Thanks be to God.

Priest (continues):

Then, when the time was fulfilled, . . . (A IB20)

THE NAMING AND THE BAPTISM

16 The sponsors . . .

A IB21, *but* his head saying, ⟨his head, and say:⟩

N., I baptize you in the name of the Father, and of the Son, and of the Holy Spirit. *Amen.*

17 The bishop shall say,

We receive this child . . . unto *his* life's end. *Amen.* (A IB22)

18 The bishop shall then mark the forehead of each candidate with the sign of the cross (or anoint him with chrism, if so allowed by the canons), or say,

The seal of the gift of the Holy Spirit.

19 And he shall add,

Blessed be the Lord God almighty; for he has turned to his people and has set them free; he has made the morning sun of heaven to rise upon them, and to shine upon those who live in darkness; according to his mercy he saves *these* his *servants* by the washing of regeneration and the renewing of the Holy Spirit, giving *them* forgiveness of all *their* sins.

Strengthen in *them*, O God, we pray, your manifold gifts of grace, the spirit of wisdom and understanding, the spirit of counsel and might, the spirit of knowledge and true godliness, and fill *them* with the spirit of your holy fear now and forever. *Amen.*

20 Then the candidates shall kneel before him and the bishop shall lay his hand on each one of them, saying,

Defend, O Lord, . . . (A C13)

21 The Lord's Prayer

22 This prayer may be added,

Almighty and everlasting God, . . . (A C15)

23 The bishop shall add one of the following sentences if the service is not followed by Holy Communion:

May the God of peace himself sanctify you wholly, . . . (1 Thess. 5.23, RSV)

Now may the God of peace who brought again . . . (Heb. 13.20, RSV)

May the God of all grace . . . 1 Pet. 5.10–11, RSV)

24 Then may follow Te Deum Laudamus, or a similar hymn of praise, as the service of Holy Communion commences and the candidates take their place with the assembled Christians,

15. *The Scottish Episcopal Rite 1967*

In 1967 this revised order for the Baptism of Infants was authorized for permissive use, for an experimental period, under Canon XXIII-8. Following this authorization the text of this new rite was first published in February 1968. No experimental rite for Confirmation has yet been produced.

I PERMISSIVE RITE FOR THE BAPTISM OF INFANTS

2 The parents and the Godparents with them shall make the answers to the questions asked in this service.

3 It is the duty of the minister to satisfy himself reasonably that a child brought for Baptism has not been baptized already. In doubtful cases the form for conditional Baptism should be used.

INTRODUCTION

4 The sacrament of Baptism is the appointed way of entrance into Christ's Church. Baptism speaks of a washing away of sin and the start of a new life. Much will depend on parents and Godparents. By their example and their teaching they must see that this child will grow up into a true and loyal member of Christ's Church, and in due time come forward for Confirmation and Communion.

5   Let us pray.

Almighty God our heavenly Father, who in every generation dost bestow new sons and daughters on thy Church, grant that this infant may be born again of water and of the Spirit; that daily increasing in the knowledge and love of thee, *he* may ever be numbered among the children of thy adoption; through Jesus Christ our Lord. Amen.

6 Hear what is written in S. Mark's Gospel; in the tenth chapter beginning at the thirteenth verse.

And they were bringing children to him, . . . (Mark 10.13–16, RSV)

7 And again in S. John's Gospel in the third chapter beginning at the fifth verse.

Jesus answered, "Truly, truly, I say to you, unless one is born of water and the Spirit, he cannot enter the Kingdom of God."

8 Let us pray for *this child* whom we bring to Baptism in the name of our Lord, and say together:

Almighty and everlasting God, heavenly Father, we give thee humble thanks that thou hast called us to the knowledge of thy grace, and to faith in thee. Increase this knowledge, and confirm this faith in us evermore. Give thy Holy Spirit to *this infant*, that *he* may be born again, and made *an heir* of everlasting salvation; through Jesus Christ our Lord. Amen.

THE PROMISES

9 You have brought this child to Baptism. You have heard that our Lord Jesus Christ wants to make *him* the child of God and a member of the Church. You must therefore make the Christian profession in which *he* is to be baptized, and in which you are to bring *him* up.

10 Will you bring up this child to reject the devil and all his works, the evil influences of the world, and all sinful desires?
R. I will.
Do you profess the Christian Faith?
R. I do.

11 Here shall be said the Apostles' Creed:

I believe in God the Father Almighty, ... (CF12)

12 Do you promise to keep God's will and commandments?
R. I do.

THE BLESSING OF THE WATER

13 The Lord be with you;
R. And with thy spirit.
Lift up your hearts;
R. We lift them up unto the Lord.
Let us give thanks unto our Lord God;
R. It is meet and right so to do.
It is indeed right and our duty always and everywhere to give thanks to thee, O Lord, Holy Father, Almighty and Eternal God, because thy Son Jesus Christ, for our forgiveness gave his life for us and commanded us to go and teach and baptize all men in the Name of the Father and of the Son and of the Holy Spirit. Therefore hear our prayer and bless

and hallow and sanctify this water, that it may be used to wash away all sin. May *this child* now to be baptized therein receive thy grace and new life and ever remain in the mystical body of thy Son, Jesus Christ, our Lord. Amen.

THE BAPTISM

14 The priest shall take each child and shall say to the sponsors,

Name this child.

Naming *him* after them he shall dip *him* three times in the water, or pour water on *him* three times saying

N., I baptize you in the name of the Father and of the Son and of the Holy Ghost. Amen.

CEREMONIES AFTER BAPTISM

15 Then shall the priest make a cross on the forehead of each child saying;

I sign you with the sign of the Cross

Here the people join in

in token that you shall not be ashamed to confess the faith of Christ crucified, and manfully to fight under his banner against sin, the world and the devil, and to continue his faithful soldier and servant unto your life's end.

16 The priest may then give to the parent or sponsor of each child a lighted candle saying to the child:

I give you this sign

Here the people join with him saying

to show that you have passed from darkness to light; that henceforth you may shine as a light in the world to the glory of God.

17 God has received you by baptism into his Church. We therefore welcome you into the Lord's family—

As a fellow member of the body of Christ
As a child of the same heavenly Father
As an inheritor with us of the kingdom of God.

18 Our Father . . .

19 O Father, we thank thee that *this infant* has been born again by thy Holy Spirit, and has been made thine own child by adoption, and has

been incorporated into thy Holy Church. Grant, O Lord, that united with Christ through his death and resurrection *he* may die to sin and live to righteousness. From darkness lead *him* to light; from death to life eternal, for Jesus' sake. Amen.

20 Let us pray for this child's home;

Almighty God, our heavenly Father, whose blessed Son did share at Nazareth the life of an earthly home; Bless we beseech thee the home of *this child*, and grant wisdom and understanding to all who have care of *him*; that he may grow up in the love of Christ our Lord. Amen.

DUTIES OF PARENTS AND GODPARENTS

21 Parents and Godparents should always remember that Baptism is the first step in the Christian Life. You must try and see that this child is brought up to live as a Christian should, loving and serving God and his fellow men. It will be your duty to teach *him* to pray, to worship with the Church, and in due time to bring *him* to the Bishop to be confirmed. *He* will then make for *himself* the promises that you have made in *his* name, and strengthened by the Holy Spirit will come to the Holy Communion to receive the sacrament of the Body and Blood of Christ, so that *he* may go forth into the world to serve God faithfully in the fellowship of his Church.

22 Will you pray for this child and help *him* to learn and to do these things?
R. I will.

16. The Church of England Rites 1968

These texts are from *Alternative Services Second Series* BAPTISM AND CONFIRMATION, authorized for experimental use in the Church of England, from 16 February 1968. The first draft of these services was contained in *Baptism and Confirmation, A Report submitted by the Church of England Liturgical Commission to the Archbishops of Canterbury and York, December 1966*, published by S.P.C.K. 1967.

Early in 1967 the Convocations of Canterbury and York gave their approval to the experimental services of Baptism and Confirmation which the 1966 Report contained. However, before these services could be used for an experimental period, the approval of the House of Laity was required. Approval for the experimental use of the Confirmation Service was given on 30 September 1967. On 16 February 1968, the House of Laity gave formal approval, for the experimental period of four years, to the service of Baptism contained in the Report.[1] The House of Laity did, however, raise two points in connection with the service of Infant Baptism, upon which further explanation or comment, if not revision, is expected before the service is considered for a further experimental period: first, in the section *The Baptism*, there was a preference for the full interrogative creed in place of the present threefold credal affirmation based upon the Prayer Book Catechism; secondly, it was requested that the giving of the candle and that which follows should be reconsidered.

I THE BAPTISM OF THOSE WHO ARE NOT OLD ENOUGH TO ANSWER FOR THEMSELVES

2 The Preface
It is the practice of the Church of England to admit to Baptism those who are not old enough to profess the Christian faith. But this is done on the understanding that they will receive a Christian upbringing. This means that they will be taught the Christian religion and encouraged to practise it, until such time as they present themselves to the Bishop for Confirmation, and publicly profess the faith in which they have been baptized.

Before proceeding to baptize a child, the Priest shall ask the parents and sponsors whether he has been baptized before. He shall also ask them:

whether they are prepared to the best of their ability to give him a Christian upbringing within the family of Christ's Church;

[1] Experimental use of these services is governed by section three of the Prayer Book (Alternative and Other Services) Measure 1965, which reads as follows: *A form or draft of a form of Service approved under either section one or section two of this Measure may not be used in any Cathedral which is a parish church or in any Church in a parish without the agreement of the Parochial Church Council of the parish or in any Guild Church without the agreement of the Guild Church Council, or in the case of Services known as Occasional Offices if any of the persons concerned objects beforehand to its use.*

whether they will help him to be regular in public worship and in private prayer, not only by their teaching, but also by their example and their prayers;

whether they will encourage him in due time to come to Confirmation and Communion.

3   The Priest shall say to the whole Congregation:

The Gospel tells us that our Lord Jesus Christ was himself baptized for our sake in the River Jordan and the Spirit came upon him. Listen to his command to his disciples after his resurrection. "Full authority in heaven and on earth has been committed to me. Go forth therefore and make all nations my disciples; baptize men everywhere in the Name of the Father and the Son and the Holy Spirit. And be assured, I am with you always, to the end of time."

On the day of Pentecost St Peter obeyed this command, saying, "Repent and be baptized, every one of you, in the name of Jesus the Messiah for the forgiveness of your sins; and you will receive the gift of the Holy Spirit."

Let us therefore thank God through our Lord Jesus Christ for our own Baptism and say together:

4   Heavenly Father, we give thee thanks that thou has called us to the knowledge of thy grace and to faith in thee. Increase this knowledge, and confirm this faith in us all our days, through the power of thy Holy Spirit, for the sake of Jesus Christ our Lord.

5   And the Priest shall continue, saying,

Our Lord Jesus Christ took children in his arms and blessed them, saying, "Let the children come to me; do not try to stop them; for the kingdom of God belongs to such as these. I tell you, whoever does not accept the kingdom of God like a child will never enter it."

Again he said, "In truth, I tell you, unless a man has been born over again he cannot see the kingdom of God. No one can enter the kingdom of God without being born from water and spirit."

Let us pray for *these children* whom we bring to Baptism in the Name of our Lord, and say together:

6   Heavenly Father, grant that by thy Holy Spirit *these children* may be born again and brought to know thee in the family of thy Church; that in newness of life *they* may overcome evil and grow in grace unto *their lives'* end; through Jesus Christ our Lord.

THE DECISION

7 The Priest shall say to the parents and sponsors,

Those who bring children to be baptized must affirm their allegiance to Christ and their rejection of all that is evil.

It is your duty to bring up *these children* to fight against evil and to follow Christ.

Therefore I ask:

8 Do you turn to Christ?
R. I turn to Christ.
Do you repent of your sins?
R. I repent of my sins.
Do you renounce evil?
R. I renounce evil.

THE BLESSING OF THE WATER

9 The Priest shall go to the font with the parents and sponsors and the children to be baptized, and shall say,

The Lord be with you;
R. And with thy spirit.

Let us pray.

We give thanks to thee, almighty Father, everlasting God, through thy most dearly beloved Son, Jesus Christ our Lord;

Because by his death and resurrection thou hast broken the power of evil, and by thy sending of the Spirit thou hast made us new men in the family of thy Church:

Bless, we pray thee, this water, that all who are baptized in it may be born again in Christ; that being baptized into his death, and receiving forgiveness of all their sins, they may know the power of his resurrection, and, may walk in newness of life;

Through the same thy Son Jesus Christ our Lord, to whom with thee and the same Spirit be all might, majesty, dominion, and power, throughout all ages, world without end. *Amen.*

THE BAPTISM

10 The Priest shall then say to the parents and sponsors,

You have brought *these children* to Baptism. You stand in the presence of God and his Church. You must now make the Christian profession in which *they are* to be baptized, and in which you will bring *them* up.

Do you believe and trust in God the Father, who made the world?
R. I believe and trust in him.
Do you believe and trust in his Son Jesus Christ, who redeemed mankind?
R. I believe and trust in him.
Do you believe and trust in his Holy Spirit, who sanctifies the People of God?
R. I believe and trust in him.

11 The Priest shall then take each child, and having asked *his* name, shall dip *him* in the water, or pour water upon *him*, saying,

N., I baptize you in the Name of the Father, and of the Son, and of the Holy Spirit. Amen.

THE SIGNING WITH THE CROSS

12 The Priest shall make a cross upon the forehead of each child, saying,

I sign you with the sign ✠ of the cross,

13 And here the People shall join with him, saying,

to show that you must not be ashamed to confess the faith of Christ crucified, and manfully to fight under his banner against sin, the world, and the devil, and to continue Christ's faithful soldier and servant unto your life's end.

14 The Priest may give to the parent or sponsor of each child a lighted candle, saying to the child,

I give you this sign,

15 And here the People shall join with him, saying,

to show that you have passed from darkness to light; that henceforth you may shine as a light in the world, to the glory of God the Father.

16 Priest and People together may then say to all the newly baptized,

God has received you by Baptism into his Church. We therefore welcome you into the Lord's family, as *fellow-members* of the Body of Christ, as *children* of the same heavenly Father, as *inheritors* with us of the kingdom of God.

6—C.I.

THE PRAYERS

17 Then shall be said,

Our Father, who art in heaven, . . . (CF9)

18 Then the Priest shall say,

We thank thee, O Father, that by thy Holy Spirit thou hast caused *these children* to be born again, to become thine own by adoption, and *members* of thy Church.

Grant that *they* may grow in the faith in which *they* have been baptized; grant that *they* themselves may profess it when *they come* to be confirmed; and
grant that all things belonging to the Spirit may live and grow in *them*; through Jesus Christ our Lord. *Amen.*

19 Bless, we pray thee, the *parents* of *these children*, give *them* the Spirit of wisdom and love, that their home may be an image of thy eternal kingdom; through Jesus Christ our Lord. *Amen.*

20 The grace of our Lord Jesus Christ, and the love of God, and the fellowship of the Holy Spirit, be with us all evermore. *Amen.*

21 When Baptism is ministered at the Holy Communion, the Priest shall proceed in the Communion service to the end of the Gospel. He shall then preach the sermon; and after that he may begin the foregoing Order at the Decision, and continue up to and including the Signing with the Cross. He shall then at once continue the Communion at the Preparation of the People or at the Preparation of the Bread and Wine. In place of the prayers at the conclusion of the Communion, he may use the foregoing prayer (18) in this Order (*We thank thee, O Father etc.*).

22 When Baptism is ministered at Morning or Evening Prayer, the Office shall be sung or said to the end of the second lesson. The Priest may then begin the foregoing Order at the Decision. And after the Signing with the Cross, the Office shall be resumed at the last canticle.

1 THE CONFIRMATION OF THOSE WHO HAVE ALREADY BEEN BAPTIZED AND ARE NOW OLD ENOUGH TO ANSWER FOR THEMSELVES

INTRODUCTION

2 The Bishop shall say,

The Lord be with you;
R. And with thy spirit.

Let us pray.

Almighty God, our heavenly Father, who by thy Holy Spirit hast called *these* thy *servants*, and made *them* thy *children* in the waters of Baptism:

Mercifully grant that, being fulfilled by the same Spirit, and strengthened by the Body and Blood of thy Son, *they* may continue thy *servants* and attain thy promises;

Through the same thy Son Jesus Christ our Lord, who with thee and the same Spirit is alive and reigns, one God, world without end. *Amen.*

3   One or more of the following lessons, or some other passage of scripture, shall then be read.

Thus says the Lord God: I will sprinkle clean water upon you, ... (Ezek. 36. 25a, 26–8, RSV)

4   Christ is like a single body with its many limbs and organs, ... (1 Cor. 12.12–13, NEB)

5   Jesus said to his disciples: "If you love me ... (John 14.15–17, NEB)

THE DECISION

6   The Bishop shall say to those who are to be confirmed,

Those who are to be confirmed must affirm their allegiance to Christ and their rejection of all that is evil. Therefore I ask:

7   Do you turn to Christ? ... (S2 IB8)

THE PROFESSION OF FAITH

8   The Bishop shall then say to them,

You have come here to be confirmed. You stand in the presence of God and his Church. You must now yourselves make the Christian profession in which you were baptized.

9   Do you believe and trust in God the Father, ... (S2 IB10)

THE CONFIRMATION

10   Then the Bishop shall at once minister Confirmation. All who are to be confirmed shall kneel before him; and he shall stand facing them, and shall say.

Our help is in the Name of the Lord:
R. Who has made heaven and earth,

Blessed be the Name of the Lord;
R. Henceforth, world without end.

11 Stretching out his hands towards those who are to be confirmed, he shall say,

Almighty and everliving God, who in Baptism hast caused thy
servants to be born again by water and the Spirit, and hast given unto
them forgiveness of all *their* sins:

Send forth upon *them* thy Holy Spirit; the Spirit of wisdom and
understanding; the Spirit of counsel and inward strength; the Spirit of
knowledge and true godliness; and fill *them*, O Lord with the Spirit
of thy holy fear.

12 And all the People shall say, *Amen.*

13 The Bishop shall then lay his hand upon the head of each one of them saying,

Confirm, O Lord, thy servant (*N.*) with thy Holy Spirit.

14 And each one shall answer, *Amen.*

15 When all have been confirmed, the Bishop and People shall say,

Defend, O Lord, *these* thy *servants* with thy heavenly grace, that *they*
may continue thine for ever, and daily increase in thy Holy Spirit more
and more, until *they* come unto thy everlasting kingdom.

THE PRAYERS

16 Then shall be said,

Our Father, who art in heaven, . . . (CF9)

17 The Bishop shall then say,

Almighty and everliving God, we make our humble supplications unto
thee for *these* thy *servants*, upon whom, after the example of thy holy
apostles, we have now laid our hands, to assure *them*, by this sign, of thy
favour and goodness towards *them*. Let thy fatherly hand, we beseech
thee, ever be over *them*; let thy Holy Spirit ever be with *them*;
strengthen *them* evermore with the Body and Blood of thy Son; and
so lead *them* in the knowledge and obedience of thy word, that in the
end *they* may obtain everlasting life; through the same Christ our Lord.
Amen.

18 The Bishop shall then give the blessing.

THE HOLY COMMUNION

19 When Confirmation is ministered at the Holy Communion, the opening prayer
may be used in place of the Collect of the Day, and the lessons in place of the

Epistle and Gospel.[1] After the Gospel and sermon, the Bishop shall proceed with the Decision, the Profession of Faith, and the Confirmation. He shall then at once begin the Preparation of the People or the Preparation of the Bread and Wine; and in place of the prayers at the conclusion of the Communion, he may use the final prayer of the Order of Confirmation (17).

[1] But if Confirmation is ministered at the Holy Communion on Christmas Day, Easter Day, the Ascension Day, or Whitsunday, the Collect, Epistle, and Gospel of the Day shall always be read.

7 THE BAPTISM AND CONFIRMATION OF THOSE WHO ARE OLD ENOUGH TO ANSWER FOR THEMSELVES

INTRODUCTION

1 At the entry of the Ministers Psalm 34.1–8 or a hymn may be sung.

2 Then shall the Bishop say,

The Lord be with you;
R. And with thy Spirit.

Let us pray.

Almighty God, who at the Baptism of thy Christ in the River Jordan didst declare him to be thine only-begotten Son: Grant that in Baptism *these* thy *servants* may be made his *members* by thy Holy Spirit, and become thy *children* in the family of thy Church; through the same thy Son Jesus Christ our Lord, who with thee and the same Spirit is alive and reigns, one God, world without end. *Amen.*

3 The following lesson may then be read.

Thus says the Lord God: I will sprinkle clean water upon you, . . . (Ezek. 36.25a, 26–8, RSV)

4 Psalm 107.1–9 or a hymn may then be sung.

5 The following lesson shall then be read. But it may be omitted if the Old Testament lesson has been read.

Christ is like a single body with its many limbs and organs, . . . (1 Cor. 12.12–13, NEB)

6 Psalm 97.9–12 or a hymn may then be sung.

7 The following lesson shall then be read; and when the Gospel is announced, the People shall answer,

Glory be to thee, O Lord.
Here begins the Gospel of Jesus Christ the Son of God. . . . (Mark 1.1–11, NEB)

8 At the end of the Gospel the People shall answer,

Praise be to thee, O Christ.

9 The sermon shall be preached after the Gospel.

THE DECISION

10 After the sermon the Bishop shall say to those who are to be baptized (and if there are any who have already been baptized and are now to be confirmed, they too shall answer),

Those who are to be baptized (and confirmed) must affirm their allegiance to Christ and their rejection of all that is evil. Therefore I ask:

11 Do you turn to Christ? . . . (S2 IB8)

12 The Bishop and other Ministers shall go to the font with those who are to be baptized; and meanwhile Psalm 42.1–7 or a hymn may be sung.

THE BLESSING OF THE WATER

13 The Bishop shall then say,

The Lord be with you;
R. And with thy spirit.

Let us pray.

We give thanks to thee, almighty Father, . . . (S2 IB9)

THE BAPTISM

14 The Minister who baptizes shall say to those who are to be baptized (and if there are any who have already been baptized and are now to be confirmed, they too shall answer),

You have come here to be baptized. You stand in the presence of God and his Church. You must now make the Christian profession in which you are to be baptized.

15 Do you believe and trust in God the Father, . . . (S2 IB10)

16 Each person to be baptized shall then come to the font, and the Minister, having asked *his* name, shall dip *him* in the water, or pour water upon *him*, saying,

N., I baptize you in the Name of the Father, and of the Son, and of the Holy Spirit. Amen.

THE SIGNING WITH THE CROSS

17 One of the Ministers shall make a cross upon the forehead of each one of them, saying,

I sign you with the sign of the cross,

18 And here the People shall join with him, saying,

to show that you must not be ashamed . . . (S2 IB13)

19 One of the Ministers may then give to each one of them a lighted candle, saying,

I give you this sign,

20 And here the People shall join with him saying,

to show that you have passed . . . (S2 IB15)

21 The Ministers and People may then say to all the newly baptized,

God has received you by Baptism into his Church. (S2 IB16)

THE CONFIRMATION

22 (S2 C10)

23 (S2 C11)

24 (S2 C12)

25 (S2 C13)

26 (S2 C14)

27 (S2 C15)

THE HOLY COMMUNION

28 The Bishop shall at once begin the Communion at the Preparation of the People or at the Preparation of the Bread and Wine; and the newly confirmed shall communicate with him. In place of the prayers at the conclusion of the Communion, he may use the final prayer (30) in this Order (*Almighty God, we thank thee etc.*)

THE PRAYERS

29 But if there is no Communion, the Bishop and People shall say,

Our Father, who art in heaven, . . . (CF9)

30 The Bishop shall then say,

Almighty God, we thank thee that by thy Holy Spirit thou hast given unto *these* thy *servants* the gift of eternal life; and we pray that *they* may be strengthened by the Body and Blood of thy Son to serve thee faithfully with all thy People; through the same Christ our Lord. *Amen.*

31 The God of peace, who brought again from the dead our Lord Jesus, that great shepherd of the sheep, through the blood of the everlasting covenant, make you perfect in every good work to do his will, working in you that which is well-pleasing in his sight, through Jesus Christ, to whom be glory for ever and ever. *Amen.*

17. The Welsh Rites 1968

In 1957 the Church in Wales published; *The Church in Wales Revised Services for Experimental Use*, HOLY BAPTISM AND CONFIRMATION. The services in this book were then introduced and authorized for experimental use. According to the Canon of September 1956, dealing with use of experimental services in the Church in Wales, such services can be used for a maximum period of ten years. While these experimental services have been in use for ten years, their permissive use is to continue until the next revision is duly authorized.

When the ten-year experimental period was approaching its end, the clergy and laity in the Church in Wales were asked to submit their criticisms and suggestions with regard to the revised services. In the light of these comments the Liturgical Commission has produced a number of revised services for Baptism and Confirmation.

As it is proposed that these revised services will replace those in the BCP and become the only lawful services for Baptism and Confirmation in the Church in Wales, it is necessary that they go through all the types of Bill Procedure. The first, formal reading, without debate, took place in April 1968, the second reading in September 1968, when there was a short debate. The third reading will take place after due consideration has been given to further proposed amendments. Following the third reading the revisions will be promulgated as a Canon of the Church in Wales.

The texts which follow are those being considered at the present time; they are shorter and simpler, both in language and structure, than those of 1957.

1   PUBLIC BAPTISM OF INFANTS
COMMONLY CALLED CHRISTENING

2   The Church teaches that Baptism, where it may be had, is generally necessary to salvation.

3   It is the duty of Christians to bring their children to Holy Baptism. Further, it is their duty to see that their children are instructed in the Catechism and brought to the Bishop to be confirmed, that they may be admitted to the Holy Communion.
   When infants are to be baptized, due notice shall be given to the Parish Priest with the names of at least two sponsors, one godfather and one godmother. Sponsors shall be baptized Christians and it is desirable that they should be regular communicants of the Church in Wales or of a Church in communion with it. If no other sponsors are available, parents may be sponsors for their own child.

4   As far as possible, Baptism shall be administered on Sundays or on other holy days in the presence of the congregation.
   When Baptism is administered at Morning Prayer or Evening Prayer, it shall follow immediately after the Second Lesson, and Morning or Evening Prayer may end at the Third Collect.
   When Baptism takes place at a celebration of the Holy Eucharist, it shall begin

after the Gospel or after the Sermon. After the Baptism, the Holy Eucharist shall continue with the Nicene Creed.

5 When a Priest cannot be present, it is lawful for a Deacon to baptize infants. In an emergency, if no Priest or Deacon is available, it is lawful for any lay person to baptize, in the Form prescribed for Private Baptism.

6 The Priest shall make certain that children brought for baptism have not already been baptized.

7 Sufficient water shall be poured into the Font immediately before the service.

THE INTRODUCTION

8 At the time appointed for the Baptism, the parents and godparents with the child shall come to the Font and the Minister shall meet them there and shall say to them:

What do you ask of the Church of God?
Answer: We ask for Holy Baptism for *this child*, that *he* may be made *a Christian.*

9 Then the Priest shall say:

You have brought this child here to be baptized, Our Saviour Christ says, No one can enter into the kingdom of God unless he is born again of water and of the Holy Spirit. In Baptism our heavenly Father will make *this child a member* of Christ, the *child* of God, and *an inheritor* of the kingdom of heaven.

You must see that *he* is brought up to worship with the Church and that *he is* taught the Creed, the Lord's Prayer, and the Ten Commandments, and *is* instructed in the Church Catechism.

You are to take care also that *he* is brought to the Bishop to be confirmed, that, strengthened by the Holy Spirit, *he* may devoutly and regularly receive the Holy Communion and serve God faithfully in the fellowship of his Church.

Will you pray for *him* and help *him* to keep the promises you will make on *his* behalf?
Answer: I will, by the help of God.

⟩ Then shall the Priest and people say this prayer:

Almighty God, our heavenly Father; Look mercifully upon *this child*; Give *him* thy Holy Spirit that *he* may be born again; Deliver *him* from the dominion of evil, and receive *him* into the family of Christ's Church; through Jesus Christ our Lord. *Amen.*

11 Then shall the Priest bless the Water in this form:

We give thanks to thee, O Lord, Holy Father, Almighty, Everlasting God, because thou hast appointed the Water of Baptism for the regeneration of mankind through thy beloved Son; who at his baptism in Jordan was anointed with the Holy Spirit; and after his saving Death and mighty Resurrection commanded his Apostles to go and make disciples of all nations, baptizing them in the Name of the Father and of the Son and of the Holy Spirit:

Hear, therefore, we beseech thee, the prayers of thy Church;

Sanctify this Water for the mystical washing away of sin, and grant that *this child*, now to be baptized therein, may receive the fulness of thy grace, and ever remain among thy faithful and elect children;

Through Jesus Christ our Lord, to whom with thee in the unity of the Holy Spirit, be all honour and glory, world without end. *Amen.*

THE PROMISES

12 Then shall the Priest ask these questions which the parents and godparents shall answer on behalf of the child.

Do you renounce the works of the devil, the vanities of the world, and the sinful desires of the flesh?
Answer: I renounce them all.
Do you believe and trust in God the Father, who made you and all the world; and in his Son Jesus Christ, who redeemed you and all mankind; and in the Holy Spirit, who sanctifies you and all the elect people of God?
Answer: I do so believe and trust.
Will you obediently keep God's holy will and commandments all the days of your life?
Answer: I will, the Lord being my helper.

THE BAPTISM

13 Then shall the Priest take the child in his arms or by the hand and shall say:

Name this child.

14 Then shall the godparents name the child and the Priest shall pour Water three times on him or dip him three times in the Water, saying:

15 *N.* I baptize thee In the Name of the Father, and of the Son, and of the Holy Spirit. Amen.

16 Then the Priest shall give back the child to one of the godparents.

THE SIGNING WITH THE CROSS

7 Then the Priest shall make the sign of the Cross on the child's forehead, saying:

Seeing that this child has now been made a member of Christ's flock, we sign *him* ✠ with the sign of the Cross, in token that *he* shall not be ashamed to confess the faith of Christ crucified, and manfully to fight under his banner, against sin, the world, and the devil; and to continue Christ's faithful soldier and servant unto *his* life's end. Amen.

8 Then he may give to one of the godparents a lighted candle, and say:

We give this lighted candle to this child as a sign of the light of Christ and of the grace of Baptism; may *he* walk before God as one of the children of light, that when our Lord comes, *he* may be worthy to go forth with all his saints to meet him and share in his eternal joy.

THE CONCLUDING PRAYERS

Then shall the Priest say:

Now that *this child* is by Baptism born again and grafted into the Body of Christ, which is his Church; let us thank God for these benefits, and together pray that *this child* may lead the rest of *his* life according to this beginning.

Then shall be said by all:

Our Father, which art in heaven, . . . (CF11)

Then shall the Priest say:

We thank thee, heavenly Father, for the mercies now given to *this child* in Baptism: Grant, we pray thee, that buried with Christ in his death and united with him in his resurrection, *he* may serve thee here in newness of life, so that finally, with all thy holy Church, *he* may come to thine everlasting kingdom; through Jesus Christ our Lord. *Amen.*

Then may follow this prayer:

Almighty God our heavenly Father, whose dearly beloved Son Jesus Christ shared with the Blessed Virgin Mary and Saint Joseph the life of an earthly home at Nazareth: Bless we beseech thee the home of *this child*; and give such grace and wisdom to all who have the care of *him*, that by their word and good example *he* may learn truly to know and love thee; through the same thy Son Jesus Christ our Saviour. *Amen.*

23 When Baptism is administered as a separate service, the Priest shall dismiss the people with this Blessing:

The Blessing of God Almighty, the Father, the Son, and the Holy Spirit, be amongst you, and remain with you always. *Amen.*

24 Immediately after the service the Priest shall enter the customary record in the baptismal register of the parish.

I   THE ORDER OF CONFIRMATION

2 All who are brought to be confirmed must have been baptized, have reached a competent age and have worshipped regularly with the Church. They must also have been instructed in the Catechism and be able to say the Creed, the Lord's Prayer, and the Ten Commandments. Everyone shall have a witness of his Confirmation.

3 The Parish Priest shall make certain that those whom he presents for Confirmation have been baptized. If there is a doubt about the Baptism of any one the Priest shall baptize him conditionally according to the Form in the Office for Private Baptism.

4 No Minister shall present for confirmation candidates who have not been instructed in his own parish unless he is certified in writing by their Parish Priest that they have been baptized and properly instructed.

5 Where the only candidates present are those whose Confirmation follows immediately on their Baptism, the service shall begin at *Our help is in the Name of the Lord.*

6 When Confirmation takes place at a celebration of the Holy Eucharist, it shall begin after the Gospel and shall end with the Laying-on of Hands. A Sermon may be preached before the Order of Confirmation or after the Laying-on of Hands. The Holy Eucharist shall continue with the Nicene Creed.

7 When Confirmation is administered as a separate service the Bishop may read a passage of Holy Scripture before his Address.

8 No one shall receive Holy Communion until he is confirmed, or is ready and desirous to be confirmed.

9 All who are to be confirmed shall stand before the Bishop, the congregation being seated, and the Minister shall present them to him, saying:

Reverend Father in God, I present unto you these persons that they may be confirmed.

10 The Bishop:

Do you assure me that they have all been baptized and properly instructed?

11 The Minister shall answer:

I do so assure you.

12 Then shall the Bishop say to the candidates:

Beloved, in order that this congregation may know that you firmly intend to confess the faith of Christ crucified and to fight manfully under his banner, and that you may have printed in your memory what your calling is and how greatly you need the continual help of the Holy Spirit, the Church requires that before you are confirmed you shall publicly declare that you are bound to believe and to do all those things to which Holy Baptism has pledged you. Are you willing to do this?

13 All the candidates shall audibly answer:

I am willing.

THE RENEWAL OF THE BAPTISMAL VOWS

14 Then shall the Bishop continue, the candidates still standing:

Do you renounce the works of the devil, . . . (W IB12)

THE CONFIRMATION

15 Here may be sung the hymn *Veni, Creator Spiritus* or there may be silent prayer, after which the Bishop shall begin the Confirmation saying:

The Lord be with you:
Answer: And with thy spirit.
Our help is in the Name of the Lord;
Answer: Who hath made heaven and earth.
Blessed be the Name of the Lord;
Answer: Henceforth world without end.

Let us pray.

Almighty and everliving God, who hast been pleased to regenerate these thy servants by Water and the Holy Spirit, for the forgiveness of all their sins; Strengthen them, we beseech thee, O Lord, with the Holy Ghost the Comforter, and daily increase in them thy sevenfold gifts of grace, the spirit of wisdom and understanding; the spirit of counsel and might; the spirit of knowledge and true godliness; and fill them, O Lord, with the spirit of thy holy fear, now and for ever; through Jesus Christ thy Son, our Lord, who liveth and reigneth with thee in the unity of the same Spirit, one God, world without end. *Amen.*

16 Then shall the candidates kneel in order before the Bishop, and the Bishop shall lay his hands upon the head of each one, saying:

Confirm, O Lord, this thy child (*or* this thy servant) with thy heavenly grace, that *he* may continue thine for ever; and daily increase in thy

Holy Spirit more and more, until *he* comes unto thy everlasting kingdom.

17   And each one shall answer: *Amen.*

18   When all have been confirmed, the Bishop shall say:

Let us pray.

Our Father, which art in heaven, ... (CF11)

19   The Bishop shall continue:

Almighty and everliving God, We make our prayers to thee for these thy servants, upon whom, after the example of thy holy Apostles, we have now laid our hands. May thy fatherly hand ever be over them; may thy Holy Spirit ever be with them; and so lead them in the knowledge and obedience of thy Word, that in the end they may obtain everlasting life; through Jesus Christ our Lord. *Amen.*

O Lord Jesus Christ, who hast given us the holy Sacrament of thy Body and Blood; Grant that these thy servants, ever partaking thereof by faith with thanksgiving, may grow in thy likeness, and be strengthened to serve thee truly all the days of their life; who with the Father and the Holy Spirit livest and reignest, one God, world without end. *Amen.*

20   Then shall the Bishop bless the newly-confirmed, saying:

The Blessing of God Almighty, ... (CF19)

21   The two prayers *Almighty and everliving God* and *O Lord Jesus Christ, who hast given us* may be used before the Blessing or Dismissal when a Confirmation takes place at the Holy Eucharist.

18. The Irish Rites 1969

In 1967 the General Synod of the Church of Ireland gave permission for the experimental use of such services as might be drafted by the Liturgical Advisory Committee. The Order of Baptism which follows was produced by this committee and submitted to the General Synod in May 1968, and revised in 1969. On the authority of the Synod, and where the permission of the Ordinary is given, the Rite can be used experimentally for a period of three years. After this experimental period, in the light of criticisms received, the Rite will undergo further examination, and possibly revision. No experimental Rite for Confirmation has yet been produced.

THE ORDER FOR
THE BAPTISM OF CHILDREN

1   The Minister of every Parish shall teach the people the meaning of Baptism and the responsibilities of those who bring children to be baptized.

2   When there are children to be baptized, the parents shall give due notice to the Minister of the Parish, who shall thereupon appoint the time for the Baptism.

3   It is desirable that parents be sponsors for their own children. Every child to be baptized shall have at least one other sponsor. Sponsors shall be baptized persons, able to make the promises required in accordance with canon 12.

4   It is desirable that members of the parish be present to support, by their faith and prayer, those who are to be baptized and received into the fellowship of the Church.

5   When this order of Baptism is used with one of the prescribed services in any church, the Minister may dispense with such parts of that service as the Ordinary shall permit.

6   The font should be so situated that Baptism may be administered in an orderly fashion.

7   The priest shall be assured that the child has not already been baptized.

INTRODUCTION

8   The priest shall say to the people:

Holy Baptism is administered to infants on the understanding that they will be brought up in the fellowship of Christ's Church; that they will be taught the Christian faith; and that, when they have publicly confessed this faith, they will be confirmed by the bishop and admitted to the Holy Communion.

9   Then turning to the sponsors the priest shall say:

I ask therefore

Will you bring up *this child* as a Christian within the family of the Church?
R. We will
Will you help *him* to be regular in public worship and in private prayer, by your teaching, by your example and by your prayers for *him*?
R. We will
Will you encourage *him* to come in due course to Confirmation and Holy Communion?
R. We will

10   The priest shall say to the people

The Lord be with you:
R. And also with you.

Let us pray.

Heavenly Father, who at the baptism of Jesus Christ in the river Jordan declared him to be your only-begotten Son; grant that by your Spirit *this infant* may be born again and made your *child* by adoption and grace, through the same Jesus Christ our Lord. *Amen.*

THE MINISTRY OF THE WORD

11   Two of the following shall be read.

Hear the words of the Epistle written by Saint Paul to the Romans in the sixth chapter, at the third verse:

All of us who have been baptized, . . . (Rom. 6.6–11, RSV)

12   or this

Hear the words of the Gospel written by Saint Matthew in the twenty-eighth chapter, at the eighteenth verse:

Jesus came and said to them, . . . (Matt. 28.18–20, RSV)

13   or this

Hear the words of the Gospel written by Saint Mark, in the tenth chapter, at the thirteenth verse:

They were bringing children to Jesus, . . . (Mark 10.13–17, RSV)

14   Here may follow a sermon.

THE DECISION

15 The priest shall say to the sponsors

Those who are brought to be baptized must affirm through their sponsors their allegiance to Christ and their rejection of all that is evil.

Therefore I ask

Do you turn to Christ?
R. I do.
Do you then renounce the Devil and all his works?
R. I do, by God's help.
Will you obey and serve Christ?
R. I will, by God's help.

AT THE FONT

16 Water shall now be poured into the font, if this has not already been done.

17 Then being at the font with the sponsors and the children to be baptized the priest shall say

We give you thanks, almighty Father, everlasting God, through your most dearly beloved Son, Jesus Christ our Lord;

Because by his death and resurrection you have broken the power of evil, and by your sending of the Spirit you have made us partakers of eternal life;

We ask you to bless this water, that *he* who is to be baptized in it may be born again in Christ; that being baptized into Christ's death *he* may receive forgiveness of sin, and that knowing the power of Christ's resurrection *he* may walk in newness of life;

And grant that being cleansed by the washing of regeneration and renewed by the Holy Spirit, *he* may so faithfully serve you in this world that finally with all your people *he* may inherit the kingdom of your glory;

Through the same your Son Jesus Christ our Lord, to whom with you and the Holy Spirit be all honour and glory for ever and ever. *Amen.*

THE BAPTISM

18 The priest shall then say to the sponsors,

You have brought *this child* to be baptized and now standing in the presence of God and his Church, you must confess the Christian faith in which *he* is to be baptized.

Do you believe in God the Father Almighty, Maker of heaven and earth?

R. I believe.

Do you believe in Jesus Christ his only Son our Lord; and that he was conceived by the Holy Spirit, born of the Virgin Mary; that he suffered under Pontius Pilate, was crucified, dead and buried; that he descended into hell, and the third day rose again from the dead; that he ascended into heaven, and is seated at the right hand of God the Father Almighty; and from thence shall come to judge the living and the dead?

R. I believe.

Do you believe in the Holy Spirit; the holy Catholic Church; the Communion of Saints; the Forgiveness of sins; the Resurrection of the body; and the Life eternal?

R. I believe.

19 Then shall the priest take the child in his arms or by the hand and shall say to the sponsors:

Name this child.

20 Then the priest shall pour water on him saying:

N. I baptize you in the Name of the Father and of the Son and of the Holy Spirit. Amen.

THE PRAYERS

21 Then shall the priest make the sign of the Cross on the forehead of each child saying:

Now that you have entered upon the Christian life, I sign you with the sign of the cross, to show that you must not be ashamed to confess the faith of Christ crucified and manfully to fight under his banner against sin, the world and the devil; and so continue Christ's faithful soldier and servant to your life's end.

22 After all have been baptized the priest and people shall say:

God has adopted you by baptism into his Church. We therefore receive you into the household of faith, As *a member* of the body of Christ, As *the child* of the same heavenly Father, And as *an inheritor* with us of the kingdom of God.

23 Then shall the priest and people say together:

Our Father, who art in heaven, . . . (CF11)

24   Then the priest shall say

Father, we thank you that *this child* has now been born again of water and the Holy Spirit, become your own *child* by adoption, and *a member* of your Church.

Grant that *he* may grow in the faith in which *he* has been baptized;

Grant that *he himself* may profess it when *he* comes to be confirmed;

Grant that *he* may bear witness to it by a life of service to *his* fellow men;

And that all things belonging to the Spirit may live and grow in *him*; through Jesus Christ our Lord. *Amen.*

25   Then the priest may say

Almighty God, bless the home of *this child* and give such grace and wisdom to all who have the care of *him*, that by their word and good example they may teach *him* to know and love you, through Jesus Christ our Lord. *Amen.*

26   The priest shall then say

May Almighty God, the Father of our Lord Jesus Christ who has given new life by water and the Holy Spirit, and has forgiven us all our sins, guard us by his grace now and evermore. *Amen.*

27   The names of those who have been baptized, with the other particulars required, shall be entered in the Parish Register of Baptisms immediately after the service.

28   The Parents may make a thankoffering.

Part 3
THE
NON-ANGLICAN
REVISIONS

1. The Book of Common Order 1611
with notes on the Genevan Service Book 1556

This text is from the *Book of Common Order*, as printed by Andro Hart (Edinburgh 1611); it was reprinted in a volume by George W. Sprott and Thomas Leishman, entitled *The Book of Common Order of the Church of Scotland, commonly known as John Knox's Liturgy* (1868), to which work we are indebted. *Knox's Liturgy*, or *the Book of Common Order*, was used in Scotland from at least 1559; in 1562 the General Assembly directed its uniform use in the administration of the Sacraments. After a number of additions and alterations it was reprinted at Edinburgh in 1564.

As a Reformed service-book, the *Book of Common Order* was favoured by the majority of English Puritans, until its replacement in 1645 by the *Westminster Directory*.

The origin of the *Book of Common Order* was *John Knox's Genevan Service Book*, which was used by Knox while a Minister of the English Congregation of Marian exiles at Geneva, over the period 1556–59. Apart from a few variations and additions "The Order of Baptism" before us is a reproduction of that found in the *Genevan Service Book*; the main variations are noted in the footnotes. For comparison we have used the text contained in W. D. Maxwell's *The Liturgical Portions of the Genevan Service Book* (1965).

I THE ORDER OF BAPTISM

2 First note, that forasmuch as it is not permitted by God's Word, that women preach or minister the Sacraments, and it is evident that the Sacraments are not ordained of God to be used in private corners, as charms, or sorceries, but left to the Congregation, and necessarily annexed to God's Word as seals of the same:* Therefore, the infant that is to be baptized shall be brought to the Church[1] on the day appointed to Common Prayer and Preaching, accompanied with the Father and Godfather, so that, after the Sermon, the child being presented to the Minister, he demandeth this question:

Do ye here present this child to be baptized, earnestly desiring that he may be ingrafted in the mystical body of Jesus Christ?

---

* The transgression of God's ordinance is called iniquity and idolatry, and is compared to witchcraft and sorcery, 1 Sam. 15. How dangerous also it is to enterprise anything rashly, or without the warrant of God's Word, the examples of Saul, I Sam. 13: of Uzzah, 2 Chron. 26: and of Nadab and Abihu, Lev. 10, sufficiently do warn us.

[1] In the *Book of Common Order*, there is no Order for Private Baptism; this was because it had to take place before the assembled congregation on preaching days. The Assembly of 1582 forbade Baptism in private houses; in 1602 the Assembly allowed it in church on other than preaching days; the Assembly of 1618 permitted it in private in cases of sickness, but this was disallowed in 1638.

3 The Answer:

Yea, we require the same.

4 The Minister proceedeth.

Then let us consider, dearly beloved, how Almighty God hath not only made us His children by adoption, and received us into the fellowship of His Church, but also hath promised that He will be our God, and the God of our children, unto the thousandth generation: Which thing, as He confirmed to His people of the Old Testament by the Sacrament of Circumcision, so hath He also renewed the same to us in His New Testament, by the Sacrament of Baptism; doing us thereby to wit, that our infants appertain to Him by covenant, and therefore ought not to be defrauded of those holy signs and badges whereby His children are known from Infidels and Pagans.

Neither is it requisite that all those that receive this Sacrament have the use of understanding and faith, but chiefly that they be contained under the name of God's people, so that the remission of sins in the blood of Jesus Christ doth appertain unto them by God's promise, which thing is most evident by St Paul, who pronounceth the children begotten and born (either of the parents being faithful) to be *clean* and *holy*. Also our Saviour Christ admitteth children to His presence, embracing and blessing them. Which testimonies of the Holy Ghost assure us, that infants be of the number of God's people, and that remission of sins doth also appertain to them in Christ. Therefore, without injury they cannot be debarred from the common sign of God's children. And yet is not this outward action of such necessity, that the lack thereof should be hurtful to their salvation, if that, prevented by death, they may not conveniently be presented to the Church. But we (having respect to that obedience which Christians owe to the voice and ordinance of Christ Jesus, who commanded to preach and baptize all without exception) do judge them only unworthy of any fellowship with Him who contemptuously refuse such ordinary means, as His wisdom hath appointed to the instruction of our dull senses.

Furthermore, it is evident that Baptism was ordained to be ministered in the element of water, to teach us, that like as water outwardly doth wash away the filth of the body, so inwardly doth the virtue of Christ's blood purge our souls from that corruption and deadly poison, wherewith by nature we were infected, whose venomous dregs, although they continue in this our flesh, yet by the merits of His death are not imputed unto us, because the justice of Jesus Christ is made ours by Baptism; not that we think any such virtue or power to be included in the visible water, or outward action, for many have been baptized, and yet never inwardly purged; but that our Saviour Christ, who commanded Baptism to be ministered, will, by the power of His Holy Spirit, effectually work in the hearts of His Elect, in time convenient, all that is meant and signified by the same. And this the Scripture calleth our Regeneration, which standeth chiefly in these two points—in mortification, that is to say, a resisting of the rebellious lusts of the flesh, and in newness of life, whereby we continually strive to walk in that pureness and perfection, wherewith we are clad in Baptism.

And although we, in the journey of this life, be encumbered with many enemies, who in the way assail us, yet fight we not without fruit; for this continual battle, which we fight against sin, death, and hell, is a most infallible argument, that God the Father, mindful of His promise made unto us in Christ Jesus, doth not only give us motions and courage to resist them, but also assurance to overcome, and obtain victory.

Wherefore, dearly beloved, it is not only of necessity that we be once baptized, but also it much profiteth oft to be present at the ministration thereof, that we (being put in mind of the league and covenant made between God and us, that He will be our God, and we His people, He our Father, and we His children) may have occasion as well to try our lives past as our present conversation, and to prove ourselves, whether we stand fast in the faith of God's Elect, or, contrariwise, have strayed from Him, through incredulity and ungodly living, whereof if our consciences do accuse us, yet by hearing the loving promises of our heavenly Father, who calleth all men to mercy, by repentance, we may from henceforth walk more warily in our vocation. Moreover, ye that be fathers and mothers may take hereby most singular comfort to see your children thus received into the bosom of Christ's Congregation, whereby ye are daily admonished, that ye nourish and bring up the children of God's favour and mercy, over whom His fatherly providence watcheth continually.

Which thing, as it ought greatly to rejoice you, knowing that nothing can come unto them without His good pleasure, so ought it to make you diligent and careful to nurture and instruct them in the true knowledge and fear of God, wherein if ye be negligent,* ye do not only injury to your own children, hiding from them the goodwill and

* What danger hangeth over those parents who neglect the bringing up of their children in godliness. 1 Sam. 2; 2 Kings 2.

pleasure of Almighty God their Father, but also heap damnation upon yourselves, in suffering His children, bought with the blood of His dear Son, so traitorously, for lack of knowledge, to turn back from Him. Therefore it is your duty, with all diligence to provide that your children, in time convenient, be instructed in all doctrine necessary for a true Christian, chiefly that they be taught to rest upon the justice of Christ Jesus alone, and to abhor and flee all superstition, Papistry, and idolatry.

Finally, to the intent that we may be assured that you, the father and the surety, consent to the performance hereof, declare here before (God, and in) the face of His Congregation, the sum of that Faith wherein ye believe, and will instruct this child.[1]

5   Then the Father, or in his absence the Godfather, shall rehearse the Articles of his Faith,[2] which done,[3] the Minister expoundeth the same as after followeth.

6   (An Exposition of the Creed.)

The Christian Faith, whereof now ye have briefly heard the sum, is commonly divided in [to] Twelve Articles; but that we may the better understand what is contained in the same, we shall divide it into four principal parts. The first shall concern God the Father; the second, Jesus Christ our Lord; the third shall express to us our faith in the Holy Ghost; and the fourth and last shall declare what is our faith concerning the Church, and of the graces of God freely given to the same.

First, of God we confess three things; to wit, that He is our Father, Almighty, maker of heaven and earth. Our Father we call Him, and so by faith believe Him to be, not so much because He hath created us (for that we have common with the rest of creatures, who are not called to that honour to have God to them a favourable Father), but we call Him Father by reason of His free adoption, by the which He hath chosen us to life everlasting in Jesus Christ, and this His most singular mercy we prefer to all things, earthly and transitory; for without this

---

[1] Those who sought baptism for children were required to repeat the Lord's Prayer, Belief, and the Ten Commandments. Any who were unable to do so had to be first instructed by the Reader.

[2] "the Articles of his Faith" refers to the Apostles' Creed, to which the Calvinists often give this title. The *Exposition of the Creed*, which follows in this service is not found in the *Genevan Service Book*, and was omitted in later editions of the *Book of Common Order*.

[3] *The Genevan Service Book* reads "*which done, the minister exhorting the people to pray saith in this manner, or such like, kneeling*". This rubric is followed by the prayer "Almighty and everlasting God, . . .", the prayer which in this text follows the *Exposition of the Creed*. The change in this rubric is important, for in the text before us the rubric which precedes this prayer reads *Then followeth this Prayer*. While the *Genevan Service Book* allows the Minister liberty to depart from the form given, no such liberty is allowed in the Scottish Book.

there is to mankind no felicity, no comfort, nor final joy; and having this, we are assured that by the same love, by the which He once hath freely chosen us, He shall conduct the whole course of our life, that in the end we shall possess that immortal Kingdom that He hath prepared for His chosen children; for from this fountain of God's free mercy or adoption springeth our vocation, our justification, our continual sanctification, and, finally, our glorification, as witnesseth the Apostle.

The same God our Father we confess Almighty, not only in respect of that He may do, but in consideration that by His power and godly wisdom are all creatures in heaven and earth, and under the earth, ruled, guided, and kept in that order that His eternal knowledge and will hath appointed them. And that is it which in the third part we do confess, that He is Creator of heaven and earth—that is to say, the heaven and the earth, and the contents thereof, are so in His hand, that there is nothing done without His knowledge, neither yet against His will; but that He ruleth them so, that in the end His godly name shall be glorified in them. And so we confess and believe that neither the devils, nor yet the wicked of the world, have any power to molest or trouble the chosen children of God, but in so far as it pleaseth Him to use them as instruments, either to prove and try our faith and patience, or else to stir us to more fervent invocation of His name, and to continual meditation of that heavenly rest and joy that abideth us after these transitory troubles. And yet shall not this excuse the wicked, because they never look in their iniquity to please God, nor yet to obey His will.

In Jesus Christ we confess two distinct and perfect natures, to wit, the eternal Godhead and the perfect Manhood joined together, so that we confess and believe, that the eternal Word who was from the beginning, by whom all things were created, and yet are conserved and kept in their being, did, in the time appointed in the counsel of His heavenly Father, receive our nature of a Virgin, by operation of the Holy Ghost, so that in His conception we acknowledge and believe that there is nothing but purity and sanctification, yea, even in so much as He is become our brother: For it behoved Him, that should purge others from their sins, to be pure and clean from all spot of sin, even from His conception.

And as we confess and believe Him conceived by the Holy Ghost, so do we confess and believe Him to be born of a Virgin, named Mary, of the tribe of Judah, and of the family of David, that the promise of God and the prophecy might be fulfilled, to wit, "That the seed of the woman shall break down the serpent's head", and that "a Virgin should conceive and bear a child, whose name should be *Emmanuel*, that is to say, *God with us*".

The name *Jesus*, which signifieth a Saviour, was given unto Him by the Angel, to assure us, that it is He alone that saveth His people from their sins. He is called *Christ*, that is to say, *Anointed*, by reason of the offices given unto Him by God His Father, to wit, that He alone is appointed King, Priest, and Prophet; King, in that, that all power is given to Him in heaven and on earth, so that there is none other but He in heaven, nor on earth, that hath just authority and power to make laws, to bind the consciences of men; neither yet is there any other that may defend our souls from the bondage of sin, nor yet our bodies from the tyranny of man. And this He doth by the power of His Word, by the which He draweth us out of the bondage and slavery of Satan, and maketh us to reign over sin, while that we live and serve our God in righteousness and holiness of our life. A Priest, and that perpetual and everlasting, we confess Him; because that by the sacrifice of His own body, which He once offered up upon the cross, He hath fully satisfied the justice of His Father in our behalf, so that whosoever seeketh any means, besides His death and passion, in heaven or on earth, to reconcile unto them God's favour, they do not only blaspheme, but also, so far as in them is, renounce the fruit and efficacy of that His only one sacrifice. We confess Him to be the only Prophet, who hath revealed unto us the whole will of His Father, in all things appertaining to our salvation. This our Lord Jesus we confess to be the only Son of God, because there is none such by nature but He alone. We confess Him also our Lord, not only by reason we are His creatures, but chiefly because He hath redeemed us by His precious blood, and so hath gotten just dominion over us, as over the people whom He hath delivered from bondage of sin, death, hell, and the devil, and hath made us kings and priests to God His Father.

We further confess and believe, that the same our Lord Jesus was accused before an earthly Judge, Pontius Pilate, under whom, albeit oft and divers times He was pronounced to be innocent, He suffered the death of the cross, hanged upon a tree betwixt two thieves: which death, as it was most cruel and vile before the eyes of men, so was it accursed by the mouth of God Himself, saying, "Cursed is everyone that hangeth on a tree." And this kind of death sustained He in our person, because He was appointed of God His Father to be our pledge, and He that should bear the punishment of our transgressions. And so we acknowledge and believe that He hath taken away that curse and malediction that hanged on us, by reason of sin.

He verily died, rendering up His spirit into the hands of His Father, after that He had said "Father, into Thine hands I commend my spirit." After His death, we confess His body was buried, and that He descended into hell. But because He was the Author of life, yea, the very life itself, it was impossible that he should be retained under the dolours of death.

And therefore the third day He rose again, victor and conqueror of death and hell, by the which His resurrection, He hath brought life again into the world, which He, by the power of His Holy Spirit, communicateth unto His lively members, so that now unto them corporal death is no death, but an entrance into that blessed life wherein our Head, Jesus Christ, is now entered: for after that He had sufficiently proved His resurrection to His disciples, and unto such as constantly did abide with Him to the death, He visibly ascended to the heavens, and was taken from the eyes of men, and placed at the right hand of God the Father Almighty, where presently He remaineth in His glory, only Head, only Mediator, and only Advocate for all the members of His body, of which we have most especial comfort, first, for that, that by His ascension the heavens are opened unto us, and an entrance made unto us that boldly we may appear before the throne of our Father's mercy. And, secondarily, that we know that this honour and authority are given to Jesus Christ our Head, in our name, and for our profit and utility; for albeit that in body He now be in the heaven, yet by the power of His Spirit he is present here with us, as well to instruct us, as to comfort and maintain us in all our troubles and adversities, from the which He shall finally deliver His whole Church, and every true member of the same, in that day when He shall visibly appear again, Judge of the quick and the dead.

For this, finally, we confess of our Lord Jesus Christ, that as He was seen visibly to ascend, and so left the world, as touching that body that suffered and rose again, so do we constantly believe that He shall come from the right hand of His Father, when all eyes shall see Him, yea, even those that have pierced Him; and then shall He gather as well those that then shall be found alive, as those that before have slept. Separation shall be made betwixt the lambs and the goats, that is to say, betwixt the elect and the reprobate; the one shall hear this joyful voice, "Come, ye the blessed of my Father, possess the Kingdom that is prepared for you before the beginning of the world": the other shall hear that fearful and irrevocable sentence, "Depart from Me, ye workers of iniquity, to the fire that never shall be quenched". And for this cause, this day in the Scriptures is called "The day of refreshing", and "of the revelation of all secrets", because that then the just shall be delivered from all miseries, and shall be possessed in the fulness of their glory. Contrariwise, the reprobate shall receive judgment, and recompense of all their impiety, be it openly or secretly wrought.

As we constantly believe in God the Father, and in Jesus Christ, as before is said; so we do assuredly believe in the Holy Ghost, whom we confess God equal with the Father and the Son, by whose working and mighty operation our darkness is removed, our eyes spiritually are illuminated, our souls and consciences sprinkled with the blood of Jesus Christ, and we retained in the truth of God, even to our lives' end. And for these causes we understand, that this eternal Spirit, proceeding from the Father and the Son, hath in the Scriptures divers names; sometimes called water, by reason of His purgation, and giving strength to this our corrupt nature to bring forth good fruit, without whom, this our nature should utterly be barren, yea, it should utterly abound in all wickedness. Sometimes the same Spirit is called fire, by reason of the illumination and burning heat of fire that He kindleth in our hearts: The same Spirit also is called oil or unction, by reason that His working mollifieth the hardness of our hearts, and maketh us receive the print of that image of Jesus Christ by whom only we are sanctified.

We constantly believe that there is, was, and shall be, even till the coming of the Lord Jesus, a Church, which is holy and universal; to wit, the Communion of Saints. This Church is holy, because it receiveth free remission of sins, and that by faith only in the blood of Jesus Christ. Secondly, because it being regenerate, it receiveth the Spirit of sanctification and power, to walk in newness of life, and in good works, which God hath prepared for His chosen to walk in. Not that we think the justice of this Church, or of any member of the same, ever was, is, or yet shall be, so full and perfect that it needeth not to stoop under mercy; but that because the imperfections are pardoned, and the justice of Jesus Christ imputed unto such as by true faith cleave unto Him. Which Church we call universal, because it consisteth and standeth of all tongues and nations, yea, of all estates and conditions of men and women, whom of His mercy God calleth from darkness to light, and from the bondage and thraldom of sin, to His spiritual service and purity of life: unto whom He also communicateth His

Holy Spirit, giving unto them one faith, one Head and Sovereign Lord, the Lord Jesus, one Baptism and right use of Sacraments, whose heart also He knitteth together in love and Christian concord.

To this Church, holy and universal, we acknowledge and believe three notable gifts to be granted; to wit, remission of sins, which by true faith must be obtained in this life; resurrection of the flesh, which all shall have, albeit not in equal condition, for the reprobate (as before is said) shall rise, but to fearful judgment and condemnation, and the just shall rise to be possessed in glory: and this resurrection shall not be an imagination, or that one body shall rise for another, but every man shall receive in his own body as he hath deserved, be it good or evil. The just shall receive the life everlasting, which is the free gift of God, given and purchased to His chosen, by Jesus Christ our only Head and Mediator: to Whom, with the Father and the Holy Ghost, be all honour, praise and glory, now and ever. So be it.

7 Then followeth this Prayer.

Almighty and everlasting God, who of Thine infinite mercy and goodness hast promised unto us that Thou wilt not only be our God, but also the God and Father of our children, we beseech Thee, that as Thou hast vouchsafed to call us to be partakers of this Thy great mercy, in the fellowship of faith, so it may please Thee to sanctify with Thy Spirit, and to receive into the number of Thy children this Infant, whom we shall baptize according to Thy Word, to the end that he, coming to perfect age, may confess Thee only, the true God, and whom Thou hast sent, Jesus Christ, and so serve Him, and be profitable unto His Church in the whole course of his life, that after his life be ended, he may be brought, as a lively member of His body, unto the full fruition of Thy joys in the heavens, where Thy Son, our Saviour Christ,[1] reigneth world without end; in whose Name we pray, as He hath taught us, saying,[2]

8 Our Father which art, &c.[3]

9 When they have prayed in this sort, the Minister requireth the Child's name, which known, he saith,

N., I baptize thee IN THE NAME OF THE FATHER, OF THE SON, AND OF THE HOLY GHOST.

---

[1] Saviour omitted in *Genevan Service Book.*
[2] saying omitted in *Genevan Service Book.*   Our father etc.

10 And as he speaketh these words, he taketh water in his hand, and layeth it upon the Child's forehead; which done, he giveth thanks, as followeth:

Forasmuch, most holy and merciful Father, as Thou dost not only beautify and bless us with common benefits, like unto the rest of mankind, but also heapest upon us most abundantly rare and wonderful gifts; of duty we lift up our eyes and minds unto Thee, and give Thee most humble thanks for Thine infinite goodness, who hast not only numbered us amongst Thy Saints, but also of Thy free mercy dost call our children unto Thee, marking them with this Sacrament, as a singular token and badge of Thy love; wherefore, most loving Father, though we be not able to deserve this so great a benefit (yea, if Thou wouldest handle us according to our merits, we should suffer the punishment of eternal death and damnation), yet, for Christ's sake, we beseech Thee that Thou wilt confirm this Thy favour more and more towards us, and take this Infant into Thy tuition and defence, whom we offer and present unto Thee, with common supplications, and never suffer him to fall into such unkindness whereby he should lose the force of Baptism, but that he may perceive Thee continually to be his merciful Father, through Thy Holy Spirit working in his heart, by whose divine power he may so prevail against Satan, that in the end, obtaining the victory, he may be exalted into the liberty of Thy Kingdom. So be it.[1]

[1] So be it omitted in *Genevan Service Book*.

2. The Westminster Directory 1644

This text is from *A Directory for the Publique Worship of God throughout the Three Kingdoms of England, Scotland, and Ireland. Together with an Ordinance of Parliament for the taking away of the Book of Common Prayer, and for establishing and observing of this present Directory throughout the Kingdom of England, and Dominion of Wales.* On the 13 March 1644 Parliament ordered that *The Directory* be printed and published, and used in the place of the Book of Common Prayer, which was thought unfit to lead the devotions of the people. The first edition of *The Directory* was printed by Evan Tyler, Alexander Fifield, Ralph Smith, and John Field (London 1644); which is reproduced here, from the text given in *The Westminster Directory* by Thomas Leishman (1901).

While *The Directory* was meant to take the place of the *Book of Common Prayer* it does not, strictly speaking, contain liturgical texts. It is rather a Manual of Directions, providing headings for prayer and preaching, to be used on different occasions, being enlarged upon at the discretion of the Minister. With regard to "*of Baptism*", we note that private and lay baptism is forbidden; godfathers, godmothers, the sign of the cross, and the wearing of the surplice, were all to be discontinued.

The Directory does not contain an Order of Confirmation.

I THE ADMINISTRATION OF BAPTISM

2 Baptism, as it is not unnecessarily to be delayed, so it is not to be administered in any case by any private person, but by a Minister of Christ, called to be the steward of the mysteries of God.

3 Nor is it to be administered in private places, or privately, but in the place of Public Worship, and in the face of the Congregation, where the people may most conveniently see and hear; and not in the places where fonts, in the time of Popery, were unfitly, and superstitiously placed.

4 The Child to be Baptized, after notice given to the Minister the day before, is to be presented by the Father, or (in case of his necessary absence) by some Christian friend in his place, professing his earnest desire that the Child may be Baptized.

5 Before Baptism, the Minister is to use some words of instruction, touching the institution, nature, use and ends of this Sacrament, showing,

"That it is instituted by our Lord Jesus Christ: That it is a Seal of the Covenant of grace, of our ingrafting into Christ, and of our union with Him, of remission of sins, regeneration, adoption, and life eternal: That the water, in Baptism, representeth and signifieth both the blood of Christ, which taketh away all guilt of sin, original and actual; and the sanctifying virtue of the Spirit of Christ against the dominion of sin, and the corruption of our sinful nature: That Baptizing, or sprink-ling and washing with water, signifieth the cleansing from sin by the blood and for the merit of Christ, together with the mortification of sin, and rising from sin to newness of life, by virtue of the death and resurrection of Christ: That the promise is made to believers and their seed; and that the seed and posterity of the faithful, born within the Church, have, by their birth, interest in the Covenant, and right to the Seal of it, and to the outward privileges of the Church, under the Gospel, no less than the children of Abraham in the time of the Old Testament; the Covenant of Grace, for substance, being the same; and the grace of God, and the consolation of believers, more plentiful than before: That the Son of God admitted little children into His presence, embracing and blessing them, saying, *For of such is the kingdom of God:* That children by Baptism, are solemnly received into the bosom of the Visible Church, distinguished from the world, and them that are with-out, and united with believers; and that all who are Baptized in the name of Christ, do renounce, and by their Baptism are bound to fight against the devil, the world, and the flesh: That they are Christians, and federally holy before Baptism, and therefore are they Baptized: That the inward grace and virtue of Baptism is not tied to that very moment of time wherein it is administered, and that the fruit and power thereof reacheth to the whole course of our life; and that outward Baptism is not so necessary, that, through the want thereof, the infant is in danger of damnation, or the parents guilty, if they do not contemn or neglect the Ordinance of Christ, when and where it may be had."

6 In these or the like instructions, the Minister is to use his own liberty and godly wisdom, as the ignorance or errors in the doctrine of Baptism, and the edification of the people, shall require.

7 He is also to admonish all that are present,

"To look back to their Baptism; to repent of their sins against their Covenant with God; to stir up their faith; to improve and make right use of their Baptism, and of the Covenant sealed thereby betwixt God and their souls."

8 He is to exhort the Parent,

"To consider the great mercy of God to him and his Child; to bring up the Child in the knowledge of the grounds of the Christian religion, and in the nurture and admonition of the Lord; And to let him know the danger of God's wrath to himself and Child, if he be negligent: Requiring his solemn promise for the performance of his duty."

9 This being done, Prayer is also to be joined with the Word of Institution, for sanctifying the Water to this spiritual use; and the Minister is to pray to this or the like effect:

"That the Lord, who hath not left us as strangers without the covenant of promise, but called us to the privileges of His ordinances, would graciously vouchsafe to sanctify and bless His own Ordinance of Baptism at this time: That He would join the inward Baptism of His Spirit with the outward Baptism of Water; make this Baptism to the Infant a Seal of Adoption, Remission of sin, Regeneration, and Eternal Life, and all other promises of the Covenant of grace: That the Child may be planted into the likeness of the Death and Resurrection of Christ; and that, the body of sin being destroyed in him, he may serve God in newness of life all his days."

10 Then the Minister is to demand the name of the Child; which being told him, he is to say (calling the Child by his name),

I BAPTIZE THEE IN THE NAME OF THE FATHER, OF THE SON, AND OF THE HOLY GHOST.

11 As he pronounceth these words, he is to Baptize the Child with Water: which, for the manner of doing of it, is not only lawful but sufficient, and most expedient to be, by pouring or sprinkling of the water on the face of the Child, without adding any other ceremony.

12 This done, he is to give thanks and pray, to this or the like purpose:

"Acknowledging with all thankfulness, that the Lord is true and faithful in keeping covenant and mercy: That He is good and gracious, not only in that He numbereth us among His saints, but is pleased also to bestow upon our children this singular token and badge of His love in Christ: That, in His truth and special providence, He daily bringeth some into the bosom of His Church, to be partakers of His inestimable benefits, purchased by the blood of His dear Son, for the continuance and increase of His Church.

"And praying, That the Lord would still continue and daily confirm more and more this His unspeakable favour: That He would receive the Infant now Baptized, and solemnly entered into the household of faith, into His fatherly tuition and defence, and remember him with the favour that He showeth to His people; that, if he shall be taken out of this life in his infancy, the Lord, who is rich in mercy, would be pleased to receive him up into glory; and if he live, and attain the years of discretion, that the Lord would so teach him by His word and Spirit, and make his Baptism effectual to him, and so uphold him by His divine power and grace, that by faith he may prevail against the devil, the world, and the flesh, till in the end he obtain a full and final victory, and so be kept by the power of God through faith unto salvation, through Jesus Christ our Lord."

3. *The Methodist Rites 1936*

These texts are from *The Methodist Book of Offices*, authorized for use in the Methodist Church by the Conference at Newcastle upon Tyne, July 1936; they are the services generally used in the Methodist churches in England at the present time.

This service book was produced for use amongst the Methodist people who had just united into one Church. Because of the diverse traditions, which had previously existed in the various Methodist churches, the Book was put forward as offering hallowed forms of service, and liturgical prayers which could be used as given or adapted at will. The Preface stresses that in many of the services there is an express place for extemporary prayer, and that there is no conflict between free prayer and liturgical prayer.

I THE ORDER OF SERVICE
FOR THE BAPTISM OF INFANTS

2 Before the administration of this Sacrament, the Minister shall ascertain whether or not the infant has been previously baptized.

3 All parents bringing their children to be baptized are to be reminded by the reading of the following address or otherwise that they thereby devote them to God, and are pledged to bring them up in the nurture and admonition of the Lord; and that the Sacrament of Baptism is administered on their promise to do so.

4 Both parents are to be present if possible.

5 The Minister shall say to the Congregation:

Dearly beloved, since it has pleased God to commit to human hands the care of this child, now brought here for holy baptism, let us recall both the promise and the warning of our Lord—the warning, how great is our offence if, by anything done or left undone, we put a stumbling-block in the way of one of His little ones; and the promise, that if we receive a little child in His Name, we receive the Lord Himself.

You know well how wide is the promise of His redeeming grace "to you and your children and to all that are afar off"; seeing that "He died for all"; how our Lord Himself gave commandment to His Church to "make disciples of all the nations, baptizing them into the Name of the Father and the Son and of the Holy Spirit"; how He commanded the children to be brought unto Him, saying, "Suffer the little children

177

to come unto Me, and forbid them not, for of such is the Kingdom of God." You recall how by His outward gesture and deed He declared His goodwill toward them, how he took them in His Arms, laid His hands upon them, and blessed them. Doubt ye not, therefore, but earnestly believe that He will likewise favourably receive this little child; that He will embrace *him* with the arms of His mercy, and will give unto *him* the Holy Spirit, to the end that *he* may be a partaker of His heavenly Kingdom.

6   Here the Congregation shall stand; and the Minister shall say to the Parents:

You are come here to acknowledge that this, your child, belongs to God, to dedicate *him* to God in holy baptism, and to receive *him* again as from the hands of God to be trained as a disciple of our Lord and Saviour Jesus Christ.

I ask you therefore:

Will you endeavour, as far as in you lies, to provide a Christian home for this child to bring *him* up in the faith of our Lord Jesus Christ, and to surround *him* with such things as are pure and true, lovely and of good report?
R. I will, God being my helper.
Will you endeavour so to order your own lives so that no stumbling-block be put in the way of this child?
R. I will, God being my helper.
Will you give this child access to the worship and teaching of the Church, that so *he* may come to the knowledge of Christ *his* Saviour, and enter into the full fellowship of them that believe?
R. I will, God being my helper.

7   Then shall the Minister say to the Congregation:

Dearly beloved, who are of the household of faith, through the high calling of God in Christ Jesus, and who are now in Christ's Name to receive this child, will you endeavour so to maintain here a fellowship of worship and service in the Church that *he* may grow up in the knowledge and love of God, and of His Son Jesus Christ our Lord?

8   The Congregation shall answer:

We will, God being our helper.

9   Afterwards the Minister shall say,

Let us pray.

Almighty and immortal God, the aid of all that need, the Helper of all that flee to Thee for succour, the life of them that believe, and the resurrection of the dead: we call upon Thee for this child, whom we bring to Thee in this Holy Sacrament. Receive *him*, O Lord, as Thou hast promised by Thy well-beloved Son, saying, Ask, and ye shall have; seek, and ye shall find; knock, and it shall be opened unto you: so give unto us that ask; let us that seek find; open the gate unto us that knock; that *this child* may become and ever remain Christ's true *disciple*, and may at last attain to the eternal Kingdom which Thou hast promised by Christ our Lord. *Amen.*

Almighty God, our heavenly Father, whose blessed Son did share at Nazareth the life of an earthly home, bless, we beseech Thee, the home of *this child*, and grant wisdom and understanding to all who have the care of *him* that *he* may grow up in Thy constant fear and love; through the same Thy Son, Jesus Christ our Lord. *Amen.*

O merciful God and heavenly Father, be pleased to give Thy Holy Spirit to the parents of *this child*, that they may have wisdom and grace to bring up their offspring in the nurture and admonition of the Lord and in the faith of Thy Holy Word; through Jesus Christ our only Mediator and Redeemer. *Amen.*

10   Here the Minister, taking the Child into his arms, shall say to the Parents or Guardians:

Name this child.

11   And, naming the Child, he shall sprinkle him with water, or pour water upon him, or dip him in water, saying:

N., I baptize thee in the Name of the Father, and of the Son, and of the Holy Spirit. *Amen.*

12   We receive *this child* into the congregation of Christ's flock, that *he* may be instructed and trained in the doctrines, privileges, and duties of the Christian religion, and trust that *he* may be Christ's faithful soldier and servant unto *his* life's end.

13   Then the following Benediction shall be said or sung:

The Lord bless thee and keep thee; the Lord make His face to shine upon thee, and be gracious unto thee; the Lord lift up His countenance upon thee and give thee peace. *Amen.*

14   Let us pray.

15 Then the Minister shall offer the following petition, the Congregation, still standing, responding by saying *Amen*.

Grant, O Lord, we beseech Thee, that *this child* may continually
partake of the Holy Spirit, and may profit thereby unto salvation.
Amen.

Grant that all things belonging to the flesh may die in *him*, and that all
things belonging to the Spirit may live and grow in *him*. *Amen.*

Grant that *he* may have power and strength to have victory, and to
triumph over the world, the flesh and the devil. *Amen.*

Grant that the parents of this child may have grace to set before *him*
the example of a godly life, and by their prayers and holy conversation
to be the ministers of God to *him* for good. *Amen.*

Grant that this Church may be so endowed with heavenly wisdom, that
it may nurture the children received by holy baptism into Thy Name,
and by loving care and godly counsel guide their feet into the way of
peace. *Amen.*

16 The grace of the Lord Jesus Christ, and the love of God, and the
fellowship of the Holy Spirit be with us all. *Amen.*

17 The officiating Minister shall see that all the necessary particulars are inserted in
the Register of Baptisms.

1 THE ORDER OF SERVICE FOR THE
PUBLIC RECEPTION OF NEW MEMBERS

2 This office may be used at the close of a shortened service on the Lord's Day.
Any persons present who are not communicating should be invited to remain
during the administration of the Lord's Supper.

3 The Congregation standing, the Minister shall say,

Dearly Beloved, we are about to receive into full communion with
the Church of our Lord Jesus Christ these persons presently to be
named.

Let us hear the words of our Lord Jesus:

If two of you shall agree on earth as touching anything that they shall
ask, it shall be done for them of My Father which is in heaven. For
where two or three are gathered together in My name there am I in
the midst.

4 Then shall be sung the following Hymn:

See, Jesu, Thy disciples see, . . . (MHB 719)

5 Then, the People still standing, the Minister shall say,

Our Lord Jesus Christ, after His Resurrection, gave commandment that His disciples should be baptized into the Name of the Father and of the Son and of the Holy Ghost. He also, after His Ascension and the outpouring of the Holy Spirit, united in His Church the multitude of believers so that they, being one Body in Him, should agree in one hope of their calling, confessing one Lord, one Faith, one Baptism, one God and Father of all, who is over all, and through all, and in all.

People: Unto Him that loveth us, and loosed us from our sins by His Blood; and made us to be a kingdom, to be priests unto His God and Father; to Him be the glory and the dominion for ever and ever. Amen.

Minister: Within the Christian Church—One, Holy, Catholic and Apostolic—the Methodist Church holds and cherishes a true place, having been raised up by God to spread Scriptural Holiness throughout the world. We therefore gather here to confess the Headship of our Lord Jesus Christ, to acknowledge the Divine Revelation recorded in Holy Scripture as the supreme rule of faith and practice, to rejoice in the inheritance of the Apostolic Faith, to seek for the constant renewal of the Holy Spirit, and to take our part in making disciples of all nations.

6 *Minister:* Let us pray.

7 Here shall follow a period of Silent Prayer.

We give thanks unto Thee, O God, for Thine only-begotten Son, Jesus Christ our Lord; for His Life and Teaching; for His Cross and Passion; for His Resurrection and Ascension, and for the gift of the Holy Spirit.

People: Thanks be unto Thee, O God.

Minister: We praise Thee for the saints and martyrs of every age; for all who have kept the faith; for our fathers in the Gospel, into whose labours we have entered, and for Thy Church on earth in which we have our place and privilege.

People: Thanks be unto Thee, O God.

Minister: We praise Thee for the forgiveness of sins, through the merits of our Lord Jesus Christ, for the ministry of Thy Holy Word and Sacraments, and for every means of Grace whereby our souls are nourished, and our bodies made temples of the Holy Spirit.

People: Thanks be unto Thee, O God.

Minister: May it please Thee, O Lord, to implant in us the mind which was in Christ Jesus, that He, ruling within His Church, may cast out all self-will and self-seeking.

People: We beseech Thee to hear us, O Lord.

Minister: We humbly beseech Thee, O Lord, that all Thy people, calling here upon Thy Holy Name, may ever be conscious of Thy presence, and worship Thee in the beauty of holiness.

People: We beseech Thee to hear us, O Lord.

Minister: May it please Thee to enrich with the gifts of Thy Spirit all who have been dedicated to Thee in this place, that they may cleave to Thee and to Thy Holy Church.

People: We beseech Thee to hear us, O Lord.

Minister: O God of unchangeable power and eternal light, look favourably upon Thy whole Church, that wonderful and sacred mystery; and by the tranquil operation of Thy perpetual providence, carry out the work of man's salvation; and let the whole world feel and see that those things which are cast down are being raised up, and those things which are grown old are being made new, and that all things are returning to perfection through Him from whom they took their origin, even through our Lord Jesus Christ. *Amen.*

Minister and People: Our Father which art in heaven, . . . (CF11)

8 Here shall be sung this Hymn:

Christ, from whom all blessings flow, . . . (MHB 720)

9 Here, all still standing, the Minister and People shall say either the Apostles' Creed,

I believe in God the Father Almighty, . . . (CF12)

10 Or this Scriptural Confession of Faith.

Minister: There is one God, the Father, of whom are all things, and we unto Him; and one Lord Jesus Christ, through whom are all things, and we through Him.

People: Our fellowship is with the Father, and with His Son Jesus Christ.

Minister: And the Word became flesh, and dwelt among us (and we beheld His glory, glory as of the only-begotten from the Father), full of grace and truth.

People: Therefore it behoved Him in all things to be made like unto His brethren.

Minister: Christ died for our sins, according to the Scriptures; and He was buried, and was raised on the third day, according to the Scriptures.

People: In whom we have our redemption through His blood, the forgiveness of our sins, according to the riches of His grace.

Minister: Ye shall receive the gift of the Holy Spirit.

People: The Spirit Himself beareth witness with our spirit, that we are children of God.

Minister: There is one body, and one Spirit, one Lord, one Faith, one Baptism.

People: In one Spirit we were all baptized into one Body.

Minister: Blessed be the God and Father of Our Lord Jesus Christ, who according to His great mercy begat us again unto a living hope by the resurrection of Jesus Christ from the dead.

People: Now unto the King eternal, immortal, invisible, the only wise God, be honour and glory, for ever and ever. *Amen.*

11 Whilst all continue standing, the Minister shall name those who are to be received and shall say to them,

Dear Brothers and Sisters in Christ, we are here present, as children of the one family of God and in His sight, to welcome you into the fellowship of His Holy Church.

Forasmuch, however, as the true fellowship of our Lord Jesus Christ is given to those who seek to be saved from their sins, and who trust in Him as their Saviour, it is meet that you who desire to live in that fellowship should confess your faith in Him.

At your baptism you were received into the congregation of Christ's flock.

You have heard the voice of Jesus saying to you, as He said to His first disciples, Follow Me.

We believe that you have already responded to His call, and that you do now sincerely desire to be saved from your sins by faith in Him.

In taking your place among the great company of those who in many generations and in every land have become His servants and His brethren, you are called with a high calling.

Our Lord Jesus offers you Himself, and in Him all the promises and gifts of God are yours. You can do all things in Him who strengthens you. He will not fail you. Having loved His own which are in the world, He loves them to the end.

In this high moment, do you now confirm your response to His gracious call, confessing Him before men, taking up your cross, and engaging yourself to continue, through good report and ill, to be His faithful soldier and servant to your life's end?

R. I do so confess Him and pledge myself to Him.

Do you now resolve, trusting in God alone for strength, to be sincere, pure and upright in thought, word and deed; to hallow your life by prayer and frequent meditation upon God's Word? Do you resolve to give attention to the means of Grace and Fellowship, to further the work of God by the dedication of yourself and your possessions, and to hasten by your service and sacrifice the coming of His Kingdom throughout the world?

R. I do so resolve, God being my helper.

In the Name of God, the giver of all grace, we now joyfully welcome you into the fellowship of Christ's Church. May He who knoweth the thoughts and desires of every heart stablish, strengthen, settle you, and so fill you with all spiritual benediction and grace that you may daily rejoice in His salvation, and be ready to do and suffer His perfect will, that finally you may become partakers of His eternal Kingdom and Glory.

12　Then shall the Minister, addressing the Church, say,

Dear Brethren in the Lord, we rejoice together, as members of Christ's Church, in welcoming into her fellowship these who now confess the Faith. Let us together with them now dedicate ourselves to the service of God, and holding nothing back, make anew our vows of loyalty to our Lord and Saviour.

13　Here shall follow a period of Silent Prayer, after which the Minister shall say,

Let us, still kneeling, sing together:

Lord, in the strength of grace, . . . (MHB 594)

Minister: Now unto Him that is able to guard you from stumbling, and to set you before the presence of His glory without blemish in exceeding joy, to the only God our Saviour, through Jesus Christ our Lord, be glory, majesty, dominion and power, before all time, and now, and for evermore. *Amen.*

14　Here shall follow the Administration of the Lord's Supper, beginning at the words: *We do not presume to come to this Thy Table . . .*

4 *The Congregationalist Rites 1936*

The *Manual for Ministers*, from which these texts are taken, was first published in 1936, and since that time has been widely used by ministers of the Congregational Church. In the Foreword it is stated that "The book is not designed to relieve ministers from the task of thinking out their own orders of service. . . . We should lose one of our distinctive qualities if our ministers used a service book like this slavishly. It is rather given to them that they may make their own selections from it, for it is in the blending of freedom and order that we shall find the best way for the conduct of the worship of our churches." This freedom of use applies to all the services in this book, including those of Baptism and The Reception of Church Members. Thus, while the services of Christian initiation can be used as given in the service-book, a minister can adapt them as he wishes.

This service-book also contains an order for *The Reception of Church Members by the Rite of Baptism*, which is to be used for adults and those who can answer for themselves. The service is to be inserted between Nos. 10–11 in *The Reception of Church Members*.

The Manual was produced by a number of Congregationalists. It is in no sense an official Manual, but is one of three used by Congregationalist ministers, the others being *A Book of Congregational Worship* and *A Book of Services and Prayers*.

1 THE BAPTISM OF CHILDREN

2 Minister.

In this service we desire to acknowledge God as the source of life and the giver of all good; to thank Him for the tender and solemn hopes which gather around the new-born; and to pray that this child may be abundantly blessed by Him, and may learn to love Him and serve His kingdom.

Inasmuch as we believe that all who are born into this world are children of God, we reverently acknowledge the Divine Fatherhood, and pray that this child may in due time manifest in character and service the gracious marks of the children of God.

Further, seeing that new responsibilities have come to the parents and to the fellowship of Christ's Church through the gift of this new life, we solemnly re-dedicate ourselves in the presence of God, and ask for His help worthily to fulfil these new and sacred duties.

THE SCRIPTURE

3 It is written, Thou shalt love the Lord thy God with all thy heart and with all thy soul and with all thy mind and with all thy strength, and thou shalt love thy neighbour as thyself.

These words shall be in your hearts, and you shall teach them diligently unto your children.

Hear the words of the Gospel of our Lord Jesus Christ.

They brought young children to Him, . . . (CF3)

4 The Minister, addressing the parents, shall then say:

You have come to present this child for Christian baptism and dedication; do you promise that *he* shall be brought up as a Christian child in the nurture and admonition of the Lord?
Answer: We do.

THE BAPTISM

5 Then the Minister shall take the child in his arms, and having been informed of the name to be given, shall baptize the child, saying;

(*Name*) —— I baptize thee in the Name of the Father, and of the Son, and of the Holy Ghost. The Lord bless thee and keep thee; the Lord make His face to shine upon thee, and be gracious unto thee; the Lord lift up His countenance upon thee and give thee peace.

6 If there be members of the church present, the Minister shall say to them:

Inasmuch as this child has been baptized in a gathering of the church, there has been laid upon us as a fellowship of Christ a special responsibility and care for *his* faith and character. We pledge ourselves, therefore, as far as may be possible to us, to help *him* to become a true member of Christ's flock, praying that *he* shall not be ashamed to confess the faith of Christ, valiantly to fight under His banner against all evil, and to continue Christ's faithful soldier and servant unto *his* life's end.

7 Here may be offered Prayer by the Minister, or some of the following may be used:

8 Heavenly Father, we pray for Thy rich blessing upon this child now solemnly baptized into the family of the Church. May *he* keep tender the hearts of those in whose care Thou hast placed *him*, and awaken them to the sacredness of their responsibilities. Endow *him* plentifully with Thy wisdom and grace that *he* may learn to love the things which are true and beautiful and right. Guide and protect *him* and bless *him*

exceeding abundantly above all that we ask or think; through Jesus Christ, our Lord. *Amen.*

9   Heavenly Father, Giver of life, we would realize afresh in the mystery and marvel of human birth the miracle of Thy presence and the token of a divine purpose; we would bow in reverence before a sign and wonder, and be conscious of a divine working beyond our understanding. Deliver us from lightly and profanely regarding that which betokens the presence of the living God; and may the new realization of the power and wisdom of the Lord of life inspire our souls with wonder and worship; through Jesus Christ, our Lord. *Amen.*

10 O Father of men, we pray that these and all parents may have a deepened sense of their responsibility for the Christian nurture of their children, and, realizing that a child's first thoughts of God come through the teaching and example of its parents, may they so live the Christian life that their children may be drawn to the Father in heaven; through Jesus Christ, our Lord. *Amen.*

11 We pray also for all who may share the responsibility of directing and shaping this young life. Grant to guardians, nurses, and teachers patience, affection, and a sense of duty, and a consciousness of the sacredness of their charge. We also remember before Thee those who work for the welfare of youth, writers for the young, and all others who are seeking to improve the conditions of child-life. Inspire their labours, enlarge their vision, and guide and sustain their zeal; through Jesus Christ, our Lord. *Amen.*

12 We pray for all children born with some defect of body or mind; for orphaned, homeless, or unwanted children; for children with loveless homes or evil surroundings; that Thou wouldst give them special gifts of heart and spirit, and lead them into the light and liberty and joy of Christ, in Whose Name we pray. *Amen.*

13 O God, Who are ever seeking to raise mankind nearer to Thy divine end and purpose, grant that the coming generation may be better than their fathers, that our weaknesses, follies, and mistakes may not be repeated, that all we have found to be right and noble and worthy may be maintained and multiplied in the days to come, and that in Thy renewal of the earth this child may be a willing instrument in Thy hand; through Jesus Christ, our Lord. *Amen.*

14　The Lord's Prayer.
15　The Benediction.

1　THE RECEPTION OF CHURCH MEMBERS

2　Minister.

It is our joy and privilege at this time to receive and welcome ——
who earnestly desire to acknowledge Christ as their Lord and Master,
and to enter into the fellowship of the Church in this place,

3　The Minister, addressing those about to be received, shall say,

Witness has been given to us of your acceptance of our Lord Jesus as
your Saviour and Friend, and with gladness of heart we receive you in
this fellowship. And together we would call to mind the sacred nature
of the Church with its obligations and privileges.

4　THE NATURE OF CHRIST'S CHURCH

We hold that wherever there is a gathered company of Christ's people
there is a church of Christ, a society of His friends, loving and serving
Him and His kingdom. We believe that the spirit of Christian fellowship uniting them to Christ and to one another also links them with
other gathered companies, forming a holy, catholic Church, continuing
from generation to generation to the glory of God and the service of
mankind.

5　THE DUTIES OF MEMBERSHIP

We would remind you that a member of a Christian church is one who
pledges himself to love and serve Christ, to help his fellows, and to
labour for the kingdom of God and His righteousness; who also sub-
mits, as far as his reason and conscience allow, to the rules of his church,
and acts in the church life in a spirit of Christian affection, courtesy,
and comradeship; and who observes as far as he is able the public
worship of his church, reveres its sacraments, loyally renders it his
practical support and service, and is jealous of its honour and reputation
in the sight of the world.

6　THE CHARGE TO THE CANDIDATES

Brethren, if any man have not the spirit of Christ, he is none of His;

but whosoever shall do the will of His Father which is in heaven, the same is His brother and sister and mother.

If ye love Christ ye will keep His commandments. The first of the commandments is: The Lord our God is one Lord, and thou shalt love the Lord thy God with all thy heart and with all thy soul and with all thy mind and with all thy strength. The second is like unto it, namely this: Thou shalt love thy neighbour as thyself.

Brethren, will you, with us, seek to manifest your discipleship of Jesus Christ by such obedience to His spirit and law?

7 Each candidate in turn shall answer:

I will so do, the Lord being my helper.

8 Minister.

Christ loved the Church, and gave Himself for it that He might present it to Himself a glorious Church, holy and without blemish. Will you, as far as in you lies, zealously serve the Church of Christ and, with all earnestness, endeavour to establish through it the kingdom of God?

9 Each candidate in turn shall answer:

I will so do, the Lord being my helper.

10 Minister:

Let us pray.

O God, Who hast taught us to keep all Thy heavenly commandments by loving Thee and our neighbour, grant us the spirit of peace and grace, that we may both be devoted to Thee with our whole heart and to each other with a pure will, We further pray for the good estate of the Church of Christ, that all who profess and call themselves Christians may be led into the way of truth, and hold the faith in unity of spirit, in the bond of peace, and in righteousness of life; through Jesus Christ, our Lord. *Amen.*

I THE RIGHT HAND OF FELLOWSHIP

Forasmuch as —— have desired to become associated with the fellow-ship of this church, and have approved themselves as conforming to our standards and traditions of church membership, in the name of the church I extend to them the right hand of fellowship and welcome.

12 SCRIPTURAL CHARGE TO NEW MEMBERS

That which we have seen and heard declare we unto you, that ye also may have fellowship with us; yea, and our fellowship is with the Father and with His Son Jesus Christ. God is light, and in Him is no darkness at all. If we say that we have fellowship with Him and walk in the darkness, we lie and do not the truth; but if we walk in the light, as He is in the light, we have fellowship one with another. He that loveth his brother abideth in the light. This is the message which we have heard from the beginning, that we should love one another. We know that we have passed out of death into life because we love the brethren.

As the body is one and hath many members, and all the members being many are one body, so also is Christ. And whether one member suffer all the members suffer with it, or one member be honoured all the members rejoice with it. Now ye are the body of Christ, and severally members thereof.

I beseech you to walk worthy of the calling wherewith ye were called, with all lowliness and meekness; with longsuffering, forbearing one another in love; giving diligence to keep the unity of the spirit in the bond of peace, Let all bitterness and wrath and anger and clamour and railing be put away from you, with all malice; and be ye kind to one another, tender-hearted, forgiving one another, even as God also in Christ forgave you. Bear ye one another's burdens and so fulfil the law of Christ.

13   Here may be offered Prayer by the Minister, or the following may be used.

Defend, O Lord, these Thy children with Thy heavenly grace, that they may continue Thine for ever; and daily increase in them Thy Holy Spirit until they come into Thine everlasting kingdom. Grant unto all them who are admitted into the fellowship of Christ's religion that they may eschew those things that are contrary to their profession, and follow all such things as are agreeable to the same; through Jesus Christ, our Lord. *Amen.*

14   Then shall follow the Communion Service.

5. The Church of Scotland Rites 1940

Work on the *Book of Common Order*, 1940, from which these texts are taken, began in 1936, following the instruction of the General Assembly of that year. The book includes much of the material contained in two previously authorized Service Books, *Prayers for Divine Service*, 1923 and 1929, and the *Book of Common Order*, 1928, and was authorized by the 1940 General Assembly for the guidance of ministers in the conduct of public worship.

Ministers of the Church of Scotland are allowed to use "free prayer", and are at liberty to adapt the Orders contained in this Book. But, states the *Preface*, "a service book is necessary to express the mind of the Church with regard to its offices of worship, in orders and forms which, while not fettering individual judgement in particulars, will set the norm for the orderly and reverent conduct of the various public services in which ministers have to lead their people" (BCO, 1928).

1 ORDER FOR THE ADMINISTRATION OF THE
SACRAMENT OF BAPTISM TO INFANTS

2 After a Baptismal hymn has been sung, the Minister shall say:

Our help is in the name of the Lord, who made heaven and earth.

3 And then he shall say:

Dearly beloved, Attend to the words of the institution of the holy Sacrament of Baptism, as delivered by our Lord and Saviour to His disciples, after His resurrection and before His ascension to the right hand of God:

All power is given unto Me . . . (Matt. 28.18–20, AV)

The Sacrament thus instituted is a sign and seal of our ingrafting into Christ; of forgiveness of sins by His blood, and regeneration by His Spirit; and of adoption, and resurrection unto everlasting life. By this Sacrament we are solemnly admitted into His Church, and are engaged to be the Lord's.

Though little children do not understand these things, yet is the promise also to them. They are heirs of the covenant of grace; and in holy Baptism God brings them into the family and household of faith, and makes them members of Christ, and citizens of the kingdom of heaven.

Consider also what is written in the Gospels:

They brought young children to Jesus, . . . (CF3)

It is the duty of those who present their children for holy Baptism to make confession of the faith wherein they are to be baptized, and to promise to bring them up in that faith, and in the nurture and admonition of the Lord.

4   Then, the Congregation standing, the Minister shall say to those who present the child:

In presenting this child for Baptism, do you receive the doctrine of the Christian Faith whereof we make confession, saying:
I believe in God the Father Almighty, . . . (CF12)
Answer: I do.
Do you promise, in dependence on Divine grace, to teach *him* the truths and duties of the Christian faith; and by prayer, precept and example, to bring *him* up in the nurture and admonition of the Lord, and in the ways of the Church of God?
Answer: I do.

5   Alternatively, the Minister may say:

In presenting this child for Baptism, do you confess your faith in God as your heavenly Father, in Jesus Christ as your Saviour and Lord, and in the Holy Spirit as your Sanctifier?
Answer: I do.
Do you promise, in dependence on Divine grace to teach *him* the truths and duties of the Christian faith; and by prayer, precept and example, to bring *him* up in the nurture and admonition of the Lord, and in the ways of the Church of God?
Answer: I do

6   Then the Minister shall say:

The Lord bless you and your *child(ren)*, and give you grace faithfully to perform these promises.

7   Let us pray.

Almighty and everlasting God, whose blessed Son, Jesus Christ our Lord, hath ordained this holy Sacrament; mercifully look upon us, we beseech Thee, and ratify in heaven that which by His appointment we do upon earth.

Sanctify this water to the spiritual use to which Thou hast ordained it, and grant that this child, now to be baptized therewith, may be born again of water and of the Holy Spirit, and ever remain in the number of Thy faithful children; through Jesus Christ our Lord. *Amen.*

O blessed Saviour, who didst take little children into Thine arms and bless them; take this child, we beseech Thee, and seal *him* for Thine own: who livest and reignest with the Father and the Holy Spirit, one God, world without end. *Amen.*

8   Then the Parent, or other Sponsor, shall present the child at the Font (the Congregation standing), and the Minister, calling the child by his Christian name or names, shall pour or sprinkle water on him, saying:

N. ——, I BAPTIZE THEE IN THE NAME OF THE FATHER, AND OF THE SON, AND OF THE HOLY GHOST. AMEN.
The blessing of God Almighty, Father, Son, and Holy Spirit, descend upon thee, and dwell in thine heart for ever. *Amen.*

9   Thereafter, the Minister shall say,

According to Christ's commandment *N*—— is now received into the membership of the holy Catholic Church, and is engaged to confess the faith of Christ crucified, and to be His faithful soldier and servant unto *his* life's end.

10   The Blessing and the Declaration above are repeated for each child that is baptized.
11   Then may be said or sung,

The Lord bless thee and keep thee; the Lord make His face to shine upon thee, and be gracious unto thee; the Lord lift up His countenance upon thee, and give thee peace. *Amen.*

12   After which the Minister shall say,

Let us pray.

Almighty and everlasting God, who of Thine infinite mercy and goodness hast promised that Thou wilt be not only our God, but also the God and Father of our children; we give Thee thanks for this child now received into the fold of Thy Church, and humbly beseech Thee that Thy Spirit may be upon *him*, and dwell in *him* for ever. Keep *him*, we entreat Thee, under Thy fatherly care and protection; guide *him* and sanctify *him* both in body and in soul. Grant that *he* may grow in wisdom as in stature, and in favour with God and man. Abundantly enrich *him* with Thy heavenly grace; bring *him* safely through the perils of childhood, deliver *him* from the temptations of youth, and lead *him* in due time to witness a good confession, and to persevere therein to the end; through Jesus Christ our Lord. *Amen.*

Almighty God, our heavenly Father, whose blessed Son did share, at Nazareth, the life of an earthly home; bless, we beseech thee, the home of this child, and grant wisdom and understanding to *his* parents and to all who have the care of *him*; that *he* may grow up in Thy constant fear and love; through the same Jesus Christ our Lord. *Amen.*

Sanctify to us all, O Lord, the ministration of this holy Sacrament. Forgive us wherein we have come short of the grace of our own Baptism, by wandering from Thy ways; and bring us back with true repentance. Quicken us anew by the power of Thy Holy Spirit, that we may walk in charity, humility, and godliness, as those who have been baptized by the same Spirit into one body; through Jesus Christ our Lord. *Amen.*

Our Father, . . . (CF9)

13   The grace of the Lord Jesus Christ, and the love of God, and the communion of the Holy Spirit, be with you all. *Amen.*

Or,

14   The peace of God, which passeth all understanding, keep your hearts and minds in the knowledge and love of God, and of His Son Jesus Christ our Lord; and the blessing of God Almighty, the Father, the Son, and the Holy Spirit, be amongst you, and remain with you always. *Amen.*

1   THE ORDER FOR THE CONFIRMATION OF
    BAPTIZED PERSONS AND FOR THEIR
    ADMISSION TO THE LORD'S SUPPER

2   The Minister addressing the Congregation shall say:

Dearly beloved,—We are about to admit to the Confirmation of their Baptism, and to participation in the Lord's Supper, these persons about to be named. They have already been under special instruction in the teaching of the Church, and are now ready to profess publicly the faith into which they were baptized.

3 Then he shall read their names, and, addressing them as they stand before the Holy Table, he shall say:

Beloved in the Lord,—In the days of your infancy you were by holy Baptism ingrafted into the Lord Jesus Christ as members of His Church, and engaged to be His. God in His mercy has brought you to years of responsibility, and you have now come to acknowledge before God and His Church the covenant then made on your behalf, to profess your faith in the Lord Jesus, to consecrate yourselves to Him, and thereby to bind yourselves anew to His service.

Our Lord Jesus Christ hath said, Whosoever shall confess Me before men, him will I confess also before My Father which is in heaven.

I charge you, therefore, to make confession of your faith, and to answer with all sincerity, and as in the presence of God, the questions which I now put to you.

4 Then, the Congregation standing, the Minister shall say,

Do you receive the doctrine of the Christian faith, whereof we make confession, saying,

I believe in God the Father Almighty, ... (CF12)

Answer: I do.

Do you promise, in dependence on Divine grace, to serve the Lord and to walk in His ways all the days of your life?

Answer: I do.

Do you promise to make diligent use of the means of grace, to share dutifully in the worship and service of the Church, and to give of your substance, as the Lord may prosper you, for the advancement of His kingdom throughout the world?

Answer: I do.

5 Alternatively the Minister may say:

Do you confess your faith in God as your heavenly Father, in Jesus Christ as your Saviour and Lord, and in the Holy Spirit as your Sanctifier?

Answer: I do.

Do you promise, in dependence on Divine grace, to serve the Lord and to walk in His ways all the days of your life?

Answer: I do.

Do you promise to make diligent use of the means of grace, to share dutifully in the worship and service of the Church, and to give of your substance, as the Lord may prosper you, for the advancement of His kingdom throughout the world?

Answer: I do.

6 Then shall the Minister say:

Let us pray.

Almighty and ever-living God, strengthen these Thy servants, we beseech Thee, with the Holy Spirit, the Comforter, and daily increase in them Thy manifold gifts of grace: the spirit of wisdom and understanding, the spirit of counsel and might, the spirit of knowledge and of the fear of the Lord; and keep them in Thy mercy unto life eternal; through Jesus Christ our Lord. *Amen.*

7 Then, the Congregation meanwhile standing, the Minister (raising his hand in blessing over the candidates, or laying his hand on the head of each as they kneel before him) shall say:

The God of all grace, who hath called you to His eternal glory, confirm you to the end, that you may be blameless in the day of our Lord Jesus Christ.

8 After which the Minister shall say to the candidates together:

God the Father, God the Son, and God the Holy Spirit bless, preserve, and keep you, now and for evermore. *Amen.*

Forasmuch as you have made confession of your faith, I do now, in the name of the Lord Jesus Christ, the great King and Head of the Church, admit you to the fellowship of the Lord's Table.

9 Then may be said or sung:

The Lord bless thee . . .

10   ### Let us pray.

Almighty God, who hast founded Thy Church upon earth, and hast promised to preserve it to the end; we thank Thee for Thy great mercy to these Thy children, and to Thy Church, to which Thou hast given the joy of receiving them into full communion. We thank Thee that by holy Baptism they have been incorporated into the body of Christ. We thank Thee for their Christian training, and for every good influence in their lives; and that Thou hast granted to them the assurance of Thy blessing and favour.

Forgive, we beseech Thee, all their sins; and graciously accept them as now they dedicate themselves to Thee. When they approach Thy

Holy Table to receive the Communion of the body and blood of Christ, grant them to behold the vision of His love and to be made partakers of His grace. Defend them, O Lord, with Thy heavenly grace, that they may continue Thine for ever, and daily increase in Thy Holy Spirit more and more, until they come unto Thy everlasting kingdom; through Jesus Christ our Lord, to whom, with Thee and the Holy Spirit, be all glory and dominion, world without end. *Amen.*

Our Father, . . . (CF9)

◀ 1   The Minister, together with representatives of the Kirk-Session, may then give the right hand of welcome to the newly-received communicants; or, this may be done after the service has ended. He may also say these, or like words:

Beloved in the Lord, now received into all the privileges of membership in the Church of Christ; consider well that you are indeed fellow-citizens with the saints, and of the household of God, and are built upon the foundation of the apostles and prophets, Jesus Christ Himself being the chief corner-stone; in whom also ye are builded together for an habitation of God through the Spirit.

If we walk in the light, as He is in the light, we have fellowship one with another.

Jesus said: If any man will come after Me, let him deny himself, and take up his cross daily, and follow Me.

To him that overcometh will I give to sit with Me in My throne, even as I also overcame, and am set down with My Father in His throne.

◀ 2   Then shall be sung a suitable Psalm or Hymn, and the Service shall end with the Benediction.

6. The Presbyterian Rites 1948

In 1944 English and Welsh Presbyterians felt a common need for a new service-book. At the time the existing service-book of 1921 was out of print and in need of revision. The Presbyterian Church of Wales proposed that the two General Assemblies might appoint members for a Joint Committee and begin work immediately; the proposal was accepted by the English Assembly. A Joint Committee was appointed, and work on a revised service-book went on for four years. The new book was published and issued by the authority of the two General Assemblies, in 1948. This was their first joint service-book and was given the title: *The Presbyterian Service Book for use in the Presbyterian Churches of England and Wales.*

The Preface of the Book states, "The General Assemblies of both Churches, in authoritatively sanctioning the publication of this book, wish it to be understood that the Orders of service herein contained are intended as guides, not as obligations, save in those portions specifically prescribed by the respective General Assemblies." This freedom of use and adaptation applies to the initiatory rites.

The rites of baptism and confirmation contained in this book are those still in general use amongst Presbyterians in England and Wales.

I THE ORDER FOR THE ADMINISTRATION OF THE SACRAMENT OF BAPTISM

2 According to the teaching of our standards, "The visible Church consists of all those throughout the world that profess the true religion, together with their children."

3 According to the teaching of the New Testament and the practice of the Church, the appointed means for making this profession, and claiming the cleansing grace of God, is found in the Sacrament of Baptism.

4 Baptism may be granted either to those of adult years who make profession of faith, or to infants for whom Baptism is sought by believing parents, with whom others may be associated as sponsors.

5 The Sacrament of Baptism is to be but once administered to any person.

6 The Sacrament is ordinarily to be administered by an ordained Minister in the Church during or after public worship, in the presence of a congregation. Should it be thought expedient to hold the Service more privately, not less than three or four witnesses should be present.

7 A register of all baptisms ought to be kept in each Congregation, each entry being attested by the officiating Minister.

8 Those who have not been baptized in infancy are to be received into the fellowship of the visible Church through Baptism, care being taken to ascertain that they have been sufficiently instructed in the Christian faith, and that they are sincerely desirous of being followers of Christ.

9 THE BAPTISM OF INFANTS

10 After the singing of a baptismal hymn the Minister says:

Our help is in the name of the Lord Who made heaven and earth, and Who redeems us in Jesus Christ His Son, our Saviour.

11 And then he says:

All born into this world are subject to sin and death, but through His grace God has given us in Jesus Christ His Son our Lord, Who died and rose again for our salvation, pardon for our sins and eternal life. Being born again of the Holy Spirit, we are brought into a new relationship with God.

Baptism is the visible sign of this new relationship and new birth. Just as water washes stains from the body, so in this Sacrament the Holy Spirit purifies our souls from sin, and enables us to be reborn into eternal life.

Let us hear now the words of the institution of the Holy Sacrament of Baptism as delivered by our Lord and Saviour to His disciples, after His resurrection and before His ascension.

All power is given . . . (Matt. 28.18–20, AV)

The Sacrament thus instituted is a sign and seal of our ingrafting into Christ; of forgiveness of sins by His blood, and regeneration by His Spirit; and of adoption, and resurrection unto everlasting life. By this Sacrament we are solemnly admitted into His Church, and are engaged to be the Lord's.

Though little children do not understand these things, yet is the promise also to them; they are heirs of the covenant of grace; and in Holy Baptism God brings them into the family and household of faith, and makes them members of Christ, and citizens of the kingdom of heaven.

Furthermore, we also read in the Gospel:

They brought young children to Jesus . . . (CF3)

Here our Lord makes known His desires to receive little children, and also the necessity for the child's virtues of simplicity, candour, and trust, in those who seek Christ's Kingdom.

12 The Congregation stands.

13 The Minister addresses the parents:

It is the duty of those who present their children for Holy Baptism to confess the faith wherein they are to be baptized, and to promise to bring them up in that faith and in the knowledge and love of the Lord. Further, by their confession of faith and promise to accept God's commandments, they speak on behalf of the child who as yet cannot speak for himself.

14 The Minister says to those who present the child:

In presenting this child for Baptism, do you confess your faith in God as your heavenly Father, in Jesus Christ as your Saviour and Lord, and in the Holy Spirit as your Sanctifier?
Answer: I do.

15 Alternatively the Minister may say:

In presenting this child for Baptism, do you receive and confess the doctrine of the Christian faith, which we declare saying:

I believe in God the Father Almighty, . . . (CF12)

Answer: I do.
Do you promise, in dependence on Divine Grace, to teach (him) the truths and duties of the Christian faith; and by prayer, precept and example, to bring (him) up in the knowledge and love of the Lord, and in the ways of the Church of God?
Answer: I do.

16 If there are sponsors present the Minister says to them:

Do you confess anew your faith in God your Father, in Jesus Christ your Lord and Saviour, and in the Holy Spirit your Sanctifier, and do you undertake, should need arise, to do all you can for this child's instruction and godly upbringing?
Answer: I do.

17 Then the Minister says:

The Lord bless you and your child(ren), and give you grace faithfully to perform these promises.

18   Let us pray.

Most merciful and loving Father, we thank Thee for the Church of Thy Son our Saviour, the ministry of Thy Word, and the Sacraments of grace. Especially do we praise Thee now for the institution of this Sacrament of Holy Baptism, wherein Thou dost give such gracious promises for our children, and dost seal them in Christ for Thine own. Do Thou sanctify this element of water for the spiritual use to which Thou hast ordained it, and grant that this child now to be baptized therewith may be born again of water and the Holy Spirit and ever remain in the number of Thy faithful children, through Jesus Christ our Lord. *Amen.*

19   The Congregation shall stand. Then the father shall present the child at the Font, and the Minister, calling the child by his Christian name, shall sprinkle water on his head, saying:

N—— I baptize thee in the name of the Father, and of the Son, and of the Holy Spirit. *Amen.*

The blessing of God Almighty, Father, Son, and Holy Spirit, descend upon thee and dwell in thy heart for ever. *Amen.*

20   Then may be sung:

The Lord bless thee and keep thee; the Lord make His face to shine upon thee and be gracious unto thee; the Lord lift up His countenance upon thee, and give thee peace. *Amen.*

21   The Blessing is repeated for each child that is baptized.

22   After the Blessing the Minister says, using the plural if more than one child has been baptized:

According to Christ's commandment this child is now received into the membership of the Holy Catholic Church, and is engaged to confess the faith of Christ crucified, and to be His faithful soldier and servant to (his) life's end. Wherefore receive ye (him) in the Lord as Christ also received us to the glory of God.

23   Let us pray.

Almighty God our Father in heaven, we bless Thee for this Holy Sacrament through which we are assured that Thou art not only our God but also the God and Father of our children, and we commend to Thy gracious keeping this little one now received into the fold of Thy Church. Guard (him) from all ill to body or soul. Grant that (he) may grow in wisdom as in stature, and in favour with God and man. Bring (him) safely through the perils of childhood; deliver (him) from the temptations of youth and lead (him) in due time to witness a good confession and to persevere therein to the end.

O Thou, whose blessed Son Jesus did share at Nazareth the life of an earthly home, bless, we pray Thee, the home upon which Thou hast bestowed this precious gift. We thank Thee for Thy goodness to this mother in preserving her life and renewing her strength. And we pray Thee that Thou wilt guide these parents as they seek to discharge the trust committed unto them, and wilt keep them faithful to the vows they have now made. Forgive us wherein we have come short of the grace of our own baptism, and help us to rededicate our lives to Thee through the vows we have heard made here.

And so sanctify to us all the ministration of this Holy Sacrament that we may never cause one of Thy little ones to stumble but in purity of living may set before them the way of Christ.

24 Our Father, . . .

25 Here a hymn or doxology may be sung.

26 Benediction,

The grace of the Lord Jesus Christ and the love of God, and the communion of the Holy Spirit, be with you all. *Amen.*

1 # THE ORDER FOR THE CONFIRMATION OF BAPTISMAL VOWS AND FOR ADMISSION TO THE LORD'S SUPPER

2 The profession of faith, on the ground of which persons who have been already baptized are admitted to the Lord's Supper, is to be made openly in the presence of the Congregation.

3 The Session, being assured that Candidates for such admission have been sufficiently instructed in the Gospel and in the duties of the Christian life, and that they desire to confirm their baptismal vows, appoints a time for the Service.

4 Normally the Service of Confirmation should take place in the presence of the Congregation at a Sunday diet of worship.

5 The Minister, addressing the Congregation, says:

Beloved, we are now to admit to the Confirmation of their Baptism, and to participation in the Lord's Supper, these persons about to be named. They have already been under special instruction in the teaching of the Church, and are now ready to profess publicly the faith into which they were baptized.

6 Then the Minister reads their names, and addressing them as they stand before the Holy Table, says:

Beloved in the Lord, in the name of this Congregation, and of the whole Church, I gladly welcome you, as you come to make profession of your faith and to enter into the full heritage of your membership in the Holy Catholic Church.

You have been in the fellowship of that Church since the day in your early childhood when you received the sacrament of Baptism. You were then solemnly engaged to be the Lord's. Prayer was made for you and promises were given that you should be trained and taught to know and love God, and God granted to you and your parents in that Sacrament the sign of His cleansing grace. For you these prayers have been answered, and these promises performed. By that grace you have been sustained and helped. God, in His mercy, has brought you to years of responsibility, and you have now come to acknowledge before God and His Church the covenant then made on your behalf, to profess your faith in the Lord Jesus, to consecrate yourself to Him, and to know yourself to be fully a member of His Church.

7 Here the congregation may stand and say:

I believe in God the Father Almighty, . . . (CF12)

I charge you now to make your personal confession of faith, and to answer with all sincerity, and as in the presence of God, the questions which I now put to you:

Do you believe in God through Jesus Christ your Saviour and Lord, and, accepting all the good things that are ours in Christ, do you promise through His grace to serve Him faithfully in his Kingdom?
Answer: I do.
Do you promise to live the Christian life, making diligent use of the means of grace—the Word, Sacraments and prayer; to seek the peace and welfare of Christ's body, the Church, and in reliance upon the grace of God, to serve Him and keep His commandments all the days of your life?
Answer: I do.

3   Let us pray.

Defend, O Lord, these Thy servants with Thy heavenly grace that they may continue Thine for ever and daily increase in Thy Holy Spirit more and more, till they come to Thine everlasting Kingdom.

Then the congregation stands and the Minister (raising his hand in blessing over the Candidates, or laying his hand on the head of each as they kneel before him) says:

The very God of peace sanctify you wholly; and I pray God your whole spirit and soul and body be preserved blameless unto the coming of our Lord Jesus Christ.

God the Father, God the Son, and God the Holy Spirit bless, preserve and keep you now and for evermore. *Amen.*

Then may be sung *The Lord bless thee,* after which the Minister says:

Dearly beloved, seeing that you have now professed your faith before

God and this people, I now declare you to be admitted to the full membership of the Church of Christ: and, in particular, into the fellowship of His congregation in this place; and in token thereof I give you the right hand of fellowship.

11   The Minister and Elders then give the right hand of fellowship to the newly-received members: after which the Minister may say:

Beloved in the Lord, now received into all the privileges of membership in the Church of Christ: consider well that you are indeed fellow-citizens with the saints, and of the household of God, and are built upon the foundation of the apostles and prophets, Jesus Christ Himself being the chief corner-stone, in Whom also you are builded together for an habitation of God through the Spirit.

If we walk in the light, as He is in the light, we have fellowship one with another.

Jesus said: If any man will come after Me, let him deny himself, and take up his cross daily and follow Me. To him that overcometh will I give to sit with Me in My throne, even as I also overcame, and am set down with My Father in His throne.

12   Let us pray.

Almighty God, Who hast founded Thy Church upon earth, and hast promised to preserve it to the end; we thank Thee for Thy great mercy to these Thy children, and to Thy Church, to which Thou hast given the joy of receiving them into the fellowship of the Lord's Table. We thank Thee that, by Holy Baptism, they have been incorporated into the Body of Christ. We thank Thee for their Christian training, for every good influence in their lives, and for the assurance of Thy blessing and favour. Forgive, we beseech Thee, all their sins; and graciously accept them as they dedicate themselves to Thee. When they approach Thy Holy Table to receive the Communion of the Body and Blood of Christ, grant them to behold the vision of His love, and to be made partakers of His grace. Sanctify to us all the ministration of his holy ordinance. Forgive us wherein we have come short of the grace of our own Confirmation, by wandering from Thy ways, and bring us back with a perfect repentance; through Jesus Christ our Lord.

13   Our Father, . . .

14   The Minister may then give an address to the newly received members.

The grace of the Lord Jesus Christ, and the love of God, and the communion of the Holy Spirit, be with you all. *Amen.*

7. *The Baptist Rites 1960*

These texts are from *Orders and Prayers for Church Worship: A Manual for Ministers*, compiled by Ernest A. Payne and Stephen F. Winward, 1960. Previous to 1960 *A Minister's Manual*, arranged by M. E. Aubrey, was used as the Baptist service-book. While the Baptist Church in England has no official service-book, in the sense that a particular service-book must be used, these two books are those most commonly used.

The Baptist Church does not, of course, have an Order for the Baptism of Infants, but it does have a service for "The Dedication of Children". But this service is in no sense sacramental. It is directed chiefly to the parents, reminding them that their child is God's gift to them, and because of this fact they have Christian responsibilities towards the child.

1 THE BAPTISM OF BELIEVERS

2 Baptism should be administered in the presence of the Congregation during Public Worship.

3 Since we are baptized into the Church, it is desirable that Baptism should, if possible, be followed by the Lord's Supper, at which the reception of the new members should take place.

4 After the singing of a Baptismal Hymn, the Minister may read a selection from the following passages of Scripture.

5 Then Jesus came from Galilee to the Jordan to John, . . . (Matt. 3.13–17, RSV)

6 (At this point the Service includes the following passages, the texts of which are given in full:)

Luke 3.21–2; *John* 3.5–8; *Acts* 2.38, 41–2; *Acts* 22.16; *Romans* 6.3–4; *Romans* 10.9–11; *1 Corinthians* 12.12–13; *Galatians* 3.26–8; *Colossians* 2.12; *1 Timothy* 6.12; *1 Peter* 3.21–2.

7 (The following additional passages are also suitable, especially for the main New Testament Lesson during the service.

Mark 1.1–13; *The Acts* 8.26–40; *The Acts* 9.1–19; *The Acts* 10.34–48; *The Acts* 16.11–15; *The Acts* 16.16–34; *The Acts* 19.1–7; *Ephesians* 4.1–6; *Ephesians* 5.21–33; *Colossians* 3.1–17; *Titus* 3.4–7; *Hebrews* 10.19–25; *1 John* 5.6–12.)

8 The Minister may conclude the selected readings as follows:

Jesus came and said to them, . . . (Matt. 28.18–20, RSV)

9   The Minister may then say:

Beloved brethren: You have just heard how our Lord Jesus Christ after his glorious resurrection and before his ascension into heaven, commanded his apostles to make disciples of all nations, baptizing them in the name of the Father, and of the Son, and of the Holy Spirit.

Let us now set forth the great benefits which we are to receive from the Lord, according to his word and promise, in this holy sacrament.

In baptism we are united with Christ through faith, dying with him unto sin and rising with him unto newness of life.

The washing of our bodies with water is the outward and visible sign of the cleansing of our souls from sin through the sacrifice of our Saviour.

The Holy Spirit, the Lord and giver of life, by whose unseen operation we have already been brought to repentance and faith, is given and sealed to us in this sacrament of grace.

By this same Holy Spirit, we are baptized into one body and made members of the holy catholic and apostolic Church, the blessed company of all Christ's faithful people.

These great benefits are promised and pledged to those who profess repentance toward God and faith in our Lord Jesus Christ. For all such believers, baptism is:

An act of obedience to the command of our Lord Jesus Christ:

A following of the example of our Lord Jesus Christ who was baptized in the river Jordan, that he might fulfil all righteousness:

A public confession of personal faith in Jesus Christ as Saviour and Lord:

A vow or pledge of allegiance to Jesus Christ, an engagement to be his for ever.

10   Addressing those who are to be baptized, the Minister shall say:

Forasmuch as you now present yourselves for Baptism, it is necessary that you sincerely give answer, before God and his Church, to the questions which I now put to you.

11   Then shall he say to each person to be baptized:

Do you make profession of repentance toward God and of faith in our Lord Jesus Christ?
Answer: I do.

Do you promise, in dependence on divine grace, to follow Christ and serve him for ever in the fellowship of his Church?
Answer: I do.

12 Then shall follow the Prayer.

Almighty and everlasting God, we give thee humble and hearty thanks for our Saviour Jesus Christ, who died for our sins, was buried, and was raised on the third day. Graciously accept, we beseech thee, these thy servants, that they, coming to thee in baptism, may by faith be united with Christ in his Church, and receive according to thy promise the forgiveness of their sins, and the gift of the Holy Spirit. Grant that they, putting on the Lord Jesus Christ, may receive out of his fullness and evermore abide in him. Keep them strong in faith, steadfast in hope, abounding in love. Bestow upon them the manifold gifts of thy grace, that they may serve thee profitably in thy Church. Defend them in all trials and temptations, and grant that, persevering to the end, they may inherit eternal life; through Jesus Christ our Lord. *Amen.*

3 As each person to be baptized stands in the water, the Minister shall pronounce his or her names, and say:

On thy profession of repentance toward God and faith in our Lord Jesus Christ, I baptize thee in the name of the Father and of the Son and of the Holy Spirit. *Amen.*

4 After each baptism the Minister may say:

The Lord bless thee and keep thee: the Lord make his face to shine upon thee, and be gracious unto thee. The Lord lift up his countenance upon thee and give thee peace.

5 Alternatively, the Choir and Congregation may sing after each baptism, or at the conclusion of the baptisms, one of the Baptismal Sentences from the Hymn Book, or the verse of a hymn or the Doxology.

6 After the baptisms, one of the following prayers may be offered:

Eternal Father, keep, we beseech thee, thy servants from falling, and present them faultless before the presence of thy glory with exceeding joy: and unto thee, the only wise God our Saviour, be glory and majesty, dominion and power, both now and for ever. *Amen.*

Teach them, good Lord, to serve thee with loyal and steadfast hearts; to give and not to count the cost; to fight and not to heed the wounds; to strive and not to seek for rest; to labour and to ask for no reward, save that of knowing that they do thy will; through Jesus Christ our Lord. *Amen.*

Grant, O Lord, that as we are baptized into the death of thy Son our Saviour Jesus Christ, so by continual mortifying our corrupt affections we may be buried with him; and that through the grave, and gate of death, we may pass to our joyful resurrection; for his merits, who died, and was buried, and rose again for us, thy Son Jesus Christ our Lord. *Amen.*

O God of hope, fill them with all joy and peace in believing, so that by the power of the Holy Spirit they may abound in hope: through Jesus Christ our Lord. *Amen.*

O God of peace, who broughtest again from the dead our Lord Jesus, the great shepherd of the sheep, by the blood of the eternal covenant, equip them with everything good that they may do thy will, and work in them that which is pleasing in thy sight: through Jesus Christ, to whom be glory for ever and ever. *Amen.*

17 If desired, a Hymn may now follow, and the normal order of public worship be continued. If it be the end of the service, the Minister may say:

Go forth into the world in peace; be of good courage; hold fast that which is good; render to no man evil for evil; strengthen the faint-hearted; support the weak; help the afflicted; honour all men; love and serve the Lord, rejoicing in the power of the Holy Spirit. *Amen.*

18 or

May God Almighty, the Father of our Lord Jesus Christ, grant you to be strengthened with power through his Spirit in the inward man; that Christ may dwell in your hearts through faith, and that you may be filled unto all the fullness of God. *Amen.*

19 or

The grace of the Lord Jesus Christ, and the love of God, and the fellow-ship of the Holy Spirit, be with you all. *Amen.*

1 THE LAYING ON OF HANDS WITH PRAYER
UPON THOSE WHO HAVE BEEN BAPTIZED

2 This order may follow baptism, either as part of the baptismal service, or as soon afterwards as convenient. It should be followed by the administration of the Lord's Supper.

3 The Minister addressing the Congregation shall say:

Beloved brethren: we are now to pray for and lay our hands upon those who have been baptized, and receive them into church membership. This rite practised by apostles is an act of acceptance and commissioning. Let us pray therefore that they, being blessed and strengthened by the Holy Spirit, may be fully equipped for their vocation and ministry as priests and servants of Jesus Christ. We also, in accepting them, commend them to your love and fellowship, and exhort you to encourage, help, and build them up in the Lord. Let us now, together with them, hear these words of Holy Scripture.

4 The Minister shall then read one or more of the following scriptures:

You are a chosen race, . . . (1 Pet. 2.9, RSV)

As each has received a gift employ it for one another, . . . (1 Pet. 4.10–11, RSV)

Never flag in zeal, . . . (Rom. 12.11–12, RSV)

You are the light of the world . . . Let your light so shine, . . . (Matt. 5.14a,16, RSV)

A new commandment I give to you, . . . (John 13.34–5, RSV)

5 Those that are baptized, kneeling in a convenient place in front of the Lord's Table, the Minister shall then offer prayer, extempore or as follows:

Almighty and everlasting God strengthen, we beseech thee, these thy servants with the Holy Spirit the Paraclete: the Spirit of wisdom and understanding, the Spirit of counsel and might, the Spirit of knowledge, piety, and godly fear. Grant that they may continue steadfastly in the apostle's teaching and fellowship, in the breaking of bread and the prayers. Enable them as royal priests of Jesus Christ to bring others to thee in prayer, and to take thee to others in witness. In all their vocation and ministry may they truly serve thee; through Jesus Christ our Lord. *Amen.*

6 Then the Minister, and one or two other appointed representatives of the Church, shall lay their hands upon the head of every one severally, the Minister praying:

Bless, O Lord, this thy servant, and strengthen *him* by the Holy Spirit, as we now in thy name commission *him* for the service and ministry of Jesus Christ our Lord. *Amen.*

7 or:

May the God of peace who brought again from the dead our Lord Jesus, the great shepherd of the sheep, by the blood of the eternal covenant, equip you with everything good that you may do his will, working in you that which is pleasing in his sight, through Jesus Christ; to whom be glory for ever and ever. *Amen.*

8 or:

The God of all grace, who called you to his eternal glory in Christ, perfect, stablish, and strengthen you. To him be the dominion for ever and ever. *Amen.*

9 The candidates now standing, the Minister may say:

So then you are no longer strangers and sojourners, but you are fellow-citizens with the saints and members of the household of God, built upon the foundation of the apostles and prophets, Christ Jesus himself being the chief corner-stone.

10 Where it is the custom, the new members may here sign the Church Covenant or the Membership Roll.

11 The Minister shall then proceed with the administration of the Lord's Supper.

8. *The Moravian Rites 1960*

The Moravian Liturgy, authorized for use in The British Province of the Moravian Church (*Unitas Fratrum*), was prepared in order to meet the growing desire and need for a single-volume service-book for use in the Moravian Church in the British Province.

In the Preface to this book, from which the following texts are taken, it is stated: "While in no way seeking to restrict or stereotype public worship, the Moravian Church values her liturgical tradition as a gift bestowed by her spiritual forefathers, since they felt that in this way full participation by the congregation and a satisfactory inclusion of the wide ranges of prayer might be assured."

While a certain amount of freedom is allowed in the use of the initiatory rites, the Questions and Answers, Baptism in the Three-fold Name, and the Laying on of Hands are invariable.

1 THE BAPTISM OF INFANTS

2 The Service may open with a Hymn, or come at a suitable point in another Service.

3 All being in order, the Infant not yet brought in, an Address may be given.

4 Then, all standing, the Minister says:

Dearly beloved, we are come together to baptize *this child* in the name of God the Father, the Son, and the Holy Ghost.

Baptism sets forth the saving work of Christ, wherein we are washed from our sins, and raised into newness of life; and in this sacrament we make confession of faith in him.

In infant baptism we declare that our children share with us these benefits of our Lord's redeeming work, and we claim them for the following of Christ as members of his body the Church.

Moreover, it is written in the Gospel that Jesus said, Suffer the little children to come unto me; forbid them not, for of such is the kingdom of God. And he took them in his arms and blessed them, laying his hands upon them.

5 Addressing the Parents or Sponsors, the Congregation still standing, the Minister says:

You have heard the words of our Saviour Christ; earnestly believe that he loves *this child*, that he is ready to receive and embrace *him*, to give *him* the blessing of eternal life, and to make *him* partaker of his everlasting kingdom.

Our Lord has promised to grant the things which we ask in his name, which promise he for his part will most surely keep and perform.

Do you, for your part, make confession of the faith wherein *this child* is to be baptized, in God as your heavenly Father, in Jesus Christ as your Saviour and Lord, and in the Holy Spirit as your Sanctifier? *Answer:* We do.

Do you promise, in reliance on divine grace, to teach *him* the truths and duties of the Christian faith, and by prayer, precept and example, to bring *him* up in the nurture and admonition of the Lord, and in the fellowship of the Church? *Answer:* We do.

The Lord preserve and bless you, and aid you to perform these promises.

6   Let us pray.

O Father of men, we praise thee for all the joy and blessing that children bring into the home and into the world. We thank thee for thy gracious providence over our homes, and especially over this home in which thou hast given deliverance to the mother, life to the child, and gladness to all. Grant that these *parents*, and all who share in the nurture of children, by receiving them in the name of Christ, may ever be enriched through their ministry of love.
R. Heavenly Father, hear us.

O thou who art the Friend of little children, and the faithful Protector of all weak and lowly things; keep, guard, and bless thy children: by the guidance of thy Spirit may they grow in strength and beauty of character, and in favour with God and man.
R. Jesus, Saviour, hear us.

O Holy Spirit, bless us all, and make all things new within us this day: help us now so to surrender ourselves to thy leading that we with our children may live together to the glory of God in the family of Jesus Christ.
R. Holy Spirit, hear us.

O Son of God, thou Saviour of the world,
R. Have mercy upon us.

By thy human birth,
By thy obedience, diligence, and faithfulness,
By all the merits of thy life, sufferings, and death,
By thy resurrection and ascension,

By thy abiding presence,
By thy word and sacraments,
R. Bless and comfort us, good Lord.

7 All stand, and during the singing of this Verse, the infant is brought in:

An infant, Lord, we bring to thee
As thy redeemed property,
And thee most fervently entreat
Thyself this child to consecrate;
Baptize *him*, and *his* soul embrace
In all the fulness of thy grace.

8 The Minister says:

The parents (sponsors) of *this child* desiring to train *him* up as a follower
of Christ, consecrate *him* to the Lord in the presence of his people; and
the Congregation receives *him* into the fold of Christ in the ordinance
of baptism, mindful of his command to the Apostle Peter, Feed my
lambs.

9   Let us pray.

Almighty and everliving God, whose blessed Son, Jesus Christ, was
carried as a child into the Temple, and who himself took little children
into his arms and blessed them; look mercifully upon us, and bless what
in thy name we do.

 Grant that *this child*, now to be baptized into the Church, the body of
Christ, may by the continual operation of thy Holy Spirit grow into
the likeness of *his* Saviour: lead *him* into full and effectual membership
of the Church; and grant that by thy grace *he* may ever remain in the
number of thy faithful children; through Jesus Christ our Lord. *Amen.*

10 The Father or Sponsor presents the Child to the Minister, who receives and
Baptizes it saying:

N., I baptize thee in the name of the Father, and of the Son, and of the
Holy Ghost. Amen.

The Lord bless thee, and keep thee; The Lord make his face to shine
upon thee, and be gracious unto thee; The Lord lift up his countenance
upon thee, and give thee peace.
R. In the name of Jesus. Amen.

11 Having handed the Child to the Mother or Sponsor, the Minister says:

We receive *this child* into Christ's Church in the trust that hereafter *he* shall not be ashamed to confess the faith of Christ, valiantly to fight under his banner, and to continue his faithful servant unto *his* life's end.

12   Let us pray.

Almighty God, our heavenly Father, whose blessed Son, Jesus Christ, did share at Nazareth the life of an earthly home; bless, we beseech thee, the home of *this child*, and grant wisdom and understanding to *his* parents and to all who have the care of *him*; that *he* may grow up in thy constant fear and love; through the same Jesus Christ our Lord. *Amen.*

Sanctify to us all, O Lord, the ministration of this holy sacrament. Forgive us wherein we have come short of the grace of our own baptism, by wandering from thy ways; and bring us back with a perfect repentance. Quicken us anew by the power of thy Holy Spirit, that we may walk in charity, humility and godliness, as those who have been baptized by the same Spirit into one body; through Jesus Christ our Lord. *Amen.*

13 A Hymn may be sung. The Service closes with the New Testament Benediction.

1 THE BAPTISM OF ADULTS AND THE
CONFIRMATION OF SUCH AS HAVE
BEEN BAPTIZED IN INFANCY

2 The Service opens with an Introit or Hymn.
3 Then, all standing, the Minister says;

Almighty God, unto whom all hearts be open, all desires known, and from whom no secrets are hid; cleanse the thoughts of our hearts by the inspiration of thy Holy Spirit, that we may perfectly love thee, and worthily magnify thy holy name; through Jesus Christ our Lord. *Amen.*

God, who at sundry times and in divers manners spake in time past unto the fathers by the prophets, hath in these last days spoken unto us by his Son. And this is the word that we have from him:

The Lord our God, the Lord is One; and thou shalt love the Lord thy God with all thy heart, and with all thy soul, and with all thy mind, and with all thy strength. This is the first and great commandment.
R. Lord, have mercy upon us, and incline our hearts to keep this law.
And the second is like it, namely this: Thou shalt love thy neighbour as

thyself. On these two commandments hang all the Law and the Prophets.

R. Lord, have mercy upon us, and write these thy laws in our hearts, we beseech thee.

Most merciful Lord, who hast caused us to hear thy wholesome and divine teaching, enlighten our souls to the understanding of thy holy Word, so that we may be not only hearers of spiritual truth, but doers of good works, following after faith, hope, love, and living without offence or blame; through Jesus Christ our Lord. *Amen.*

4 Then follow the reading of Scripture, a Hymn or Canticle, and an Address.

5 The Te Deum (Canticle 7) or another Hymn is sung.

6 All standing, the Minister says:

With the heart man believeth unto righteousness, and with the mouth confession is made unto salvation; for Jesus said, Everyone who shall confess me before men, him will I also confess before my Father which is in heaven.

7 Naming the Candidates, the Minister continues:

You are here to declare before God, and in the presence of this Congregation, your faith in Christ, and your steadfast purpose to fulfil, with the help of his Holy Spirit, the duties to which your acceptance of the christian call pledges you.

8 The Minister asks these Questions, and the Candidates answer severally:

Do you believe in Jesus Christ, who loved you and gave himself for you?
Answer: I do.
Is it your set will and purpose, denying ungodliness and worldly lusts, to live soberly, righteously, and godly in this present world, following and serving Christ?
Answer: It is.
Is it your earnest wish to continue steadfastly in the teaching and fellowship of the Church?
Answer: It is.

9 At a Baptism the Candidate kneels, and the Minister prays:

Almighty and everliving God, whose blessed Son, Jesus Christ, was baptized of John the Baptist in the Jordan, and saw the heavens rent asunder, and the Spirit as a dove descending upon him; look mercifully upon us, and bless what in thy name we do.

Grant that this thy servant, now to be baptized into the Church, the body of Christ, may by the continual operation of thy Holy Spirit grow into the likeness of *his* Saviour; lead *him* into full and effectual membership of thy Church, and grant that by thy grace *he* may ever remain in the number of thy faithful people; through Jesus Christ our Lord. *Amen.*

10 Laying his hands on the head of the Candidate, the Minister recites a suitable text of Scripture, and thereafter Baptizes him, saying:

N., I baptize thee in the name of the Father, and of the Son, and of the Holy Ghost. *Amen.*

11 At a Confirmation, the Minister, standing before the Candidates and naming them, lays his hands on the head of each, and recites a suitable text of Scripture.

12 This Blessing is pronounced over each person Baptized or Confirmed:

The Lord bless thee, and keep thee; The Lord make his face to shine upon thee, and be gracious unto thee; The Lord lift up his countenance upon thee, and give thee peace.
R. In the name of Jesus. *Amen.*

13 The Minister gives to each the Right Hand of Fellowship in token of Reception into the Communion of Christ's Church, and when all have been received, says:

We receive you into this Congregation of Christ's Church in the trust that hereafter you shall not be ashamed to confess the faith of Christ, valiantly to fight under his banner, and to continue his faithful servant unto your life's end.

You have confessed a good confession in the sight of many witnesses. I charge you in the sight of God who quickeneth all things, and of Christ Jesus, who before Pontius Pilate witnessed a good confession, that you keep the commandment, without spot, without reproach, until the appearing of our Lord Jesus Christ.

14   Let us pray.

Defend, O Lord, these thy servants with thy heavenly grace, that they may continue thine for ever; and daily increase in them thy Holy Spirit more and more, until they come into thy everlasting kingdom. *Amen.*

O righteous Lord, thou hast opened unto us the gates of righteousness, and thou callest us to walk in the ways of holy living; that thy servants may partake of this blessedness, guide them with thy truth, and sustain them by thy love. *Amen.*

Almighty Lord ...

CF18, *but* now and ever ⟨here and ever⟩

Now unto him that is able to keep us from falling, and to set us before the presence of his glory without blemish in exceeding joy, to the only God our Saviour, be glory, majesty, dominion and power, now and for evermore. *Amen.*

15 The Service closes with a Hymn, and the following:

Go forth into the world in peace; ...

1928 C20, *but* Holy Spirit ⟨Holy Ghost⟩

9. *The Lutheran Rites 1962*

These texts are from *The Occasional Services and Additional Orders*, which was jointly prepared by the Lutheran Churches in America, and published in 1962, for the use of the Lutheran Churches co-operating in The Commission on the Liturgy and Hymnal. As the services in this service-book are also used in the English speaking Lutheran churches, and occasionally in the National Lutheran churches in this country, these Rites may be said to represent the use of Lutherans in England.

1 ## ORDER FOR THE BAPTISM OF INFANTS

2 Baptism shall ordinarily be administered in the Church at any time of the stated services, or at a specially appointed service. At Matins or Vespers, the Order here given may follow the Lessons or the Sermon; at the Service it may follow the Sermon.

3 When circumstances demand, Baptism may be administered privately, and public announcement thereof shall afterward be made. Infants should be brought to the Church for Holy Baptism as soon as possible after birth.

4 The names of the Parents, of the Sponsors, of the Child, and of the Minister, with the date and place of birth and of baptism, shall be entered in the Record of the Congregation, and a proper certificate issued.

5 Only members of the Church shall be accepted as Sponsors, and they shall be instructed as to their spiritual responsibility to the Child.

6 This Order may be preceded and followed by a Hymn.

7 The Sponsors (and the Assistant), together with the Congregation, shall say *Amen* at the end of each prayer.

8 The Minister shall say:

In the Name of the Father, and of the Son, and of the Holy Ghost. *Amen.*

9 Dearly Beloved: Forasmuch as all men are born in sin, and our Saviour Jesus Christ hath said, Except a man be born of Water and of the Spirit, he cannot enter into the kingdom of God: Let us call upon God the Father, through our Lord Jesus Christ, that of his goodness and mercy he will receive *this Child* by Baptism, and make *him* a living member of his holy Church.

10 Then may the Minister make the sign of the Cross on the Child's forehead saying:

Receive the sign of the holy Cross, in token that henceforth thou shalt know the Lord, and the power of his Resurrection, and the fellowship of his sufferings.

11 The Congregation shall stand until the end of the Lord's Prayer.

12 The Minister shall say:

Let us pray.

Almighty and everlasting God, the Father of our Lord Jesus Christ: We call upon thee for *this Child*, and beseech thee to bestow upon *him* the gift of thy baptism and thine everlasting grace by the washing of regeneration. Receive *him*, O Lord, as thou hast promised by thy well-beloved Son, saying: Ask, and it shall be given unto you; seek, and ye shall find; knock, and it shall be opened unto you; through the same Jesus Christ, thy Son, our Lord. *Amen.*

13 Then shall the Minister say:

Hear the Holy Gospel, which saith: They brought young children to him that he should touch them; . . . (CF3)

14 Then shall all say the Lord's Prayer.

15 During the Prayer the Minister may lay his hand upon the head of the Child.

Our Father, who art in heaven, . . . (CF11)

16 Then shall the Minister say to those who present the Child:

Since in Christian love you present *this Child* for Holy Baptism, I charge you that you diligently and faithfully teach *him* the Ten Commandments, the Creed, and the Lord's Prayer; and that, as *he* grows in years, you place in *his* hands the Holy Scriptures, bring *him* to the services of God's House, and provide for *his* instruction in the Christian Faith; that, abiding in the covenant of *his* Baptism and in communion with the Church, *he* may be brought up to lead a godly life until the day of Jesus Christ. I therefore call upon you to answer in *his* stead:

17 Then may the Minister say:

Do you renounce the devil, and all his works, and all his ways? *Answer:* I renounce them.

18 Then shall the Minister say:

Do you believe in God the Father Almighty, Maker of heaven and earth? *Answer:* I believe.

Do you believe in Jesus Christ his only Son our Lord, Who was conceived by the Holy Ghost, Born of the Virgin Mary, Suffered under Pontius Pilate, Was crucified, dead, and buried: Descended into hell;

The third day rose again from the dead; Ascended into heaven, and sitteth on the right hand of God the Father Almighty; Whence he shall come to judge the quick and the dead?

Answer: I believe.

Do you believe in the Holy Ghost; The Holy Christian (*or*, catholic) Church, the Communion of Saints; The Forgiveness of sins; The Resurrection of the body, And the Life everlasting?

Answer: I believe.

19   Then shall the Minister say to those who present the Child:

Do you present *this Child* to be baptized into this Christian Faith? *Answer:* I do.

20   The Congregation shall rise, and the Minister shall say:

Let us pray.

Almighty, everlasting God, whose dearly beloved Son, Jesus Christ, hath said to his disciples: All power is given unto me in heaven and in earth, and hath commanded them to go and teach all nations, baptizing them in the Name of the Father, and of the Son, and of the Holy Ghost; and hath promised to be with them alway, even unto the end of the world: Regard the prayers of thy people, and grant unto *this Child* now to be baptized, the fulness of thy grace, that *he* may ever remain in the number of thy faithful and elect children; through the same Jesus Christ our Lord. *Amen.*

21   The Minister may now ask,

How shall this Child be named?

and shall then baptize him by applying water three times as he saith:

N., I baptize thee: In the Name of the Father, and of the Son, and of the Holy Ghost. Amen.

22   Then the Minister, laying his hand on the head of the Child, shall say:

Almighty God, the Father of our Lord Jesus Christ, who hath begotten thee again of Water and the Holy Ghost, and hath forgiven thee all thy sin, strengthen thee with his grace unto life everlasting. Amen.

Peace be with thee.

23   Then shall the Minister say:

Let us pray.

Almighty and most merciful God and Father: We thank thee that thou

dost graciously preserve and extend thy Church, and that thou hast
granted to *this Child* the new birth in Holy Baptism, and received *him*
as thy *Child* and *heir* to thy Kingdom; and we humbly beseech thee to
defend and keep *him* in this grace, that *he* may never depart from thee
but always live according to thy will, and finally receive the fulness
of thy promise in thine eternal kingdom; through Jesus Christ, thy
Son, our Lord, who liveth and reigneth with thee and the Holy Ghost,
one God, world without end. *Amen.*

24 Then shall the Minister say:

The Blessing of Almighty God, the Father, the Son, and the Holy
Ghost, be with you alway. *Amen.*

I ORDER FOR CONFIRMATION

2 Candidates for Confirmation shall be instructed in the Christian Faith as it is set
forth in the Small Catechism, and be approved in such manner as may be deemed
satisfactory by the Pastor and the Church Council.

3 Confirmation shall be administered at a public service of the Congregation. In case
of serious illness or pressing necessity, it may be administered privately in the
presence of members of the Church. In such case the Confirmation shall be publicly
announced to the Congregation.

4 When Confirmation is administered at The Service, and there be no Communion,
this Order shall follow the Prayer of the Church.

5 If the Holy Communion be administered, this Order shall follow the Sermon; and
at the conclusion of this Order, The Service shall be continued with the Offering,
the Offertory, and the Prayer of the Church.

6 Before the Epistle and the Gospel for the Day, one or more of the following
Lessons may be read: Acts 8.14–17; Romans 10.8–11 (Begin: *The word is nigh thee*);
Ephesians 2.13–22; Ecclesiastes 12.1–7; John 15.1–16.

7 The Hymn, *Come, Holy Ghost, our souls inspire*, (117), or another Hymn of Invocation
of the Holy Ghost, shall be sung.

8 The Minister shall say:

The following persons, having been instructed in the Christian Faith
and approved by the Church, are now presented for the Rite of
Confirmation.

9 Then shall the Minister announce the names of the persons to be confirmed, after
which they shall come to the Altar.

10 Then shall the Minister say:

Dearly Beloved: In Holy Baptism you were received by our Lord Jesus
Christ and made members of his holy Church. In accordance with our
Lord's command, you have been instructed in the Word of God and
led to the knowledge of his will and his gracious Gospel; and you now

desire to make public profession of your faith, and to be confirmed. I therefore ask each of you:

11   The Minister may then say:

Do you renounce the devil, and all his works, and all his ways?
Answer: I renounce them.

12   Then shall the Minister say:

Do you believe in God the Father Almighty?
Answer: I believe in God the Father Almighty, Maker of heaven and earth.
Do you believe in Jesus Christ?
Answer: I believe in Jesus Christ his only Son our Lord, Who was conceived by the Holy Ghost, Born of the Virgin Mary. Suffered under Pontius Pilate, Was crucified, dead and buried: He descended into hell; the third day he rose again from the dead; He ascended into heaven, And sitteth on the right hand of God the Father Almighty; From thence he shall come to judge the quick and the dead.
Do you believe in the Holy Ghost?
Answer: I believe in the Holy Ghost; The holy Christian (*or* catholic) Church, the Communion of Saints; The Forgiveness of sins; The Resurrection of the body, and the Life everlasting.
Do you promise to abide in this Faith, and in the covenant of your Baptism, and as a member of the Church to be diligent in the use of the Means of Grace and in prayer?

13   Then shall each candidate answer in turn:

I do, by the help of God.

14   Then shall the Minister say:

Let us pray.

Almighty and everlasting God, who hast vouchsafed to regenerate these thy servants by Water and the Spirit, and hast forgiven them all their sins: Strengthen them, we beseech thee, with the Holy Ghost, the Comforter; and daily increase in them thy manifold gifts of grace: the spirit of wisdom and understanding; the spirit of counsel and might; the spirit of knowledge and of the fear of the Lord, now and forever; through Jesus Christ, thy Son, our Lord. *Amen.*

15   Then shall the candidates kneel, and the Minister shall lay his hand, or hands, on the head of each and say the Prayer of Blessing.

The Father in heaven, for Jesus' sake, renew and increase in thee the gift of the Holy Ghost, to thy strengthening in faith, to thy growth in grace, to thy patience in suffering, and to the blessed hope of everlasting life.

16 Each one confirmed shall say:

Amen.

17 Then shall they rise, and the Minister shall say:

Forasmuch as you have made confession of your faith and have received Holy Baptism, I do now, in the Name of the Lord Jesus Christ, the great King and Head of the Church, admit you to the fellowship of the Lord's Table, and to participation in all the spiritual privileges of the Church.

God the Father, God the Son, and God the Holy Ghost, bless, preserve, and keep you, now and for evermore. *Amen.*

18 Then shall the Congregation rise, and the Minister shall say:

The Lord be with you.
R̂. And with thy spirit.

Let us pray.

Almighty and merciful God, heavenly Father, who only workest in us to will and to do the things that please thee: Confirm, we beseech thee, the work which thou hast begun in these thy servants; that, abiding in the communion of thy Church and in the faith of thy Gospel, no false doctrine, no lust of the flesh, nor love of the world may lead them away from thee, nor from the truth which they have confessed; but that in joyful obedience to thy Word, they may ever know thee more perfectly, love thee more fervently, and serve thee in every good word and deed, to the blessing of their fellow men, the edification of thy people and the glory of thy Name; through Jesus Christ, thy Son, our Lord, who liveth and reigneth with thee and the Holy Ghost, one God, world without end. *Amen.*

19 Then shall all say:

Our Father, who art in heaven, . . .

20 Then shall the Minister dismiss them, saying:

The Blessing of Almighty God, the Father, the Son, and the Holy Ghost, be with you alway. *Amen.*

10. The Roman Catholic Rites 1964

The Baptismal text is from *The Small Ritual, Being Extracts from The Rituale Romanum in Latin & in English. The Small Ritual* was issued in 1964, after the Vatican Council had issued its decree on the liturgy; it "has been approved *ad interim* as the official English text in England and Wales. That is to say, whatever English is used will be taken from this book until such time at least as the present *Rituale Romanum* is replaced, as the original Latin text, with a new *Rituale* produced under the direction of the Post-Conciliar Liturgical Commission."[1]

The text of *The Rite of Confirmation* reproduces the authorized text published by the Catholic Truth Society, in 1965. A revised Rite of Confirmation is soon to be introduced.

I THE RITE OF INFANT BAPTISM

2 When all is ready the priest washes his hands and puts on, over his cassock, a surplice and a purple stole. If assistants are available he should take one or more with him, and they too should be vested in surplices. He proceeds to the church door where those who have brought the child await his arrival.

3 He asks first (unless he already knows) whether the child is from his own or another parish, whether it is a boy or a girl, whether for any reason it has already been baptized at home, and if so by whom and how. He enquires who are to be the godparents, and instructs them in what to do during the ceremony, and how to make the responses.

4 He should make sure that the name chosen for the child is not frivolous and unworthy of a Christian, but rather the name of one of the saints of God whom the child can learn, later on, to imitate and look to for protection.

BAPTISM OF A SINGLE INFANT[2]

5 The child, having been named, is held, if a child in arms, on the right arm of whoever carries it during the ceremony.

6 The priest then addresses the child by name, and asks:

N. What do you ask of the Church of God?
The godparent replies: Faith.
Priest: What does Faith offer you?
Godparent: Life everlasting.

---

[1] From the Preface to *The Small Ritual*.
[2] *The Small Ritual* provides a second Rite, for the Baptism of Several Infants.

Priest: If then you desire to enter into life, keep the commandments. "Thou shalt love the Lord thy God with thy whole heart and with thy whole soul, and with thy whole mind; and thy neighbour as thyself."

7 He blows gently with his breath into the face of the child and says:

Go forth from *him*, unclean spirit, and give place to the Holy Spirit, the Paraclete.

8 He traces the sign of the cross with his thumb upon the forehead and upon the breast of the child, saying:

Receive the sign of the cross upon your fore ✠ head and upon your ✠ heart. Know that you are bound now by a heavenly rule of life, and let your conduct henceforth prove you fit to be a living temple of God.

Let us pray.

Hear our prayer, Lord God, and guard this chosen servant *N.* May thy strength never fail *him* now, for we have traced upon *him* the sign of Christ's cross. May *he* always remember what *he* learns of thy greatness and thy glory. May *he* keep thy commandments and be worthy, *he* too, to have glory, the glory of new life in thee. Through Christ our Lord. *Amen.*

9 He places his hand on the child's head saying:

Let us pray.

Almighty, everlasting God, Father of our Lord Jesus Christ, look upon this thy servant *N.*, whom thou hast called to the first lessons of the Faith. Drive out of *him* all blindness of heart; break the bonds of Satan which have bound *him*. Open to *him*, O Lord, the door of thy mercy. Steeped in this symbol of thy wisdom may *he* no longer be tainted with evil desires, but rather spread about *him* the fragrance of thy commandments, as *he* serves thee happily in thy Church and grows holier with each passing day. Through the same Christ our Lord. *Amen.*

10 Then he blesses the salt. Once blessed it may be kept for use on further occasions.

I adjure thee in the name of God the Father ✠ almighty, in the love of Jesus Christ ✠ our Lord, in the power of the Holy ✠ Spirit. I adjure thee through the living, ✠ true ✠ and holy ✠ God, the God ✠ who made thee for the well-being of the human race, and commanded thee to be hallowed by his servants for the use of those who come to the knowledge of him by faith. In the name of the Holy Trinity, through thee may Satan be put to flight. Wherefore, O Lord our God, we beseech thee, sanctify ✠ this salt and bless ✠ it; and make of it a sovereign remedy to linger within the inmost being of all who partake of it. In the name of that same Lord Jesus Christ, who is to come to judge the living and the dead and the world by fire. *Amen.*

11   He puts a little of the blessed salt into the mouth of the child, and says:

N. Receive this salt, learning from it how to relish what is right and good. May it make your way easy to eternal life. *Amen.*

℣. Peace be with you.

℞. And with you.

Let us pray.

God of our fathers, O God with whom all truth begins, look upon thy servant *N.* who now has tasted salt as the first nourishment at thy table. Do not leave *him* hungry. Give to *his* soul food in abundance, that *he* may be eager, hopeful and lighthearted in the service of thy Name. Lead *him* we pray thee, to the waters of new Life, that, with all who are faithful to thee, *he* may merit the eternal rewards thou hast promised. Through Christ our Lord. *Amen.*

I adjure thee, unclean spirit, in the name of the Father ✠ and of the Son ✠ and of the Holy ✠ Ghost to depart and remain far away from this servant of God *N.* He commands thee now who walked dry-shod upon the waters, and when Peter would have perished in the sea stretched out to him his saving hand. And so, accursed spirit, give heed to the sentence passed upon thee. Give honour to Jesus Christ his son, and to the Holy Ghost, and begone from this servant of God *N.*; for God and our Lord Jesus Christ in his goodness has called *him* to his holy grace and blessing and to the waters of baptism.

12   He traces the sign of the cross upon the forehead of the child saying:

And this sign of the holy Cross ✠, which we put upon *his* forehead, do thou, foul spirit, never dare to violate. Through the same Christ our Lord. *Amen.*

13   He places his hand upon the child's head and says:

Let us pray.

Holy Lord and Father, almighty and eternal God, author of light and of truth, we ask thy neverfailing and kind fatherly love for this thy servant *N.* Enlighten him in thy goodness with the light of thy own understanding. Cleanse *him* and sanctify *him*; give *him* true knowledge; that made worthy by the grace of thy Baptism *he* may be endowed with unwavering hope, sound judgement and a firm grasp of holy doctrine. Through Christ our Lord. *Amen.*

14 The priest places the left-side of his stole upon the child and leads him into the church, saying as he does so:

N. Come into the temple of God, that your lot may be with Christ in life eternal. *Amen.*

15 When they have entered the church, the priest leads the way to the font, saying aloud meanwhile together with the godparents:

I believe in God the Father Almighty, Creator of heaven and earth; and in Jesus Christ his only Son our Lord, who was conceived by the Holy Ghost, born of the Virgin Mary; suffered under Pontius Pilate, was crucified, dead, and buried; he descended into hell; the third day he rose again from the dead; he ascended into heaven, sitteth at the right hand of God the Father Almighty; from thence he shall come to judge the living and the dead. I believe in the Holy Ghost; the holy Catholic Church; the communion of saints; the forgiveness of sins; the resurrection of the body, and life everlasting. Amen.

Our Father, who art in heaven, . . . (CF9)

16 Before entering the Baptistery he stands with his back to the baptistery gates and says:

I adjure you, each and every unclean spirit, in the name of God the Father ✠ almighty, in the name of Jesus Christ ✠ his Son, our Lord and our Judge, and by the power of the Holy ✠ Spirit, to be gone from this image of God N., whom our Lord in his goodness has called to his holy temple that *he himself* may become a temple of the living God, and the Holy Ghost may dwell in *him*. Through the same Christ our Lord, who will come to judge the living and the dead and the world by fire. *Amen.*

17 The priest touches the ears and the nostrils of the child with his thumb (moistened with saliva[1]) and as he touches first the right and then the left ear he says:

Ephpheta, which is: Be thou open.

18 Then as he touches the nostrils he says:

To the sweet fragrance about you. As for thee, evil spirit, get thee gone; for God's judgement is upon thee.

---

[1] It is no longer obligatory to moisten the thumb with saliva.

19   The priest questions the child saying:

N. Do you renounce Satan?
Godparent: I do renounce him.
Priest: And all his works?
Godparent: I do renounce them.
Priest: And all his pomp?
Godparent: I do renounce them.

20   The priest dips his thumb into the oil of catechumens and anoints the child upon the breast and between the shoulders in the form of a cross, saying:

I anoint you with this ✠ saving oil in Christ Jesus our Lord, that you may have eternal life.
℟. Amen.

21   With cotton wool he wipes his thumb and the places anointed.

22   He lays aside the purple stole and takes a white one. Then he enters the baptistery followed by the godparents with the child.

23   There at the font he addresses the child by name:

N. Do you believe in God the Father almighty, creator of heaven and earth?
Godparent: I do believe.
Priest: Do you believe in Jesus Christ his only Son, our Lord, who was born into this world and who suffered for us?
Godparent: I do believe.
Priest: Do you believe in the Holy Ghost, the Holy Catholic Church, the communion of Saints, the forgiveness of sins, the resurrection of the body and life everlasting?
Godparent: I do believe.

24   And then again calling the child by name, the priest asks:

N. Are you willing to be baptized?
Godparent: I am.

25   While the godparent (or godparents) hold the child, the priest takes baptismal water and pours it thrice over the head of the child in the form of a cross, at the same time saying once only, distinctly and with attention:

N. I baptize thee in the name of the ✠ Father *he pours once* and of the ✠ Son *he pours again* and of the Holy ✠ Ghost *he pours a third time.*

26   If there should be a doubt whether or not the child has been baptized, the following form is used:

N. If thou art not baptized, I baptize thee in the name of the ✠ Father and of the ✠ Son and of the Holy ✠ Ghost.

27   The priest dips his thumb into the sacred Chrism and anoints the child on the crown of the head in the form of a cross saying:

May Almighty God, the Father of our Lord Jesus Christ, who has given you new life through water and the Holy Ghost, and forgiven you all your sins

here he anoints the child

himself anoint you with saving ✠ Chrism in the same Jesus Christ our Lord, that you may have eternal life. *Amen.*
Priest: Peace be with you.
R̲. And with you.

28   With cotton wool he wipes his thumb and the place anointed. He places upon the child's head the white linen cloth representing a white garment, saying:

Take this white garment, and see that you carry it without stain before the judgement seat of our Lord Jesus Christ, that you may have eternal life. *Amen.*

29   He gives a lighted candle either to the child or to the godparent saying:

Take this burning light and keep true to your baptism throughout a blameless life. Keep the commandments of God; that when the Lord shall come like a bridegroom to his marriage feast you, in company with all the Saints, may meet him in the heavenly courts, and there live for ever. *Amen.*

30   When all is done he says:

Go in peace N. and the Lord be with you. *Amen.*

I   THE RITE OF CONFIRMATION[1]

2   The Bishop, vested in white stole and cope, and mitre of cloth of gold, will be seated on the faldstool while he addresses the candidates for Confirmation.

3   The mitre is removed and the Bishop stands, with joined hands, facing the candidates who kneel with their hands joined while he says or sings:

May the Holy Ghost come down upon you, and may the power of the Most High God keep you free from every sin.
R̲. Amen.
V̲. Our help is in the name of the Lord.

---

[1] In the Instruction on putting into effect the Constitution on the Sacred Liturgy issued by the Sacred Congregation of Rites in September 1964 it is stated that the sacrament of Confirmation may be administered during Mass, after the Gospel and Homily. If the Mass is celebrated by the Bishop himself, he will administer Confirmation wearing the Mass vestments.

℞. Who made heaven and earth.

℣. Lord, hear my prayer.

℞. And let my cry come to thee.

℣. The Lord be with you.

℞. And with you.

4 Then, stretching out his hands towards those to be confirmed, he says or sings:

Let us pray.

Almighty, everlasting God, who hast given new life through water and the Holy Ghost to these thy servants, and granted them forgiveness of all their sins, send down upon them from heaven thy Holy Spirit the Paraclete with his sevenfold gifts. *Amen.*

℣. The Spirit of wisdom and of understanding.

℞. Amen.

℣. The Spirit of counsel and of fortitude.

℞. Amen.

℣. The Spirit of knowledge and of piety.

℞. Amen.

Fill them with the Spirit of reverent fear of thyself and in thy goodness mark them out for eternal life with the sign of the Cross ✠ of Christ. Through the same Jesus Christ thy Son our Lord; who lives with thee in the unity of the same Holy Spirit, God for ever. *Amen.*

5 The Bishop sits down and the mitre is put on. A linen veil is spread over his lap and fastened, and the sacred chrism is brought to him.

6 The candidates now come forward, hands ungloved, each having a card on which his or her name is written, to be handed to the assistant on the Bishop's right. Each kneels in turn before the Bishop and the god-parent lays his or her right hand, ungloved, on the candidate's right shoulder. The Bishop, having dipped the thumb of his right hand in the chrism, makes the sign of the cross with it, once on the forehead of each one, his hand laid on the head, saying:

N. I sign thee with the sign of the ✠ Cross and I confirm thee with the Chrism of salvation. In the name of the Father, ✠ and of the Son and of the Holy Ghost. *Amen.*

7 While these last words are said he makes the sign of the cross three times over the candidate and then strikes him lightly on the left cheek, saying:

Peace be with you.

8 The candidate moves away and the chrism is removed by a priest with a piece of cotton wool.

9 When all have been confirmed the Bishop washes his hands while the following antiphon is said or sung:

Confirm, O God, what thou hast wrought in us, from thy holy temple in Jerusalem.

℣. Glory be to the Father, and to the Son, and to the Holy Ghost.

℟. As it was in the beginning, is now and ever shall be, world without end. Amen.

Confirm, O God, what thou hast wrought in us, from thy holy temple in Jerusalem.

10 After this the mitre is removed and the Bishop rises, turns towards the altar, and, with joined hands, says or sings:

℣. Show us, O Lord, thy mercy.

℟. And grant us thy salvation.

℣. Lord, hear my prayer.

℟. And let my cry come to thee.

℣. The Lord be with you.

℟. And with you.

Let us pray.

O God who didst give thy holy Spirit to the Apostles and didst will that through them and through those who should come after them, he should be given to the rest of the faithful; look favourably upon this humble fulfilment of our office, and grant that the same Holy Spirit, coming into the hearts of those whose foreheads we have marked with Sacred Chrism and signed with the sign of the holy Cross, may dwell therein and make of them a living temple of his glory. Who with the Father and the same Holy Spirit lives and reigns, God for ever. *Amen.*

11 Then, still facing the altar, he says:

Thus shall every man be blessed who fears the Lord.

12 Turning towards the persons confirmed, he makes the sign of the cross over them, once, saying:

May the Lord bless ✠ you from Sion, and all the days of your earthly life keep before your eyes the treasures of the heavenly Jerusalem. And may eternal life be yours. *Amen.*

13 The Bishop may then sit and resume the mitre to give an exhortation or the service may close with Benediction of the Blessed Sacrament.

11. *The Methodist Rites 1967*

These texts, *Baptism of Infants*; *Public Reception into Full Membership, or Confirmation*; and *The Baptism of those who are able to Answer for Themselves with the Public Reception into Full Membership, or Confirmation* are from *Baptism and Confirmation (or Recognition) Services*. This small service-book was prepared by the Methodist Faith and Order Committee and authorized for use by the English Methodist Conference of 1967. While the revised services in this book are authorized for experimental use for a period of three years, this does not mean that all Methodist Churches in England must use these services, but that they can be used wherever local churches and Ministers desire to use them. After the period of experimental use further revision is envisaged.

I BAPTISM
GENERAL DIRECTIONS

2 The Font should, when possible, stand prominently in a space apart.

3 The Society Stewards shall see that all necessary arrangements are made for the administration of the Sacrament of Baptism, after due notice has been given to the Minister, in the case of children by the parents or guardians, in other cases by the candidate for Baptism.

4 Before or during the service water shall be poured into the Font.

5 The Minister shall enquire beforehand whether each candidate has already been baptized.

6 No one shall be baptized who is known to have been baptized already.

7 (If it is uncertain whether a candidate has already been baptized or not, the following form of words is to be used at the Baptism:
   N., if thou art not already baptized, I baptize thee in the Name of the Father, and of the Son, and of the Holy Spirit. Amen.)

8 It is fitting that water should be poured or sprinkled upon the candidate three times or that he should be dipped in the water three times, once at the mention of each Person of the Trinity, but it is sufficient that it be done once.

9 The officiating Minister shall see that Baptisms, whether public or private, are entered in the Register of Baptisms.

I THE BAPTISM OF INFANTS
GENERAL DIRECTIONS

2 A solemn obligation rests upon parents to present their children to Christ in Baptism, which claims for them the benefits of his redeeming work, and signifies their admission into the visible community of his Church. Parents thereby dedicate them to God, and are pledged to bring them up in the nurture and admonition of the Lord; and the Sacrament of Baptism is administered on their promise to do so.

3 Before every administration of Baptism at least seven days' notice (save in exceptional circumstances) should be required of the parents or guardians to the Minister, in order to permit of interview and preparation.

4 As soon as possible after notice has been given, full enquiry should be made and all necessary instruction and exposition of the service given by the Minister, a Deaconness, or some other competent and instructed Leader. For this purpose the parents or guardians may be visited in their home, or they should be asked to attend at the church at a convenient hour. Instruction should be regarded as particularly necessary in the case of a first child, or of the first Baptism from the home according to the Methodist rite. If the parents or guardians cannot pledge themselves to give the promises contained in the Service of Baptism, the Minister may defer the Baptism of the child.

5 Two sponsors may be appointed to assist the parents in carrying out their promises: one chosen by the parents and the other, who shall normally be a member of the Society in which the Baptism takes place, by the Minister.

6 It is the privilege and responsibility of the sponsors to support the parents in the Christian upbringing of the children; to help them to carry out the promises and so to act as a link between the family and the larger family of the Church; and regularly to pray for the children.

7 Normally the Sacrament of Baptism should be administered in the Church by an ordained Minister, at a service of public worship. Where administration by an ordained Minister is impracticable, the Sacrament may be administered, after consultation with the Superintendent or one of his colleagues, by a Probationary Minister in pastoral charge, by an ordained Deaconess, by a Probationary Deaconess in pastoral charge, or by a fully accredited Local Preacher.

This procedure shall be varied only where strong pastoral considerations require that a child presented without proper notice or preparation should not be refused Baptism.

8 Baptism should take place at home or in hospital only in cases of prolonged or serious illness. The Minister, or in emergency any person present, should then name the child and pour or sprinkle water upon him or dip him in water saying:
N., I baptize thee in the Name of the Father, and of the Son, and of the Holy Spirit. Amen.
This is sufficient for Baptism, but it is fitting that all who are present should then say the Lord's Prayer, and that other prayers should be offered as opportunity allows.

9 If the Baptism is administered by any person other than the Minister, notice shall be given at once to the Minister, who shall make the entry in the Register of Baptisms.

10 If the child recovers he should be brought to the church in order that the congregation may publicly welcome him, preferably at the time when other children are to be baptized. The parents may make the usual answers, except the request for his Baptism. The Baptism shall be omitted, and the Minister shall explain to the people that the child has already been received into the congregation of Christ's flock by Baptism. The blessing and the final prayer may be used.

11 The Baptism of infants may be administered in any of these ways:

1. It should normally be administered at a main service of public worship, after the reading and exposition of scripture.

(a) Public worship may retain its own lessons, and this it shall always do on special days such as Christmas Day, Easter Day, Ascension Day, and Whitsunday. If there are frequent Baptisms, this may well be done on other days also.

(b) Public worship may, except on special days, have lessons related to Baptism, such as Genesis 17.1,7–8, Exodus 19.3–8a, Psalm 42.1–2, Jeremiah 31.31–4, Ezekiel 36.24–8, Acts 2.38–42, Romans 6.3–11 and the Gospel passages in the order of service, viz. Matthew 28.18–20, Mark 10.13–16. If one of these Gospels passages is read, the other may, but need not, be read during the service of Baptism itself.

2. It may be publicly administered, for good reason, at a service other

than the main service of public worship; and then one or more of the lessons suggested above may be read before the Gospel passages in the Order of Baptism.

2   One of these Collects for Baptism may be used, either before the Collect for the Day or before the lessons in the Order of Baptism.

Almighty God, our heavenly Father, from whom every family in heaven and earth is named, and who didst promise faithful Abraham that in him should every family on earth be blessed: Grant to *these* thy *children* whom we present to thee that *they* may be enrolled with thy faithful people, and with them inherit the promises and receive the fulness of thy grace, through Jesus Christ our Lord. *Amen.*

Almighty God, our heavenly Father, who in every generation dost give new sons and daughters to thy Church: Grant that *these children* now to be received by Baptism may daily grow in the knowledge and love of thee, through Jesus Christ thy Son our Lord. *Amen.*

3   The Introduction to the service provides for a hymn, the Lord's Prayer, a collect, and a fuller ministry of the Word. Any of these may be used at this point in any service of Baptism, but they are intended chiefly for use when Baptism is administered at a service other than the main service of public worship.

4   If the service is the Holy Communion, the Creed in the Communion Service shall be omitted.

5   Regular pastoral care shall be given by the local church and its Minister to all who have been baptized, and regular prayer shall be offered for them. A Baptism Roll shall be kept of all baptized children associated with the Church. The officiating Minister shall see that the parents receive a Certificate of Baptism and that particulars of the Baptism are given to the Baptismal Roll Secretary. The Leaders' Meeting, in conjunction with the Minister, is responsible for the maintenance and periodical review of the Baptismal Roll. The Leaders' Meeting shall satisfy itself that all possible care is given to such children and suitable instruction provided, as they are able to receive it, to equip them for Christian discipleship.

Children who are not yet old enough to answer for themselves may be baptized with the same form of service as is used for infants.

1 **THE BAPTISM OF INFANTS**
THE SERVICE

2 **THE INTRODUCTION**

Here may be sung a Hymn.

3   The Minister may say:

Let us pray.

Our Father, which art in heaven, . . . (CF11)

4   One of the Collects for Baptism may be said.

5   One or more of the Lessons for Baptism, other than the Gospel passages, may be read.

THE GOSPEL

6   Here shall be read one or both of these Gospel passages, except as provided in the General Directions:

The Gospel according to Matthew, the twenty-eighth chapter, beginning at the eighteenth verse.

Jesus came and said to them, . . . (Matt. 28.18–20, RSV)

The Gospel according to Mark, the tenth chapter, beginning at the thirteenth verse.

They were bringing children to him, . . . (Mark 10.13–16, RSV)

7   The Minister shall say:

Beloved in Christ, we learn from the Gospels that our Lord Jesus Christ was himself baptized in the River Jordan, that he died and rose again to give us eternal life, and that he commanded his Church to make disciples of all the nations and to baptize them. We remember how he received little children, took them in his arms and blessed them, saying: "To such belongs the kingdom of God."

Thus the children of Christian parents are brought to be baptized with water as a sign of cleansing and by Baptism to be made members of God's family the Church. We, therefore, bring *these children* whom God has entrusted to us, and claim for *them* all that Christ has promised in the new covenant. Christ loves *them* and is ready to receive *them*, to embrace *them* with the arms of his mercy, and to give *them* the blessing of eternal life.

THE GREAT PRAYER OF BAPTISM

8 The Minister, standing at the Font, shall say, the people standing and responding:

• Let us pray.

Blessed art thou, O Lord, holy Father, almighty, everlasting God;

For thou hast created all things and made man in thine own image;

And when we had fallen into sin, thou didst not leave us in our darkness, but didst send thy only Son Jesus Christ to be our Saviour;

We thank thee that he took our nature upon him, that he was baptized in Jordan and anointed with the Holy Spirit and went about doing good, that he died on the cross and rose again for our salvation, and that after his ascension he poured forth his Holy Spirit upon his people to make of them a new creation;

R. Thanks be to thee, O God.

Be present with us, O Father, in the power of thy Spirit to fulfil thy promises:

Grant that *these children* now to be baptized in this water may die to sin and be raised to the new life in Christ. *Amen.*

Grant that *they* may learn to trust Jesus Christ as *their* Lord and Saviour. *Amen.*

Grant that through the power of the Spirit *they* may have victory over evil. *Amen.*

From darkness lead *them* to light, from death lead *them* to eternal life, through Jesus Christ our Lord. *Amen.*

THE PROMISES AND THE PROFESSION OF FAITH

9 The Minister shall say to the Congregation:

Members of the household of faith, who are now in Christ's name to receive *these children*, will you so maintain the common life of worship and service that *they* and all the children in your midst may grow up in the knowledge and love of God and of his Son Jesus Christ our Lord? R. With God's help, we will.

0 The Minister shall say to the parents of the children:

Minister: You have brought *your children* to be baptized, and you will receive them again from the hands of God to be trained in the doctrines, privileges and duties of the Christian religion. I ask you therefore:

Will you provide for *these your children* a Christian home of love and faithfulness?

9—C.I.

Answer: With God's help, we will.

Minister: Will you help *them* by your words, prayers and example to renounce all evil and to put *their* trust in Jesus Christ *their* Saviour?

Answer: With God's help, we will.

Minister: Will you encourage *them* to enter into the full membership of the Church, and to serve Christ in the world?

Answer: With God's help, we will.

11 If there are sponsors, the Minister shall say:

Minister: Will you, who have come to support these parents, help them in the Christian upbringing of *these children*?

Answer: With God's help, we will.

12 The Minister shall say:

Let us confess the faith of the Church:

13 Then all shall say the Apostles' Creed:

I believe in God the Father Almighty, . . . (CF12; descended into hell[1])

14 Then shall the Minister say to the parents:

Do you then present *these your children* to be baptized?
Answer: We do.

THE BAPTISM

15 The Minister, taking each child into his arms, shall say to the parents or guardians: Name this child; and, naming *him* accordingly, he shall pour or sprinkle water upon *him*, or dip *him* in the water, saying:

N., I baptize thee in the Name of the Father, and of the Son, and of the Holy Spirit. *Amen.*

16 The Minister, making the sign of the cross on the forehead of the child, shall say:

By Baptism we receive this child into the congregation of Christ's flock, and pray that *he* may not be ashamed to hold fast the faith of Christ crucified, to fight against evil, and to persevere as Christ's faithful soldier and servant to the end of *his* life. *Amen.*

17 This blessing shall be said or sung:

The Lord bless thee and keep thee; the Lord make his face to shine upon thee, and be gracious unto thee; the Lord lift up his countenance upon thee and give thee peace. *Amen.*

[1] *Meaning here,* the place of the departed.

THE FINAL PRAYERS

18 The Minister shall say:

Let us pray.

We thank thee, most merciful Father, that it has pleased thee to receive *these children* for thine own within thy family the Church.

May *they* learn to show forth by *their lives* what *they* now *are* by thy call, and so bear witness to thy love for all the world. *Amen.*

Bless the home(s) of *these children*, and grant wisdom and true affection to *their* parents that they may lead *them* in the way of perfect love. *Amen.*

Strengthen thy Church in the Holy Spirit that through our worship and ministry to the world *these children* may learn to follow Christ. *Amen.*

19 Or he shall pray in his own words.

20 The Minister, whether proceeding with the service of public worship, or else dismissing the people, shall say:

The grace of the Lord Jesus Christ, and the love of God, and the fellowship of the Holy Spirit, be with us all. *Amen.*

I PUBLIC RECEPTION
INTO FULL MEMBERSHIP
OR CONFIRMATION
GENERAL DIRECTIONS

2 At the Baptism of infants their parents and the Church claim God's promises on behalf of the children. The children are constantly to be taught to look forward to their reception into the full membership of the Church, when they will claim for themselves these promises and God will strengthen them for his service in the world.

3 When children sincerely desire to serve Jesus Christ, and are receiving regular instruction in the Bible and the Faith, their names shall be brought before the Leaders' Meeting. If they are approved, they shall be entered as "Members in Training", so as to distinguish them from older people who are "on Trial". Before such children are admitted into full membership, the classes in which they have been meeting shall take the form of, or be supplemented by, a Preparation Class.

4 The names of candidates for full membership, other than Members in

Training, shall be brought before the Leaders' Meeting. If they are approved as Members on Trial, the Leaders' Meeting shall arrange for a Preparation Class.

5 In the Preparation Classes, the Catechisms should be used.

6 Full membership is open to all who sincerely desire to be saved from their sins through faith in the Lord Jesus Christ, who evidence the same in life and conduct, and who give assurance that they seek fellowship with Christ and his people by taking up the duties and privileges of the Methodist Church.

7 When those "on Trial" or "in Training" have thus been on probation for not less than three months, their names shall again be brought before the Leaders' Meeting, and those then approved shall be admitted to full membership by the Leaders' Meeting and shall at the earliest opportunity afterwards be publicly received by the Minister in the presence of the Society at a service which shall include the Sacrament of the Lord's Supper. Such a service should be held at least once a year either for a local Society or a group of Societies.

8 If any have not received Christian Baptism, that Sacrament should be administered either before or in connection with the Service of Public Reception into Full Membership or Confirmation. In this Service those who desire to be saved from their sins through faith in the Lord Jesus Christ and who evidence the same in their life and conduct, and who desire to have fellowship with the Methodist people, having been baptized, and having been approved by a Leaders' Meeting, are publicly received into full membership, with all its duties and privileges, of the Methodist Church, which is within the Holy Catholic Church. As they commit themselves to Jesus Christ, their Lord and Saviour, prayer is made that the Holy Spirit, who alone makes them new creatures in him, may strengthen them by confirming the gifts which he has given.

THE SERVICE

1 This order is to be used when all those who are to be confirmed have already been baptized.

THE MINISTRY OF THE WORD

2 Here may be sung this or some other Hymn:

Being of beings, God of love, . . . (MHB 383)

3   The Minister shall say this prayer, or pray in his own words:

Let us pray.

Almighty God, our heavenly Father, who by the preaching of the Gospel has led *these thy servants* to the knowledge of thy truth; Grant that the good work which thou hast begun in *them* may be confirmed by the continued working of thy Holy Spirit, through Jesus Christ our Lord. *Amen.*

4   This Lesson from the Old Testament shall be read:

The Book of Jeremiah, the thirty-first chapter, beginning at the thirty-first verse.
Behold, the days are coming, . . . (Jer. 31.31–4, RSV)

5   This Epistle shall be read:

The letter of Paul to the Romans, the eighth chapter, beginning at the twelfth verse.
So then, brethren, . . . (Rom. 8.12–17, RSV)

6   Here may be sung this or some other Hymn:

What shall I render to my God . . . (MHB 399)

7   This Gospel shall be read:

The Gospel according to Mark, the first chapter, beginning at the fourteenth verse.
Now after John was arrested, . . . (Mark 1.14–20, RSV)

8   The Sermon shall be preached.

9   Then may be sung this or some other Hymn:

O thou who camest from above . . . (MHB 386)

10   Announcements may be made here, and the gifts of the people, which the Minister is later to receive at the Offertory, may be collected.

11   Those who wish to leave shall do so now.

12   Those who are to be confirmed shall stand, and the Minister shall say to them:

Beloved in Christ, at your Baptism you were received into God's family the Church. You have grown in the knowledge and love of our Lord. You have heard Christ saying to you, as he said to his first disciples, Follow me. You have already responded to his call, and you come now by your own choice publicly to renounce evil and profess your faith in him. You are now to be confirmed as *members* of a chosen race, a royal priesthood, a holy nation, God's own people, sent forth as Christ's *servants* and *witnesses* into the world. For all this God will strengthen you by his Holy Spirit.

THE PROMISES AND THE PROFESSION OF FAITH

13   The Minister shall proceed to ask these questions, and those who are to be confirmed shall all answer, the people also standing:

Minister: I ask you therefore: Do you repent of your sins and renounce all evil?

Answer: With God's help, I do.

Minister: Do you trust in Jesus Christ as your Lord and Saviour?

Answer: I do.

Minister: Will you obey Christ and serve him in the world?

Answer: With his help, I will.

14   The Minister shall say:

Let us profess together the faith of the Church:

15   Then all shall say the Apostles' Creed:

I believe in God the Father Almighty, ... (CF12; descended into hell[1])

THE CONFIRMATION AND RECEPTION

16   Those who are to be confirmed shall kneel, but the people shall remain standing, and the Minister shall say:

Almighty God, our heavenly Father, who in Baptism hast received *these* thy *children* into thy family: Establish *them* in faith, we pray thee, by the Holy Spirit, and daily increase in *them* thy manifold gifts of grace,

the spirit of wisdom and understanding. *Amen.*

the spirit of counsel and might. *Amen.*

the spirit of knowledge and true godliness and the fear of the Lord. *Amen.*

and keep them in thy mercy for ever, *Amen.*

Either

17   The Minister shall lay his hand upon the head of each one of them, saying:

Confirm, O Lord, thy servant N. (or this thy servant) by thy Holy Spirit that *he* may continue thine for ever.

18   And each one shall answer: *Amen.*

19   All shall stand and the Minister shall say to those who have been confirmed:

We welcome you into the full membership of the Christian Church and the Society in this place (*or*, the Societies of this Circuit).

20   Then the Minister and another representative member of the Society may give the right hand of fellowship to each of them.

[1] *Meaning here*, the place of the departed.

21 A Bible or a Book of Offices may be given here.

Or

22 The Minister shall say:

Confirm, O Lord, *these* thy *servants* by thy Holy Spirit that *they* may continue thine for ever. *Amen.*

23 All shall stand, and the Minister shall welcome each one severally, giving to him the right hand of fellowship, and saying:

N. We welcome you into the full membership of the Christian Church and the Society in this place (*or*, the Societies of this Circuit).

24 Then another representative member of the Society may give the right hand of fellowship to each of them.

25 A Bible or a Book of Offices may be given here.

26 The Minister and congregation standing shall say together:

O God, Father of our Lord Jesus Christ, we are not our own but thine. As thou didst send thy Son into the world to save the world, so send us to serve our neighbours and to bring them to believe in him. Amen.

27 Here shall be sung this Hymn:

Lord, in the strength of grace, . . . (MHB 594)

THE LORD'S SUPPER

28 The Minister shall proceed to the Lord's Supper, beginning at the Offertory. Before the dismissal this or some other Hymn may be sung:

Ye servants of God, . . . (MHB 426)

29 If this service is used on Christmas Day, Easter Day, Ascension Day or Whitsunday, then the Collect, Epistle and Gospel of the Day shall be read in place of those given in this order of service.

1 THE BAPTISM OF THOSE WHO ARE ABLE
TO ANSWER FOR THEMSELVES WITH THE
PUBLIC RECEPTION INTO FULL MEMBERSHIP
OR CONFIRMATION
GENERAL DIRECTIONS

2 Those who are able to answer for themselves, if they have not already received Christian Baptism, should first be instructed. The Senior Catechism may be used for this purpose. When the Minister is satisfied

as to their repentance, faith, and desire for Baptism, he shall proceed to baptize them, preferably at a service of public worship. Two sponsors may be appointed by the Minister, in consultation with the candidate, to assist the candidate in carrying our his promise.

3 When those who are able to answer for themselves are baptized together with their children, the order for the Baptism of those who are able to answer for themselves shall be used, with such additions as are necessary, and after the parents have made their own promises they shall make those that relate to the upbringing of their children.

4 If a person who is of age to answer for himself is in danger of dying unbaptized, the Minister, if he is satisfied as to his repentance, faith and desire for Baptism, may baptize him in the same way in which infants are baptized in an emergency; and if he recovers he may come to the Church in order that the congregation may publicly welcome him; and he should be further instructed in order that he may be received as a full member as soon as possible.

5 Those who are to be baptized when they are able to answer for themselves will normally have fulfilled the requirements for full membership, and the Leaders' Meeting, being satisfied of this, shall receive them into the full membership of the Methodist Church. Thus, when they are baptized, they shall normally proceed at once to the Public Reception into Full Membership, or Confirmation. Therefore, the order of service for their Baptism includes also their Public Reception or Confirmation: nevertheless for good reason this service may be used without Public Reception or Confirmation, which should then follow after an interval of time.

6 If at a service for Public Reception, or Confirmation, some have already been baptized and others have not, then the order of service for the Baptism of those who are able to answer for themselves with Public Reception into Full Membership, or Confirmation, shall be used.

7 The General Directions for Public Reception into Full Membership or Confirmation should also be consulted.

THE SERVICE
THE MINISTRY OF THE WORD

1 Here may be sung this or some other Hymn:

Being of beings, God of love, . . . (MHB 383)

2 The Minister shall say this Collect, or pray in his own words:

Let us pray.

Almighty God, our heavenly Father, who hast given us the Sacrament of Holy Baptism; Grant that by Baptism *these* thy *servants* may be made *members* of the Body of thy son, and may share his death and resurrection, through the same Jesus Christ our Lord. *Amen.*

3 This lesson from the Old Testament shall be read:

The Book of Ezekiel, the thirty-sixth chapter, beginning at the twenty-fifth verse.

I will sprinkle clean water upon you, . . . (Ezek. 36.25–8, RSV)

4 This Epistle shall be read:

The Letter of Paul to the Romans, the sixth chapter, beginning at the third verse.

Do you not know, . . . (Rom. 6.3–11, RSV)

5 Here may be sung this or some other Hymn:

Come, Father, Son and Holy Ghost, . . . (Tune: Breslau)

6 This Gospel shall be read:

The Gospel according to John, the third chapter, beginning at the first verse.

Now there was a man of the Pharisees, . . . (John 3.1–7, RSV)

7 The Sermon shall be preached.

8 Here may be sung this or some other Hymn:

O thou who camest from above . . . (MHB 386)

9 The Minister and those who are to be baptized, with their sponsors, shall come to the Font; and the Minister shall say:

Beloved in Christ, we learn from the Gospels that our Lord Jesus Christ, when he was baptized in the River Jordan, received the Holy Spirit. He taught us that we must be born again if we are to enter the kingdom of God. He died and rose again for our sins, and commanded his Church to make disciples of all the nations, baptizing them in the Name of the Father, and of the Son, and of the Holy Spirit. He has poured out this Spirit upon his Church, and those who are baptized into him share his death and resurrection.

Thus we know that God will receive *these persons* who *turn* to him in repentance and faith, and will forgive *their* sins. He will bestow on *them* new life through the Holy Spirit and make *them* members of his Church.

THE GREAT PRAYER OF BAPTISM

10 The Minister shall say, all standing:

Let us pray.

Blessed art thou, O Lord, Holy Father, almighty, everlasting God; For thou has created all things and made man in thine own image; And when we had fallen into sin, thou didst not leave us in darkness, but didst send thy only Son, Jesus Christ, to be our Saviour;

We thank thee that he took our nature upon him, that he was baptized in Jordan and anointed with the Holy Spirit, and went about doing good, that he died on the cross and rose again for our salvation, and that after his ascension he poured forth his Holy Spirit upon his people to make of them a new creation;

R. Thanks be to thee, O God.

Be present with us, O Father, in the power of thy Spirit to fulfil thy promises:

Grant that *these* who *are* now to be baptized in this water having professed their faith in Christ and being born again of the Spirit, may ever receive through Christ the forgiveness of their sins. *Amen.*

Grant that, sharing Christ's death and resurrection, *they* may die to sin and be raised to the new life of righteousness in Christ. *Amen.*

Grant that *they* putting off the old nature may be a new creation in Christ Jesus. *Amen.*

Grant that, being baptized into Christ's Body the Church, *they* may ever remain among the number of his people. *Amen.*

From darkness lead *them* to light, from death lead *them* to eternal life, through Jesus Christ our Lord. *Amen.*

THE PROMISES AND THE PROFESSION OF FAITH

11 The Minister shall say to the congregation:

Members of the household of faith, who are now in Christ's name to receive *these persons,* will you so maintain the common life of worship and service that *they* may grow in grace and in the knowledge and love of God and of his Son Jesus Christ our Lord?

R. By God's help, we will.

12 The Minister shall speak to those who are to be baptized, and also to any who, having already been baptized, are now to be confirmed; and they all shall answer:

Minister: You have heard Jesus saying to you, as he said to his first disciples, Follow me. You have already responded to his call, and you sincerely desire to be saved from your sins through faith in him. I ask you therefore:

Do you repent of your sins and renounce all evil?
Answer: With God's help, I do.
Minister: Do you trust in Jesus Christ as your Lord and Saviour?
Answer: I do.
Minister: Will you obey Christ and serve him in the world?
Answer: With his help, I will.

13 The Minister shall say:

Let us profess together the faith of the Church.

14 Then all the congregation shall say the Apostles' Creed.

I believe in God the Father Almighty, . . . (CF12; descended into Hell[1])

15 Then the Minister shall say to those who are to be baptized:

Do you then wish to be baptized in this faith?
Answer: I do.

THE BAPTISM

16 The Minister shall ask the sponsors or other witnesses to give the Christian name or names of the person to be baptized, and then, naming the person accordingly, shall pour or sprinkle water upon *him*, or dip *him* in water, saying:

17 I baptize thee in the Name of the Father, and of the Son, and of the Holy Spirit. *Amen.*

THE CONFIRMATION AND RECEPTION

18 Those who are baptized when they are able to answer for themselves shall normally proceed at once to Confirmation; but if there be no Confirmation, then that which follows shall be omitted, and the Minister shall proceed to the Final Prayers.

19 When there are others to be confirmed who have been baptized previously, the Minister shall say to them:

Beloved in Christ, . . .

M 12, *but* and have by your own choice publicly renounced evil and professed your faith in him ⟨and you come now . . . faith in him⟩

20 Those who are to be confirmed shall kneel, but the people shall remain standing, and the Minister shall say:

[1] *Meaning here*, the place of the departed.

20–30 Almighty God, . . . (M 16–26)

31 Here shall be sung this Hymn:

Lord, in the strength of grace . . . (MHB 594)

THE LORD'S SUPPER

32 The Minister shall proceed to the Lord's Supper, beginning at the Offertory. Before the dismissal this or some other Hymn may be sung:

Now thank we all our God, . . . (MHB 10)

THE FINAL PRAYERS

33 These prayers are to be used if, in exceptional circumstances and for good reason, Confirmation does not immediately follow the Baptism of those who are able to answer for themselves.

34 The Minister, making the sign of the cross on the forehead of the person, shall say:

By Baptism we receive *this person* into the congregation of Christ's flock, and pray that *he* may not be ashamed to hold fast the faith of Christ crucified, to fight against evil, and to persevere as Christ's faithful soldier and servant to the end of *his* life. *Amen.*

35 This blessing shall be said or sung:

The Lord bless thee and keep thee; the Lord make his face to shine upon thee, and be gracious unto thee; the Lord lift up his countenance upon thee and give thee peace. *Amen.*

36 The Minister shall say:

Let us pray.

We thank thee, most merciful Father, that it has pleased thee to receive *these* thy *servants* for thine own within thy family the Church.

May *they* learn to show forth by *their lives* what *they* now *are* by thy call, and so bear witness to thy love for all the world, through thy Son, Jesus Christ, our Lord. *Amen.*

37 Or he shall pray in his own words.

38 The Minister, whether proceeding with the service of public worship or dismissing the people, shall say:

The grace of the Lord Jesus Christ, and the fellowship of the Holy Spirit, be with us all. *Amen.*

39 If this service is used on Christmas Day, Easter Day, Ascension Day or Whitsunday, then the Collect, Epistle and Gospel of the day shall be read in the place of those given in this order of service.

12. *The Presbyterian Rites 1968*

In 1964 texts of the *Order for the Baptism of Infants* and of the *Order for the Confirmation of Baptized Persons and Admission to the Lord's Supper* were printed and published for members of the Presbyterian General Assembly. These services were put forward for experimental use in the Presbyterian Churches of England and Wales, so that the comments of the whole Church could be considered, before these, and other experimental services, were included in a revised Presbyterian Service Book.

The *Presbyterian Service Book* for use in the Presbyterian Churches of England and Wales, issued by authority of the General Assembly, in 1968, included the revised experimental initiatory rites put forward in 1964, which are now the official rites of the Presbyterian Church, and are here reproduced.

I ORDER FOR THE ADMINISTRATION OF THE SACRAMENT OF BAPTISM

2   Baptism is to be administered to the infant children of parents or guardians who are communicant members of Christ's Church, and to adults who, not having been baptized in infancy, desire to make their profession of faith and to be admitted to church membership.

3   The Baptism of Adults will normally include, in one rite, admission to communicant membership and to participation in the Lord's Supper.

4   In the Baptism of Infants, if parents or guardians so wish, others may be associated with them in undertaking a responsibility for the Christian upbringing of their child, but this is not essential. Such godparents, having responsibility to share in the Christian upbringing of the child, should for the fulfilment of their vows be communicant members of the Christian Church.

5   Care should be taken to ascertain that those bringing infants for Baptism, and those seeking Adult Baptism, have been sufficiently instructed in the Christian Faith and that they are sincerely desirous of following Christ.

6   The Sacrament shall be administered by an ordained Minister of the Church at a public service of the Church, a congregation being present to witness and participate in the reception of the baptized into the fellowship of the Church. In special circumstances, should it be expedient to hold the service privately, two or three witnesses, including an Elder of the congregation, should be present.

7   The Sacrament of Baptism is to be but once administered to any person.

8   A register of all Baptisms shall be kept in each congregation, each entry being attested by the officiating Minister. It is desirable that a Baptismal Certificate be issued. The recommended form of certificate is that which also has a place for a record of reception into communicant membership.

9   Attention is drawn to the Declaration on the Sacrament of Baptism in the Book of Order of the Presbyterian Church of Wales, which is commended as the authoritative statement for that Church and should be consulted, particularly with regard to the categories of those eligible for Baptism.

10 ORDER FOR THE BAPTISM OF INFANTS

11 After a Baptismal hymn has been sung, the Minister shall say:

Our help is in the Name of the Lord
Who made heaven and earth.
Dearly beloved—The Sacrament of Baptism is now to be administered
to the child of A. and B.Z. From the early days of the Church this
sacrament has been administered according to the command in
Scripture:
"Go ye, therefore, and teach all nations, . . . (Matt. 28.19–20, AV)

12 Then the Minister shall expound the meaning of Baptism in his own words or as
follows:

In the Sacrament of Baptism, Christ receives believers and their children
into his Church. Baptism is administered with water in the Name of
the Father and of the Son and of the Holy Spirit, and signifies the
graciousness of God to all who repent and put their trust in him, the
washing away of their sin through the death of Christ, and the gift to
them of newness of life in the family of God. It signifies also God's
promise and assurance to them that in their new life thus begun his
grace will be sufficient for every need.

In Infant Baptism the same grace is given and promised to the child
of believing parents. The child is received into the Church in the
confidence that, nurtured and trained in a Christian home and in the
fellowship of Christ's people, he will be led by the Holy Spirit in due
time to make his own profession of faith in Christ as his Saviour and
Lord. (*Statement of the Christian Faith*, 1956.)

Furthermore, we read in the gospel:

They brought young children to him, . . . (Mark 10.13–16, AV)

In this Sacrament those who present their children for Baptism are
required to profess their faith and to make solemn promise to bring up
their children within the family of Christ's Church.

13 The Apostles' Creed may then be said by all and the Minister shall then ask:

Do you confess your faith in God as we have just declared it?
R̷. I do.

14 Or if the Creed be not said the Minister shall say:

I call upon you to profess your faith and to make your vows before
God and his people.

15 The parents stand and the Minister shall say:

In presenting your child for Baptism do you confess your faith in God, Father, Son and Holy Spirit?
Ry. I do.
Do you promise, by God's help, to provide a Christian home for this child and bring *him* up in the worship and teaching of the Church, that *he* may come to know Christ as Lord and Saviour?
Ry. I do.
Do you promise to encourage *him* in due time to make *his* own profession of faith so that, received into the full fellowship of the Church, *he* may go out into the world to serve God faithfully?
Ry. I do.

16 The Minister shall then say:

The Lord bless you and your child and give you grace faithfully to perform these promises.

17 If there are godparents present, the Minister shall ask them to stand and shall say to them:

As godparents of this child, do you profess your faith in God, Father, Son and Holy Spirit? Do you undertake to help these parents in every way you can to bring up this child in the faith of the gospel and in the ways of the Church of Christ, to set before *him* a Christian example and to lead *him*, in due time, to make *his* own profession of faith?
Ry. I do.

18 The Minister shall then say:

The Lord bless you and keep you faithful to this trust.

19 The congregation standing, the Minister or an appointed member of the congregation shall say:

And we, representing the whole Church of Christ, undertake to provide, for this child, instruction in the gospel of God's love, the example of Christian faith and character, and the strong support of the family of God in fellowship, prayer and service.

20   Let us pray.

Almighty and everlasting God, Who, of thine infinite mercy, Hast revealed thyself as the Father of all men, We thank thee for thy providential care of this family; for the love which has bound them together; for the blessed gift of this child; and the renewal of the mother's strength. We thank thee that thou hast safely brought them to this hour. Send down thy Holy Spirit to sanctify this water to the spiritual use to which thou hast ordained it and grant that this child, now to be baptized with this water, may receive thy blessing, and be led by thy Holy Spirit to know thee as Father, and to love and obey Jesus Christ as Lord and Saviour, so that *he* may faithfully serve thee all the days of *his* life. *Amen.*

21   The congregation shall stand and the Minister shall take the child from the father and, calling him by his Christian name(s), shall sprinkle water on him, saying:

N. —— I baptize you in the Name of the Father and of the Son and of the Holy Spirit.

22   The blessing of God almighty, Father, Son and Holy Spirit, descend upon you and dwell in your heart for ever.

23   The congregation may sing the blessing. (RCH 727)

The Lord bless thee and keep thee; the Lord make his face to shine upon thee and be gracious unto thee; the Lord lift up his countenance upon thee and give thee peace.

24   Then the Minister shall say:

According to Christ's commandment, this child is now received into the membership of the holy catholic Church and is engaged to confess the faith of Christ crucified, and to be his faithful soldier and servant to *his* life's end.

Wherefore receive ye *him* in the Lord as Christ also received us to the glory of God.

25   Then the Minister shall return the child to the parents.

26   Let us pray.

Almighty and everlasting God, we give thee thanks for this child now received into the fold of thy Church. We humbly beseech thee, to keep *him* under thy care and guidance; to grant that *he* may grow in wisdom as in stature, and in favour with God and man; to write thy law in *his* heart and suffer *him* not to fall away from thee. Bless this family, and keep these parents faithful to their vows and to the trust committed unto them; guide them with thy counsel in the Christian nurture of their child, and grant them ever deeper knowledge and love of Jesus Christ. O God, the Father of our Lord Jesus Christ, of whom the whole family in heaven and earth is named, We commend to thee all the families of this congregation, help us in our homes to honour thee and in love to serve one another, And now unto him that loved us,

and washed us from our sins in his own blood and hath made us kings
and priests unto God and his Father, to him be glory and dominion
for ever and ever. *Amen.*

27   Here the Lord's Prayer may be said.

28   Then a hymn or doxology may be sung.

29   Thereafter the Minister shall pronounce a Benediction:

The grace of the Lord Jesus Christ, the love of God, and the communion
of the Holy Spirit be with you all. Amen.

1   ACT OF CONFIRMATION

2   The profession of faith, on the ground of which persons who have been already
baptized are admitted to the Lord's Supper, is to be made openly in the presence
of the congregation.

3   The Session, being assured that candidates for such admission have been sufficiently
instructed in the Gospel and in the duties of the Christian life, and that they desire
to confirm their baptismal vows, appoints a time for the service.

4   Normally the Service of Confirmation should take place in the presence of the
congregation at a Sunday diet of worship.

5   The Minister, addressing the congregation, says:

Dearly beloved, we are now to admit to communicant membership of
the holy catholic Church A.B., C.D. —— They have been under
instruction in the teaching of the Church and are now ready to profess
publicly their faith in Jesus Christ.

6   Inviting them to stand before the Holy Table he shall say:

Beloved in the Lord, in the name of this congregation, and of the whole
Church, I gladly welcome you, as you come to make profession of
your faith and to enter into the full heritage of your membership of
the holy catholic Church.

You have been in the fellowship of that Church since the day in
your early childhood when you received the sacrament of Baptism.
You were then solemnly engaged to be the Lord's. Prayer was made
for you and promises were given that you should be trained and
taught to know and love God, and God granted to you and your
parents in that sacrament the sign of his cleansing grace. For you these
prayers have been answered, and these promises performed. By that
grace you have been sustained and helped. God, in his mercy, has
brought you to years of responsibility, and you have now come to
acknowledge before God and his Church the covenant then made on
your behalf, to profess your faith in the Lord Jesus, to consecrate yourself to him, and to know yourself to be fully a member of his Church.

I charge you now to make your personal profession of faith, and to answer, before God and his people, the questions I now put to you:

Do you profess your faith in God, Father, Son and Holy Spirit?
Answer: I do.
Do you repent of your sins with a humble and contrite heart, and do you promise, in entire dependence on the grace of God in Christ, to fight against sin both within yourself and in the world? And do you, as a member of the Christian Church, promise to make use of the means of grace by being faithful in Bible reading and prayer, and joining regularly in public worship and in the sacrament of the Lord's Supper?
Answer: I do.
Do you promise to dedicate your daily life to God, glorifying him in your work, using your time and talents for the advancement of his kingdom, seeking the peace and unity of the Church and supporting its work and witness throughout the world?
Answer: I do.

7   Then the Minister may say:

I invite you to say after me:

I take God the Father for my Father:
I take God the Son for my Saviour and Lord:
I take God the Holy Spirit for my Comforter and Guide:
I take God's word for my rule of faith and conduct:
I take God's people for my people:
And so doing I give myself to him in the service of his kingdom.
And this I do deliberately, sincerely, freely and for ever:
God being my helper.

8   Then the Minister shall say:

Having taken these solemn vows will you kneel.

9   The candidates kneel.

10   Then the Minister shall say:

Defend, O Lord, these thy servants with thy heavenly grace that they may continue thine for ever, and daily increase in the Holy Spirit, till they come to thine everlasting kingdom.

11   Then the congregation stands and the Minister (raising his hand in blessing over the candidates, or laying his hand on the head of each as they kneel before him) shall say:

The God of all grace, who hath called you to his eternal glory, confirm you to the end, that you may be blameless in the day of our Lord Jesus Christ.

12 or

The very God of peace sanctify you wholly; and I pray God your whole spirit and soul and body be preserved blameless unto the coming of our Lord Jesus Christ. God the Father, God the Son, and God the Holy Spirit bless, preserve and keep you now and ever more. *Amen.*

13 Then may be sung (RCH 727).

The Lord bless thee and keep thee; the Lord make his face to shine upon thee and be gracious unto thee; the Lord lift up his countenance upon thee and give thee peace. *Amen.*

14 The candidates now standing, the Minister shall say:

Dearly beloved, seeing that you have professed your faith before God and this people, I now declare you to be admitted to communicant membership of the Church of Jesus Christ: and in particular, into the fellowship of his congregation in this place; and in token thereof I give you the right hand of fellowship.

15 The Minister and one, or more, Elders then give the right hand of fellowship to the newly-received members; after which, addressing the congregation, the Minister shall say:

Brethren, I commend to your love and care these persons whom we today receive into the membership of this congregation. Be kindly affectioned one to another with brotherly love. Bear ye one another's burdens and so fulfil the law of Christ.

16   Let us pray.

Almighty God who by the gracious guidance of thy Holy Spirit hast brought these thy servants to put their trust in thee and who hast promised to perfect in us the work thou hast begun, we thank thee that they have been made members of the Body of Christ. We thank thee for their Christian training, for every good influence in their lives and for the assurance of thy continual blessing and favour. Nourish them continually by the communion of the precious Body and Blood of thy Son and keep them faithful to the end. Bless our fellowship one with another, that all of us here, both old and young, may learn at the feet of Christ our common task and brotherhood, and be lifted up into stronger faith and wider knowledge and deeper consecration to his service, through Jesus Christ our Lord. *Amen.*

Now unto him that is able to keep you from falling, and to present you faultless before the presence of his glory with exceeding joy, to the only wise God our Saviour, be glory and majesty, dominion and power, both now and for ever. *Amen*.

17 If the act of Confirmation takes place in a service of Holy Communion, the celebration of the Lord's Supper shall then proceed.

13. The Church of Scotland Rites 1968

While *The Book of Common Order*, 1940, is still the official service-book of the Church of Scotland, a number of revised initiatory rites have now been authorized for experimental use.

Following the instruction of the General Assembly of 1961, a Committee began work on the revision of the service for the administration of Holy Baptism. Their work resulted in a draft revised service being presented to the General Assembly of 1963, which authorized its experimental use. Further revisions of this service were submitted to the General Assemblies of 1965, 1967, and 1968. The General Assembly of 1968 resolved to "receive the revised draft service *Order for the Administration of Holy Baptism* and authorize its experimental use in the Church".

On receiving the report *The Doctrine and Practice of Confirmation* the General Assembly of 1967 instructed "the Committee on Public Worship and Aids to Devotion to prepare suitable orders of service for the Confirmation and Admission to the Lord's Supper of those baptized in infancy, and for Baptism and Admission to the Lord's Supper of adults".[1] In response to this direction two services were produced: *Confirmation and Admission to the Lord's Supper*, and *Holy Baptism, Confirmation and Admission to the Lord's Supper*. The second of these services was produced to provide a service for the growing number of people now seeking baptism and admission to Communion, in the Church of Scotland, in adult years.

The *Vows of Church Membership* are not experimental but have been officially authorized for use in the Church of Scotland.

I HOLY BAPTISM

ORDER FOR THE ADMINISTRATION OF HOLY BAPTISM

2 During the singing of a suitable hymn, the infants shall be brought into the church, and the Minister, standing at the Font, shall then say:

Beloved in the Lord, hear the words of our Lord Jesus Christ who, after His Resurrection and before His Ascension, commanded His disciples saying:

All power is given unto Me . . . (Matt. 28.18–20, AV)

In the days of His flesh, our Lord Jesus Christ, taking upon Himself the sins of the world, was baptized by John in the river Jordan, and

---

[1] Quoted from the Preface in the Booklet: *Holy Baptism and Confirmation and Admission to the Lord's Supper*, 1969, from which the following services are taken.

anointed by the Holy Spirit for His saving work which He accomplished by His Cross and Resurrection.

On the day of Pentecost, as He had promised, the Church was baptized with the Holy Spirit, and the Apostle Peter called upon the people, saying:

Repent, and be baptized . . . (Acts 21.38-9, AV)

Holy Baptism is administered according to our Lord's institution and command. The pouring or sprinkling of water is a sign of cleansing from sin by the Blood of Christ, renewal by the Holy Spirit, adoption, and resurrection unto everlasting life. In this Sacrament believers and their children are received by name into the Church and sealed as members of the Body of Christ.

[(Consider what is written in the Gospels:

They brought young children to Jesus . . . (CF3)]

3 [Then a Hymn may be sung.]

It is the duty of those who present their children for Baptism to confess the faith wherein they are to be baptized, and to promise to bring them up in that faith, and in the way of Christ and His Church.

4 Then, the parents or other sponsors standing, the Minister shall say to them:

Do you present *this child* to be baptized, earnestly desiring that *he* may be grafted into Christ as a member of His Body the Church?
Answer: I do.
Do you believe in one God, Father, Son and Holy Spirit; and do you confess Jesus Christ as your Saviour and Lord?
Answer: I do.
Do you promise, depending on the Grace of God, to teach *this child* the truths and duties of the Christian Faith; and by prayer and example to bring *him* up in the life and worship of the Church?
Answer: I do

5 Then the Minister shall say:

The Lord bless you and your *child* and enable you faithfully to keep these promises.

6 Then, addressing the congregation, he shall say:

This Sacrament lays solemn obligations upon you the People of God. Will you be faithful to your calling as members of the Church of Christ, so that *this child*, and all other children in your midst, may grow up in the knowledge and love of Christ? In acceptance of this responsibility, let all stand.

7   The Minister shall then say:

Let us confess the Faith.
I believe in God the Father Almighty, . . . (CF12)

8   Then the Minister shall call the people to prayer, saying:

Lift up your hearts.
R. We lift them up unto the Lord
Blessed art Thou, O God the Father, Creator of all things.
Blessed art Thou, O Lord Jesus Christ, Son of God, baptized in Jordan,
    crucified at Calvary, risen and glorified.
Blessed art Thou, O Holy Spirit of God, Lord and Giver of Life.

Send forth Thy Holy Spirit, O God, to sanctify us all and to bless this
water that *this child*, being born anew of water and the Holy Spirit,
may receive the fulness of Thy grace, and ever be found in the number
of Thine elect. Grant that *his* name may be written in the Lamb's Book
of Life and that, buried with Christ in Baptism, *he* may rise with Him
into newness of life, and be numbered with Thy saints in glory everlasting; through the same Jesus Christ our Lord. *Amen.*

9   Then the parent, or other sponsor, presenting the child at the Font (the Congregation standing) shall give the child's name to the Minister: and the Minister, who may then take the child into his arms, shall call him by his Christian name or names and shall pour or sprinkle water on his head, saying:

N. —— I BAPTIZE THEE IN THE NAME OF THE FATHER, AND OF THE
SON, AND OF THE HOLY GHOST. *Amen.*

The blessing of God Almighty, Father, Son, and Holy Spirit, descend
upon thee, and dwell in thine heart for ever. *Amen.*

10   This formula and blessing shall be repeated for each child.

11   [Then may be said or sung:

The Lord bless thee and keep thee; the Lord make His face to shine
upon thee, and be gracious unto thee; the Lord lift up His countenance
upon thee, and give thee peace. *Amen.*]

12   Thereafter the Minister, using the Christian name(s) and surname of each child baptized, shall say:

According to Christ's commandment N —— M —— *is* now received
into the membership of the One Holy Catholic and Apostolic Church,

and *is* engaged to confess the faith of Christ crucified, and to be His faithful soldier and servant unto *his* life's end.

13 [Here may be read:

Jesus said: "Whoso shall receive one such little child . . ." (Matt. 18.5–6, 10, AV]

14 After which the Minister shall say:

Let us pray.

O God our heavenly Father, whose Son Jesus Christ took little ones into His arms and blessed them: we give Thee thanks that Thou hast received *this child* into Thy Church and sealed *him* as Thine own. Let Thy Holy Spirit rest upon *him*, that, grafted into Christ, the True Vine, *he* may abide in Him for ever, growing in wisdom as in stature, and in favour with God, and man. Lead *him* through the perils of this earthly life, and bring *him* in due time to Thy Holy Table to receive the Communion of the Body and Blood of Christ, that by grace *he* may witness a good confession, and persevere therein to the end; through Jesus Christ our Lord.

Almighty God, we thank Thee for Thy love and mercy to *this mother* whom Thou hast delivered to rejoice over *her* little *one*. Hallow, we beseech Thee, the *home* enriched by the birth of *this* child. Grant Thy help to the parents that in gratitude and faith they may order their family life in the way of Thy commandments, serving one another in love; for the sake of Jesus Christ our Lord.

Most merciful God, in whose Church there is but one Lord, one Faith, and one Baptism, grant us grace ever to acknowledge the Lordship of Thy Son Jesus Christ, to confess with our whole lives the one true faith, and to dwell in love and unity with all who have been baptized into His Name; through the same Jesus Christ Thy Son our Lord, who taught His Church ever to pray and say:

Our Father . . . *Amen.*

15 Or, alternatively

Let us pray.

Most merciful Father, we give Thee thanks that it has pleased Thee to receive *this child* into Thy Church and to call *him* Thine own in Christ Jesus. Let Thy Holy Spirit rest upon *him*, that, grafted into Christ the True Vine, *he* may abide in Him for ever, growing in wisdom as in stature, and in favour with God and man. As *he is* made *partaker* of the death of Thy Son, so may *he* be made *partaker* of His resurrection, and finally obtain everlasting life; through Jesus Christ our Lord.

O God, whose blessed Son shared at Nazareth the life of an earthly home: bless, we beseech Thee, the *home* of *this child*, and grant wisdom and understanding to all who have the care of *him*, that *he* may grow up in Thy constant fear and love; through the same Thy Son Jesus Christ our Lord.

Most merciful God, in whose Church there is but one Lord, one Faith, and one Baptism, grant us grace ever to acknowledge the Lordship of Thy Son Jesus Christ, to confess with our whole lives the one true faith, and to dwell in love and unity with all who have been baptized into His Name; through the same Jesus Christ Thy Son our Lord, who taught His Church to pray and say:

Our Father . . . *Amen.*

16 Then may be sung a hymn or doxology.

17 Thereafter, the Minister shall pronounce the Benediction:

The peace of God, which passeth all understanding, keep your hearts and minds in the knowledge and love of God, and of His Son Jesus Christ our Lord; and the blessing of God Almighty, the Father, the Son, and the Holy Spirit, be amongst you, and remain with you always. *Amen.*

18 NOTES

1. It is assumed that Administration of Holy Baptism normally follows the preaching of the Word.
2. The Form and Order of Service to precede Baptism is for the guidance of ministers and may be used in whole or in part according to local needs.
3. The parts of the Service, including the items of praise, contained in square brackets may be omitted at the discretion of the minister.
4. Suitable metrical Psalms for the occasion include Psalm 8; Psalm 65.1–4; Psalm 68.18–20; and Psalm 102 (2).13–18.
5. Suitable Scripture Lessons include:
   Old Testament: Genesis 6.9–22; Exodus 14.19–31; 2 Kings 5.9–14; Jeremiah 31.27–34; Ezekiel 36.25–8.
   New Testament: *Epistles:* Romans 6.3–14; 1 Corinthians 10.1–13; Ephesians 4.1–7; Hebrews 9.11–14.
   Gospels: St Matthew 3.13–17; St Mark 10.35–40; St Luke 12.49–53; St John 3.1–6.

1 CONFIRMATION AND ADMISSION TO THE LORD'S SUPPER

2 The Kirk Session shall be constituted prior to this Service and the Minister shall submit the names of those who have been instructed in the Faith and prepared for their first Communion. Being satisfied of their knowledge and character the Kirk Session shall resolve to receive them publicly into the fellowship of the Lord's Table.

3 The Congregation being assembled, the Minister shall say:

Let us worship God.

4 A metrical Psalm or Hymn shall be sung, after which, the people still standing, the Minister shall say:

Our help is in the name of the Lord, who made heaven and earth. Know ye not, that so many of us as were baptized into Jesus Christ were baptized into His death? Therefore we are buried with Him by baptism into death: that like as Christ was raised up from the dead by the glory of the Father, even so we also should walk in newness of life.

By grace are ye saved through faith; and that not of yourselves: it is the gift of God.

Let us pray.

Almighty God, our heavenly Father, who in Christ hast purchased a people for Thyself, and hast promised to dwell among them for ever; look in mercy upon us thy children in this holy place.

Holy Lord God, we acknowledge before Thee our many sins. We confess that we have neglected the grace of our baptism into Jesus Christ. Remember not, Lord, the sins of our youth, nor our transgressions: but according to Thy mercy remember Thou us and forgive all our sins, for Jesus' sake.

Grant, O Lord, to Thy people pardon and peace, that they may be cleansed from all their sins and serve Thee with a quiet mind; through Jesus Christ our Lord.

5 Here may be added appropriate supplications and petitions.

Almighty and eternal God, so draw our hearts to Thee, so possess our minds, so control our wills, that we may be wholly Thine. Use us, we pray Thee, as Thou wilt, always to Thy glory and the welfare of Thy people; through our Lord and Saviour Jesus Christ, who liveth and reigneth, and is worshipped and glorified with Thee, O Father, and the Holy Spirit, one God, blessed for ever. *Amen.*

6 Then a Lesson from the Old Testament shall be read; after which a Prose Psalm shall be sung or read, or a Hymn or Anthem sung.

7   Then a Lesson or Lessons from the New Testament shall be read.

8   Then a Hymn shall be sung.

9   The Sermon shall be preached, concluding with an Ascription of Praise.

10 Then the Offerings shall be received, and when they are presented the Minister shall say:

Let us pray.

Almighty God, Giver of all good, accept in Thy mercy these gifts which we offer unto Thee; and grant us grace, with them to present ourselves a living sacrifice, holy and acceptable to Thee, which is our reasonable service; for the sake of Jesus Christ our Lord. *Amen.*

11 A Hymn shall be sung, and thereafter the Minister, standing before the Holy Table and addressing the Congregation, shall say:

Dearly beloved—The Kirk Session, being satisfied of the Christian knowledge and character of the persons now to be named, has resolved to admit them to participation in the Lord's Supper. They will profess publicly the faith into which they were baptized, be confirmed by the Holy Spirit, and be received into the fellowship of the Lord's Table.

12 Those named shall come forward and stand before the Minister, who shall address them, saying:

Beloved in the Lord—In the days of your infancy you were by Holy Baptism grafted into the Lord Jesus Christ as members of His Church. Now, having reached years of responsibility, you come of your own choice to acknowledge before God and His Church the covenant of grace of which you were made heirs; to profess your faith in the Lord Jesus; to offer yourself to Him in the service of the Church and the world; and to receive the gifts and strengthening power of the Holy Spirit.

It is written: The fruit of the Spirit is love, joy, peace, patience, kindness, goodness, faithfulness, gentleness, self-control. If we live by the Spirit, let us also walk by the Spirit.

As a confession of your faith, we now ask you to answer these questions, remembering the words of our Lord Jesus Christ who said: Whosoever shall confess me before men, him will I confess also before my Father which is in heaven.

Do you believe in one God, . . .

(Here follow the Vows of Church Membership as authorized in 1968; see p. 269 below.)

13 Then the Minister shall say:

The Lord bless you and enable you faithfully to keep these promises.

Let us pray.

O Lord our God, confirm these Thy servants with the Holy Spirit, the Comforter. Daily increase in them the gifts of Thy grace; the spirit of wisdom and understanding, the spirit of counsel and might, the spirit of knowledge and of the fear of the Lord; and keep them in Thy mercy unto life eternal; through Jesus Christ our Lord. *Amen.*

14 Then, the Congregation meanwhile standing, as those being confirmed kneel separately or together, the Minister, laying his hand on the head of each, or raising his hand in blessing over them, shall say:

The God of all grace, who hath called you to His eternal glory, confirm you by His Spirit that you may be established in His Covenant and be blameless in the day of our Lord Jesus Christ. *Amen.*

15 When all have been confirmed the Minister may say:

Defend, O Lord, these Thy servants with Thy heavenly grace, that they may continue Thine for ever; and daily increase in Thy holy Spirit more and more, until they come unto Thy everlasting kingdom. *Amen.*

16 Those confirmed shall stand, and the Minister shall say:

In the name of the Lord Jesus Christ, the great King and Head of the Church, and by authority of this Kirk Session, I now admit you to the fellowship of the Lord's Table, in token of which we give you the right hand of fellowship.

17 When all have returned to their places, the Minister shall say:

Let us stand and confess the Faith.

I believe in God the Father Almighty, . . . (CF12)

18 Then the Minister shall say:

Let us pray.

Bless the Lord, O my soul; and all that is within me, bless His holy name.

O God most glorious, we thank Thee for Thy Church, One, Holy, Catholic, and Apostolic. We bless Thee for the light of the Gospel and the ministries of Word and Sacrament. We praise Thee for the good and holy lives which have enriched Thy people, and proclaimed Thy grace. We thank Thee for Thy great mercy to Thy children confirmed this day by Thy Holy Spirit; for their Baptism into Christ; and for every influence which has led them to faith in Him,

Grant, O Lord, that they, with all who shall receive the Communion of the Body and Blood of the Lord Jesus Christ, may approach that holy Mystery in charity and true penitence, and by faith feed on Him who giveth life unto the world, even Jesus Christ our Lord.

Remember, O Lord, the whole congregation of the faithful, Thy Holy Catholic Church. Draw them nearer to Thee and to one another, in the bonds of a living faith; and cause them to abound in truth and love, in unity and peace, as servants of the same Lord.

Gracious God, have mercy upon all mankind. So move men's hearts by Thy Holy Spirit that every nation may seek the way of peace. Bless our Queen and all the Royal House; guide with thy wisdom the Queen's ministers; establish the peoples of this land and Commonwealth in faith, righteousness, and liberty. Visit with Thy love every heart and home where there is sickness, sorrow, or any kind of trouble; for the sake of Jesus Christ our Saviour.

O God, receive our thanksgiving for all dear to us who, being hidden from our mortal sight, now live in Thee, and for the redeemed of all ages who have entered into the heavenly rest. Keep us one with the whole family in heaven and on earth who abide in Thee and with Thee for ever; through Jesus Christ our Lord.

19 Our Father. . . . *Amen.*

20 A Psalm or Hymn shall be sung. Thereafter the Minister shall dismiss the people saying:

Go forth into the world in peace; be of good courage; hold fast that which is good; render to no man evil for evil; strengthen the fainthearted; support the weak; help the afflicted; honour all men; love and serve the Lord, rejoicing in the power of the Holy Spirit.

And the blessing of God Almighty, the Father, the Son, and the Holy Spirit, be amongst you and remain with you always. *Amen.*

21 NOTE

Appropriate Scripture Lessons include:
Old Testament: Joshua 24.14–18; Isaiah 58.8–12; Jeremiah 31.31–4;
                Ezekiel 36.25–8.
New Testament: *Epistles:* Romans 8.11–17; Romans 12.1–12;
                  1 Corinthians 12.12–20; Ephesians 6.10–18.
                  Gospels: St Matthew 20.20–8; St Luke 9.57–62;
                  St John 15.1–12.

1 HOLY BAPTISM, CONFIRMATION,
AND ADMISSION TO THE LORD'S SUPPER

2 The Kirk Session shall be constituted prior to this Service and the Minister shall submit the names of those who have been instructed in the Faith and prepared for their first Communion. Being satisfied of their Christian knowledge and character, the Kirk Session shall resolve to receive them publicly into the fellowship of the Lord's Table.

3 The Congregation being assembled, the Minister shall say:

Let us worship God

4 A metrical Psalm or Hymn shall be sung, after which, the people still standing, the Minister shall say:

Our help is in the name of the Lord, . . . (S C4)

5 [Here may be added appropriate supplications and petitions]

Almighty and eternal God, . . . (S C5)

6 Then a Lesson from the Old Testament shall be read, after which a Prose Psalm may be read or sung, or a Hymn or Anthem sung.

7 Then a Lesson, or Lessons from the New Testament shall be read.

8 The Sermon shall be preached, concluding with an Ascription of Praise.

9 The Offerings shall be received, and when they are presented the Minister shall say:

Let us pray.

Almighty God, . . . (S C10)

10 A Hymn shall be sung, and thereafter the Minister, standing before the Holy Table and addressing the Congregation, shall say:

Dearly beloved—The Kirk Session, being satisfied of the Christian knowledge and character of the persons now to be named has resolved to admit them to participation in the Lord's Supper, and to the full rights and privileges of membership of the Church.

11 Those named shall come forward and stand before the Minister, who shall address them, saying:

In Holy Baptism believers and their children are received by name into the Church and sealed as members of the Body of Christ. Some of you were baptized in infancy; others of you are now presenting yourselves for baptism. All of you come of your own choice to profess your faith in the Lord Jesus, to offer yourselves to Him in the service of the Church and the world, and to receive the gifts and strengthening power of the Holy Spirit.

It is written:

The fruit of the Spirit is love, joy, peace, patience, kindness, goodness, faithfulness, gentleness, self-control. If we live by the Spirit, let us also walk by the Spirit.

Galatians 5.22,23,25

As a confession of your faith we now ask you to answer these questions, remembering the words of the Lord Jesus:

Whosoever therefore shall confess me before men, him will I confess also before my Father which is in heaven.

St Matthew 10.32

Do you believe in one God, . . .

(Here follow the Vows of Church Membership as authorized in 1968; see p. 269 below.)

2 Then the Minister shall say:

The Lord bless you, and enable you faithfully to keep these promises.

3 Then, addressing those who have not been baptized, the Minister shall say:

Do you repent of your sins with a humble and contrite heart, and acknowledge your dependence on the grace and mercy of God which are in Christ Jesus?
Answer: I do.
Do you present yourself to be baptized, earnestly desiring that you may be grafted into Christ as a member of His Body the Church?
Answer: I do.

Let us pray.

Almighty God, who didst so love the world that Thou gavest Thine Only Son to save us from sin and eternal death, we thank Thee for Him, for His Baptism in the Jordan and in His own blood on the Cross, for His Resurrection and Exaltation, and for His gift of the Holy Spirit. We thank Thee for His command to His Church to make disciples of all nations, baptizing them and teaching them, and pray that those baptized may be born anew of water and the Holy Spirit, and receive the fulness of Thy grace, Grant that their names may be written in the Lamb's Book of Life, and that, buried with Christ in Baptism, they may rise with Him into newness of life and be numbered with Thy saints in glory everlasting.

O Lord our God, confirm all these Thy children with the Holy Spirit, the Comforter. Daily increase in them the gifts of Thy grace;

the spirit of wisdom and understanding, the spirit of counsel and might, the spirit of knowledge and of the fear of the Lord: and keep them in Thy mercy unto life eternal; through Jesus Christ our Lord. *Amen.*

14 [Then may be sung the Hymn: *Come, Holy Ghost, our souls inspire.*]

BAPTISM

15 Then those to be baptized shall kneel, and the Minister, calling each by his Christian name, or names, shall pour or sprinkle water on his head, saying:

N —— I BAPTIZE THEE IN THE NAME OF THE FATHER, AND OF THE SON, AND OF THE HOLY GHOST. *Amen.*

CONFIRMATION

16 Then the Minister shall lead the newly baptized to the front of the Holy Table, where they shall kneel, and the Minister laying his hands on the head of each, or raising his hands in blessing over them, shall say:

The God of all grace, . . . (S C14)

17 Thereafter those who were baptized in infancy shall come forward and kneel before the Holy Table, and the Minister shall confirm them in the same manner, and with the same words.

18 When all have been confirmed, the Minister shall say:

Defend, O Lord, . . . (S C15)

ADMISSION

19 Those confirmed shall stand, and the Minister shall say:

In the name of the Lord Jesus Christ, the only King and Head of the Church, and by authority of this Kirk Session, I now admit you to the fellowship of the Lord's Table, in token whereof we give you the right hand of fellowship.

20 When all have returned to their places, the Minister shall say:

Let us stand and confess the faith.

I believe in God the Father Almighty, . . . (CF12)

21 Then the Minister shall say:

Let us pray.

O God, most glorious, we thank Thee for Thy Church, One, Holy, Catholic, and Apostolic. We bless Thee for the light of the Gospel and for the ministries of Word and Sacrament. We praise Thee for the good and holy lives which have enriched Thy people, and proclaimed

Thy grace. We thank Thee for Thy great mercy to Thy children baptized and confirmed this day.

Grant, O Lord, that they, with all who shall receive the Communion of the Body and Blood . . . (S C18)

22 Our Father, . . . *Amen.*

23 A hymn of discipleship or of thanksgiving shall then be sung.

24 Thereafter the Minister shall dismiss the people, saying:

Go forth into the world in peace; . . . (S C20)

25 NOTE

Appropriate Scripture Lessons include:
Old Testament: Genesis 6.9–22; Exodus 14.19–31; 2 Kings 5.9–14;
                Jeremiah 31.27–34; Ezekiel 36.25–8.
New Testament: *Epistles:* Romans 6.3–14; 1 Corinthians 10.1–13;
                Ephesians 4.1–7; Hebrews 9.11–14; Revelation 7.9–17.
               Gospels: St Matthew 3.13–17; St Mark 10.35–40;
                St Luke 12.49–53; St John 3.1–6.

VOWS OF CHURCH MEMBERSHIP
EDINBURGH 27 MAY 1968

The General Assembly authorize for use in the Service of Confirmation and Admission to Holy Communion the new vows of Church membership:

1 Do you believe in one God, Father, Son, and Holy Spirit; and do you confess Jesus Christ as your Saviour and Lord?
   Answer: I do.

2 Do you promise to join regularly with your fellow-Christians in worship on the Lord's Day?
   Answer: I do.

3 Do you promise to be faithful in reading the Bible, and in prayer?
   Answer: I do.

4 Do you promise to give a fitting proportion of your time, talents, and money for the Church's work in the world?
   Answer: I do.

5 Do you promise, depending on the grace of God, to confess Christ before men, to serve Him in your daily work, and to walk in His ways all the days of your life?
   Answer: I do.

10+ C.I.

14. *The Congregationalist Rites 1969*

The first edition of *A Book of Services and Prayers* was published in 1959, and was produced by a committee appointed by the Congregational Union of England and Wales. After ten years of use the book was revised and republished. The rites which follow are taken from this revised 1969 edition.

The Preface of the 1959 edition, which was reproduced in that of 1969, gives some indication as to how its compilers intended it to be used. "It is neither designed nor intended to be used as a book of common prayer. Its purpose is to provide ministers and lay preachers with guidance in the ordering and conduct of worship and to make material available for use throughout the Christian Year and on special occasions." In the services the use of extempore prayer is both allowed and encouraged.

I THE BAPTISM OF CHILDREN

2 The Sacrament should be administered in the presence of the Congregation during Public Worship.

3 After the singing of a suitable Hymn, the Minister says:

The mercy of the Lord is from everlasting to everlasting upon them that fear him, and his righteousness unto children's children, to such as keep his covenant, and to those that remember his commandments to do them.

He shall feed his flock like a shepherd: he shall gather the lambs with his arm, and carry them in his bosom,

The promise is to you, and to your children, and to all that are afar off, even as many as the Lord our God shall call.

4 Hear now the words of the Gospel of our Lord and Saviour Jesus Christ:

Jesus came and spake unto his disciples, . . . (Matt. 28.18–20, AV)

They brought young children to him . . . (CF3)

5 Dearly beloved: This holy sacrament is a sign and seal of the covenant of grace, which God has made with us through our Lord Jesus Christ, and which unites us in the life of his Church. It declares the redeeming love of God for all mankind, signifies the claim of Christ upon those for whom he died and rose again, and pledges the gift of the Holy

Spirit by whose power we are renewed and sanctified. Through baptism we are received into the family and household of God.

You have heard how our Lord encouraged parents of Galilee to bring their children to him, how he received them in his arms, laid hands on them and blessed them. In his grace and love he is the same yesterday, today, and for ever; and so we bring this child (or these children) to him in the assurance that he will receive *him* into the arms of his mercy, and give *him* the blessing of eternal life.

6 Then addressing the parents the Minister says:

I ask you therefore, in presenting this child for baptism, do you confess your faith in Jesus Christ as Saviour and Lord; and do you promise, depending on divine help, to teach this child the truths and duties that belong to the Christian life, and to bring *him* up in the nurture and admonition of the Lord and in the fellowship of the Church?

7 The parents answer:

We do.

8 Then the Minister says:

Let us pray.

Almighty God, our heavenly Father, who hast given thy people this holy sacrament to be a sign and seal of the covenant of grace which thou hast made with us in Jesus Christ our Lord: grant, we beseech thee, that this child, who, we shall now baptize according to thy Word, may receive the fullness of thy grace, and become a true and faithful member of thy Church; through Jesus Christ our Lord. *Amen.*

9 The Congregation standing, the Minister receives the child and inquires the name. Then pronouncing the name, he sprinkles water on the head of the child, saying:

(Name) —— I baptize thee in the name of the Father, and of the Son, and of the Holy Spirit. *Amen.*

0 The Lord bless thee and keep thee. The Lord make His face to shine upon thee, and be gracious unto thee, The Lord lift up His countenance upon thee and give thee peace. *Amen.*

I Then addressing the Congregation the Minister says:

We receive this child into the congregation of Christ's flock, in the trust that hereafter *he* shall not be ashamed to confess the faith of Christ, valiantly to fight under his banner against all evil, and to continue Christ's faithful soldier and servant unto *his* life's end. *Amen.*

12 Here the child is returned to the parents, and the Minister offers Prayers, using, if he wishes, the following:

Most gracious Father, we thank thee for the encouragement of the Gospel that we should present our children to that kind and tender Shepherd, who loved them and gave himself for them, that he may gather them in his arms and carry them in his bosom, We pray thee to take this child into thy loving care. Grant *him* deliverance from all dangers and evils; surround *him* with thy grace and defend *him* by thy mercy. May *he* possess in abundant measure the gift of thy Holy Spirit, leading *him* to the knowledge of thy great salvation, and to an abiding faith in Jesus Christ as *his* Saviour. In the days of *his* youth grant that *he* may remember *his* Creator, and by that knowledge be preserved from the seductions of the world and from the despair that attends the life without faith and love.

We thank thee for thy goodness to these parents, and especially that thou hast moved them to bring their child into thy house, thus acknowledging thy claim to the life thou hast given. We pray that they may have grace and understanding to lead *him* in the ways of life which are acceptable to thee, and that their godly example may inspire *him* to loving service and obedience to thy will. And may the blessing of God rest upon their home, and his peace abide with them evermore.

We would bring before thee our hopes and prayers for all our children and for the young people of all the nations. Deliver them from the sin, the confusion and dismay which afflict our world today; save them from selfishness and pride, from errors and false thought of life, and from attempting to find fulfilment and joy in those things which bring only pain and disillusion. Grant them thy heavenly light, and the presence and power of thy Spirit, that there may rise up in all the earth a seed to serve thee, and a generation to call thee blessed: through Jesus Christ our Lord. *Amen.*

13 The Minister and People may say together the Lord's Prayer.

14 A Hymn may be sung.

15 If the Service is concluded, the Minister pronounces the Benediction.

1 THE RECEPTION OF CHURCH MEMBERS ON PROFESSION OF FAITH

2 The Members who are to be received sit together, at the front of the Congregation.

3 Addressing the Congregation, the Minister says:

In the name of the Lord Jesus Christ, and in accordance with the

decision of the Church Meeting, we are now to receive into full communion with the Church . . .

(here the Minister reads the full names of those to be received).

4   Addressing those to be received, the Minister continues:

Dearly beloved, in your baptism you were received into the fellowship
of Christ, sealed as members of the family and household of God, and
engaged to be the Lord's. Now you come, of your own choice, to
profess your faith in the Lord Jesus Christ, to consecrate yourselves to
him, and to accept the privileges and responsibilities of membership
in his Church.

5   Or he may say:

Dearly beloved, we have heard with joy of your decision to live the
Christian life, and of your desire to be joined to the family and household of God. Now you come, after careful thought and prayer, to
profess your faith in the Lord Jesus Christ, to consecrate yourselves to
him, and to accept the privileges and responsibilities of membership
in his Church.

6   Hear, then, the words of Holy Scripture:

Jesus said: Abide in me, and I in you. . . . (John 15.4–11, RV)

7   or

I beseech you therefore, . . . (Rom. 12.1–2, RV)

8   or

I therefore, the prisoner in the Lord, . . . (Eph. 4.1–6, RV)

9   The Minister, having invited the Congregation to stand, addresses by name each of
those to be received:

Do you acknowledge Jesus Christ as your Lord and Saviour, and do you
confess the Christian faith as it is taught in the Holy Scriptures?
Response: I do.
Do you promise to obey God's holy will, and to walk according to his
commandments all the days of your life? Do you resolve to fulfil the
duties of membership in the Church, joining regularly in public
worship, in the Communion of the Lord's Supper, and in the Church
Meeting; and, being faithful in Bible reading and in prayer, in giving
and in service?
Response: I do.

Do you promise to live and witness as a Christian believer, to seek the peace and welfare of Christ's Church, and, with all the followers of Christ, to work and pray for the coming of his kingdom in the world? *Response:* I do.

10   The Minister then says to each of the Members to be received:

In the name of the Lord Jesus Christ, we receive and welcome you to membership of the Church, to share in all its privileges and responsibilities: and in token thereof we now give you the right hand of fellowship.

The Father of our Lord Jesus Christ grant you, according to the riches of his glory, to be strengthened with might by his Spirit in the inner man, that Christ may dwell in your hearts by faith; that ye, being rooted and grounded in love, may be filled with all the fullness of God.

11   or

The God of all grace, who hath called us unto his eternal glory by Christ Jesus, make you perfect, stablish and strengthen you: to him be glory and dominion for ever and ever. *Amen.*

12   or

The God of hope fill you with all joy and peace in believing, that ye may abound in hope, in the power of the Holy Spirit.

13   The Minister then leads the Congregation in Prayer, extempore, or as follows:

Let us pray.

Eternal God, our heavenly Father, who hast given thy Son to be the Saviour of mankind; we thank thee that thou hast granted thy servants to know thy love in Christ Jesus and to acknowledge him as their Lord. Send down upon them the gift of thy Holy Spirit; deepen their faith in the Gospel; establish them in the fellowship of thy Church; give them joy in thy service; and keep them steadfast unto the end.

We confess, O Lord our God, that we have not loved thee as we ought. Forgive us, we beseech thee, and grant us grace that we may all renew our vows, give ourselves again to thy obedience, and in our lives bear witness to the mercy wherewith thou hast redeemed us; through Jesus Christ our Lord. *Amen.*

14   Then follows the Sacrament of the Lord's Supper.

15. *The Roman Catholic Rite 1969*

The Second Ecumenical Council of the Vatican in its *Constitution on the Sacred Liturgy*: Chapter 3, Nos. 62–3, 67–71, declares the need for revision in the rites of the sacraments and sacramentals. Such revisions are to be carried out in order that they may meet the requirements of our time. To this end they are, in future, to be administered in the vernacular language.

On the rite, for the Baptism of Infants, the *Constitution* directs that revision of the rite should clearly express that those to be baptized are, in fact, infants. The duties of the parents, who are to be given a full and meaningful place in the new rite, and the godparents, are to be brought out more fully.

The text which follows the *Rite of Baptism for Several Children*, is from *The Roman Ritual*, revised by decree of the Second Vatican Ecumenical Council and published by authority of Pope Paul VI; *Rite of Baptism for Children*, published by the International Committee on English in the Liturgy, December 1969.

The new Rite of Confirmation referred to in the *Constitution*, 3.71, is not yet available. [December 1969.]

Omission marks, in the text, indicate reference to alternatives outside the present text.

I RITE OF BAPTISM
FOR SEVERAL CHILDREN
RECEPTION OF THE CHILDREN

2　If possible, baptism should take place on Sunday, the day on which the Church celebrates the paschal mystery. It should be conferred in a communal celebration for all the recently born children, and in the presence of the faithful, or at least of the relatives, friends and neighbours, who are all to take an active part in the rite.

3　It is the role of the father and mother, accompanied by the godparents, to present the child to the Church for baptism.

4　If there are very many children, and if there are several priests or deacons present, these may help the celebrant in the parts referred to below.

5　The people may sing a psalm or hymn suitable for the occasion. Meanwhile the celebrating priest or deacon, vested in alb or surplice, with a stole (with or without a cope) of festive colour, and accompanied by the ministers, goes to the entrance of the church or to that part of the church where the parents and godparents are waiting with those who are to be baptized.

6　The celebrant greets all present, and especially the parents and godparents, reminding them briefly of the joy with which the parents welcomed their children as gifts from God, the source of life, who now wishes to bestow his own life on these little ones.

7 First the celebrant questions the parents of each child.

Celebrant: What name do you give to your child ? (or: have you given ?)
Parents: N.
Celebrant: What do you ask of God's Church for *N* ?
Parents: Baptism.

8 The celebrant may choose other words for this dialogue.

9 The first reply may be given by someone other than the parents if local custom gives him the right to name the child.

10 In the second response the parents may use other words, e.g.: "faith", "the grace of Christ", "entrance into the Church", "eternal life".

11 If there are many children to be baptized, the celebrant asks the names from all the parents together, and each family replies in turn. The second question may also be asked of all together.

12 *Celebrant:* What name do you give each of these children ? (or, have you given ?)
Parents: N., N., etc.
Celebrant: What do you ask of God's Church for your children ?
All: Baptism.

13 The celebrant speaks to the parents in these or similar words:

You have asked to have your children baptized. In doing so you are accepting the responsibility of training them in the practice of the faith. It will be your duty to bring them up to keep God's commandments as Christ taught us, by loving God and our neighbour. Do you clearly understand what you are undertaking ?
Parents: We do.

14 This response is given by each family individually. But if there are many children to be baptized, the response may be given by all together.

15 Then the celebrant turns to the godparents and addresses them in these or similar words:

Are you ready to help these parents in their duty as Christian mothers and fathers ?

All the godparents: We are.

16 The celebrant continues:

N. and N. (or, My dear children), the Christian community welcomes you with great joy. In its name I claim you for Christ our Saviour by the sign of his cross. I now trace the cross on your foreheads, and invite your parents (and godparents) to do the same.

17 He signs each child on the forehead, in silence. Then he invites the parents and (if it seems appropriate) the godparents to do the same.

18 The celebrant invites the parents, godparents, and the others to take part in the liturgy of the word. If circumstances permit, there is a procession to the place where this will be celebrated, during which a song is sung, e.g. Psalm 84.7, 8, 9ab.

19 The children to be baptized may be carried to a separate place, where they remain until the end of the liturgy of the word.

THE CELEBRATION OF GOD'S WORD

SCRIPTURAL READINGS AND HOMILY

20 One or even two of the following gospel passages are read, during which all may sit if convenient.

John 3.1–6   The meeting with Nicodemus.

Matthew 28.18–20   The Apostles are sent to preach the gospel and to baptize.

Mark 1.9–11   The baptism of Jesus.

Mark 10.13–16   Let the little children come to me.

21 The passages listed . . . may be chosen, or other passages which better meet the wishes or needs of the parents. Between the readings responsorial psalms or verses may be sung as given. . . .

22 After the reading, the celebrant gives a short homily, explaining to those present the significance of what has been read. His purpose will be to lead them to a deeper understanding of the mystery of baptism and to encourage the parents and godparents to a ready acceptance of the responsibilities which arise from the sacrament.

23 After the homily, or in the course of or after the litany, it is desirable to have a period of silence while all pray at the invitation of the celebrant. If convenient, a suitable song follows. . . .

INTERCESSIONS (PRAYER OF THE FAITHFUL)

24 Then the prayer of the faithful is said:

Celebrant: My brothers and sisters,★ let us ask our Lord Jesus Christ to look lovingly on these children who are to be baptized, on their parents and godparents, and on all the baptized.

(★ At the discretion of the priest, other words which seem more suitable under the circumstances, such as friends, dearly beloved, brethren, may be used. This also applies to parallel instances in the liturgy.)

Leader: By the mystery of your death and resurrection, bathe these children in light, give them the new life of baptism and welcome them into your holy Church.

All: Lord, hear our prayer.

Leader: Through baptism and confirmation, make them your faithful followers and witnesses to your gospel.

All: Lord, hear our prayer.

10★

Leader: Lead them by a holy life to the joys of God's kingdom.
All: Lord, hear our prayer.
Leader: Make the lives of their parents and godparents examples of faith
to inspire these children.
All: Lord, hear our prayer.
Leader: Keep their families always in your love.
All: Lord, hear our prayer.
Leader: Renew the grace of our baptism in each one of us.
All: Lord, hear our prayer.

25 Other forms may be chosen. . . .

26 The celebrant next invites all present to invoke the saints. At this point, if the children have been taken out, they are brought back.

Holy Mary, Mother of God   pray for us.
Saint Joseph   pray for us.
Saint John the Baptist   pray for us.
Saint Peter and Saint Paul   pray for us.

27 The names of other saints may be added, especially the patrons of the children to be baptized, and of the church or locality. The litany concludes:

All you saints of God   pray for us.

PRAYER OF EXORCISM AND ANOINTING BEFORE BAPTISM

28 After the invocations, the celebrant says:

(a) Almighty and ever-living God, you sent your only Son into the world to cast out the power of Satan, spirit of evil, to rescue man from the kingdom of darkness, and bring him into the splendour of your kingdom of light. We pray for these children: set them free from original sin, make them temples of your glory, and send your Holy Spirit to dwell within them. (We ask this) through Christ our Lord.

All: Amen.

29 Another form of the prayer of exorcism:

(b) Almighty God, you sent your only Son to rescue us from the slavery of sin, and to give us the freedom only your sons and daughters enjoy. We now pray for these children who will have to face the world with its temptations, and fight the devil in all his cunning. Your Son died and rose again to save us. By his victory over sin and death, bring these children out of the power of darkness. Strengthen them with the grace of Christ, and watch over them at every step in life's journey. (We ask this) through Christ our Lord.

All: Amen.

30   The celebrant continues:

We anoint you with the oil of salvation in the name of Christ our Saviour; may he strengthen you with his power, who lives and reigns for ever and ever.

All: Amen.

31   He anoints each child on the breast with the oil of catechumens. If the number of children is large, the anointing may be done by several ministers.

32   If, for serious reasons, the conference of bishops so decides, the anointing before baptism may be omitted. In that case the celebrant says once only:

May you have strength in the power of Christ our Saviour, who lives and reigns for ever and ever.

All: Amen.

33   And immediately he lays his hand on each child in silence.

34   If the baptistry is located outside the church or is not within view of the congregation, all go there in procession.

35   If the baptistry is located within view of the congregation, the celebrant, parents, and godparents go there with the children, while the others remain in their places.

36   If, however, the baptistry cannot accommodate the congregation, the baptism may be celebrated in a suitable place within the church, and the parents and godparents bring the child forward at the proper moment.

37   Meanwhile, if it can be done suitably, an appropriate song is sung, e.g. Psalm 22.

CELEBRATION OF THE SACRAMENT

38   When they come to the font, the celebrant briefly reminds the congregation of the wonderful work of God whose plan it is to sanctify man, body and soul, through water. He may use these or similar words:

My dear brothers and sisters, we now ask God to give these children new life in abundance through water and the Holy Spirit.

39   or:

My dear brothers and sisters, God uses the sacrament of water to give his divine life to those who believe in him. Let us turn to him, and ask him to pour his gift of life from this font on the children he has chosen.

BLESSING AND INVOCATION OF GOD OVER BAPTISMAL WATER

40   Then, turning to the font, he says the following blessing (outside the Easter season):

(*a*) Father, you give us grace through sacramental signs, which tell us of the wonders of your unseen power.

In baptism we use your gift of water, which you have made a rich symbol of the grace you give us in this sacrament.

At the very dawn of creation your Spirit breathed on the waters, making them the wellspring of all holiness.

The waters of the great flood you made a sign of the waters of baptism, that make an end of sin and a new beginning of goodness.

Through the waters of the Red Sea you led Israel out of slavery, to be an image of God's holy people, set free from sin by baptism.

In the waters of the Jordan your Son was baptized by John and anointed with the Spirit.

Your Son willed that water and blood should flow from his side as he hung upon the cross.

After his resurrection he told his disciples: "Go out and teach all nations, baptizing them in the name of the Father, and of the Son, and of the Holy Spirit."

Father, look now with love upon your Church, and unseal for her the fountain of baptism.

By the power of the Spirit give the water of this font the grace of your Son.

You created man in your own likeness: cleanse him from sin in a new birth to innocence by water and the Spirit.

41   The celebrant touches the water with his right hand and continues:

We ask you, Father, with your Son to send the Holy Spirit upon the water of this font. May all who are buried with Christ in the death of baptism rise also with him to newness of life. (We ask this) through Christ our Lord.

All: Amen.

42   Other forms of the blessing:

(*b*) *Celebrant:* Praise to you, almighty God and Father, for you have created water to cleanse and give life.

All: Blessed be God.

(or some other suitable acclamation by the people).

Celebrant: Praise to you, Lord Jesus Christ, the Father's only Son, for you offered yourself on the cross, that in the blood and water flowing from your side, and through your death and resurrection, the Church might be born.

All: Blessed be God.

Celebrant: Praise to you, God the Holy Spirit, for you anointed Christ at his baptism in the waters of Jordan, so that we might all be baptized into you.

All: Blessed be God.

Celebrant: Come to us, Lord, Father of all, and make holy this water which you have created, so that all who are baptized in it may be washed clean of sin, and be born again to live as your children.

All: Hear us, Lord.

(or some other suitable invocation).

Celebrant: Make this water holy, Lord, so that all who are baptized into Christ's death and resurrection by this water may become more perfectly like your Son.

All: Hear us, Lord.

The celebrant touches the water with his right hand and continues:

Lord, make holy this water which you have created, so that all those whom you have chosen may be born again by the power of the Holy Spirit, and may take their place among your holy people.

All: Hear us, Lord.

If the baptismal water has already been blessed, the celebrant omits the invocation *Come to us, Lord* and those which follow it, and says:

You have called your children, *N., N.,* to this cleansing water that they may share in the faith of your Church and have eternal life. By the mystery of this consecrated water lead them to a new and spiritual birth. (We ask this) through Christ our Lord.

All: Amen.

(c) *Celebrant:* Father, God of mercy, through these waters of baptism you have filled us with new life as your very own children.

All: Blessed be God.

(or some other suitable acclamation by the people)

Celebrant: From all who are baptized in water and the Holy Spirit, you have formed one people, united in your Son Jesus Christ.

All: Blessed be God.

Celebrant: You have set us free and filled our hearts with the Spirit of your love, that we may live in your peace.

All: Blessed be God.

Celebrant: You call those who have been baptized to announce the Good News of Jesus Christ to people everywhere.

All: Blessed be God.

Celebrant: You have called your children, *N., N.,* to this cleansing
water and new birth that by sharing the faith of your Church
they might have eternal life. Bless ✠ this water in which they
will be baptized. We ask this in the name of Christ our Lord.
All: Amen.

If the baptismal water has already been blessed, the celebrant omits this last
prayer and says:

You have called your children, *N., N.,* to this cleansing water that
they may share in the faith of your Church and have eternal
life. By the mystery of this consecrated water lead them to a
new and spiritual birth. (We ask this) through Christ our Lord.
All: Amen.

43 During the Easter season, if there is baptismal water which was consecrated at the
Easter Vigil, the blessing and invocation of God over the water are nevertheless
included, so that this theme of thanksgiving and petition may find a place in the
baptism. The forms of this blessing and invocation are those found in . . ., with
the variation indicated at the end of each text.

RENUNCIATION OF SIN AND PROFESSION OF FAITH

44 The celebrant speaks to the parents and godparents in these words:

Dear parents and godparents: You have come here to present these
children for baptism. By water and the Holy Spirit they are to receive
the gift of new life from God, who is love.

On your part, you must make it your constant care to bring them up
in the practice of the faith. See that the divine life which God gives
them is kept safe from the poison of sin, to grow always stronger in
their hearts.

If your faith makes you ready to accept this responsibility, renew now
the vows of your own baptism. Reject sin; profess your faith in Christ
Jesus. This is the faith of the Church. This is the faith in which these
children are about to be baptized.

45 The celebrant questions the parents and godparents:

Celebrant: Do you reject Satan?
Parents and godparents: I do.
Celebrant: And all his works?
Parents and godparents: I do.
Celebrant: And all his empty promises?
Parents and godparents: I do.

46   Or,

Celebrant: Do you reject sin, so as to live in the freedom of God's
     children?

Parents and godparents: I do.

Celebrant: Do you reject the glamour of evil, and refuse to be mastered
     by sin?

Parents and godparents: I do.

Celebrant: Do you reject Satan, father of sin and prince of darkness?

Parents and godparents: I do.

47   According to circumstances, this second form may be expressed with greater
     precision by the conference of bishops, especially in places where it is necessary
     for the parents and godparents to reject superstitious and magical practices used
     with children.

48   Next the celebrant asks for the threefold profession of faith from the parents and
     godparents:

Celebrant: Do you believe in God, the Father, almighty, creator of
     heaven and earth?

Parents and godparents: I do.

Celebrant: Do you believe in Jesus Christ, his only Son, our Lord, who
     was born of the Virgin Mary, was crucified, died, and was buried,
     rose from the dead, and now is seated at the right hand of the
     Father?

Parents and godparents: I do.

Celebrant: Do you believe in the Holy Spirit, the holy catholic Church,
     the communion of saints, the forgiveness of sins, the resurrection
     of the body, and the life everlasting?

Parents and godparents: I do.

49   The celebrant and the congregation give their assent to this profession of faith:

Celebrant: This is our faith. This the faith of the Church. We are
     proud to profess it, in Christ Jesus our Lord.

All: Amen.

50   If desired, some other formula may be used instead, or a suitable song by which the
     community expresses its faith with a single voice.

BAPTISM

51   The celebrant invites the first of the families to the font. Using the name of the
     individual child, he questions the parents and godparents:

Celebrant: Is it your will that N. should be baptized in the faith of the
     Church which we have all professed with you?

Parents and godparents: It is.

52 He baptizes the child saying:

N., I baptize you in the name of the Father,

53 He immerses the child or pours water upon it.

and of the Son,

54 He immerses the child or pours water upon it a second time.

and of the Holy Spirit.

55 He immerses the child or pours water upon it a third time.
56 He asks the same question and performs the same action for each child.
57 After each baptism it is appropriate for the people to sing a short acclamation.
58 If the baptism is performed by the pouring of water, it is preferable that the child be held by the mother (or father). Where, however, it is felt that the existing custom should be retained, the godmother (or godfather) may hold the child. If baptism is by immersion, the mother or father (godmother or godfather) lifts the child out of the font.
59 If the number of children to be baptized is large, and other priests or deacons are present, they may baptize some of the children in the way described above, and with the same form.

ANOINTING WITH CHRISM

60 Then the celebrant says:

God the Father of our Lord Jesus Christ has freed you from sin, given you a new birth by water and the Holy Spirit, and welcomed you into his holy people. He now anoints you with the chrism of salvation. As Christ was anointed Priest, Prophet, and King, so may you live always as members of his body, sharing everlasting life.
All: Amen.

61 Next, the celebrant anoints each child on the crown of the head with chrism, in silence.
62 If the number of children is large and other priests or deacons are present, these may anoint some of the children with chrism.

CLOTHING WITH WHITE GARMENT

63 The celebrant says:

(N., N.,) you have become a new creation, and have clothed yourselves in Christ. See in this white garment the outward sign of your Christian dignity. With your family and friends to help you by word and example, bring that dignity unstained into the everlasting life of heaven.
All: Amen.

64 The white garments are put on the children. A different colour is not permitted unless demanded by local custom. It is desirable that the families provide the garments.

LIGHTED CANDLE

65 The celebrant takes the Easter candle and says:

Receive the light of Christ.

66 Someone from each family (e.g. the father or godfather) lights the child's candle from the Easter candle.

67 The celebrant then says:

Parents and godparents, this light is entrusted to you to be kept burning brightly. These children of yours have been enlightened by Christ. They are to walk always as children of the light. May they keep the flame of faith alive in their hearts. When the Lord comes, may they go out to meet him with all the saints in the heavenly kingdom.

EPHPHETHA OR PRAYER OVER EARS AND MOUTH

68 If the conference of bishops decides to preserve the practice, the rite of Ephphetha follows. The celebrant touches the ears and mouth of each child with his thumb, saying:

The Lord Jesus made the deaf hear and the dumb speak. May he soon touch your ears to receive his word, and your mouth to proclaim his faith, to the praise and glory of God the Father.
All: Amen.

69 If the number of children is large, the celebrant says the formula once, but does not touch the ears and mouth.

CONCLUSION OF THE RITE

70 Next there is a procession to the altar, unless the baptism was performed in the sanctuary. The lighted candles are carried for the children.

71 A baptismal song is appropriate at this time, e.g. *You have put on Christ, in him you have been baptized. Alleluia, alleluia.*

72 Other songs may be chosen from . . .

LORD'S PRAYER

73 The celebrant stands in front of the altar and addresses the parents and god-parents, and the whole assembly in these or similar words:

Dearly beloved, these children have been reborn in baptism. They are now called children of God, for so indeed they are. In confirmation they will receive the fullness of God's Spirit, In holy communion they will share the banquet of Christ's sacrifice, calling God their Father in the midst of the Church. In their name, in the Spirit of our common son-ship, let us pray together in the words our Lord has given us:

74 All present join the celebrant in singing or saying:

Our Father in heaven, holy be your Name, your kingdom come, your
will be done, on earth as in heaven. Give us today our daily bread.
Forgive us our sins as we forgive those who sin against us. Do not bring
us to the test but deliver us from evil.

BLESSING

75 The celebrant first blesses the mothers, who hold the children in their arms, then
the fathers, and lastly the entire assembly:

(a) *Celebrant:* God the Father, through his Son, the Virgin Mary's
child, has brought joy to all Christian mothers, as they see the
hope of eternal life shine on their children. May he bless the
mothers of these children. They now thank God for the gift
of their children. May they be one with them in thanking him
for ever in heaven, in Christ Jesus our Lord.

All: Amen.

Celebrant: God is the giver of all life, human and divine. May he
bless the fathers of these children. With their wives they will
be the first teachers of their children in the ways of faith. May
they be also the best teachers, bearing witness to the faith by
what they say and do, in Christ Jesus our Lord.

All: Amen.

Celebrant: By God's gift, through water and the Holy Spirit, we
are reborn to everlasting life, In his goodness, may he continue
to pour out his blessings upon all present, who are his sons and
daughters. May he make them always, wherever they may be,
faithful members of his holy people. May he send his peace
upon all who are gathered here, in Christ Jesus our Lord.

All: Amen.

Celebrant: May almighty God, the Father, and the Son, ✠ and the
Holy Spirit, bless you.

All: Amen.

76 Other forms of the final blessing:

(b) *Celebrant:* May God the almighty Father, who filled the world with
joy by giving us his only Son, bless these newly-baptized
children. May they grow to be more fully like Jesus Christ our
Lord.

All: Amen.

Celebrant: May almighty God, who gives life on earth and in heaven, bless the parents of these children. They thank him now for the gift he has given them. May they always show that gratitude in action by loving and caring for their children.

All: Amen.

Celebrant: May almighty God, who has given us a new birth by water and the Holy Spirit, generously bless all of us who are his faithful children. May we always live as his people, and may he bless all here present with his peace.

All: Amen.

Celebrant: May almighty God, the Father, and the Son, ✠ and the holy Spirit, bless you.

All: Amen.

(c) *Celebrant:* May God, the source of life and love, who fills the hearts of mothers with love for their children, bless the mothers of these newly-baptized children. As they thank God for a safe delivery, may they find joy in the love, growth, and holiness of their children.

All: Amen.

Celebrant: May God, the Father and model of all fathers, help these fathers to give good example, so that their children will grow to be mature Christians in all the fullness of Jesus Christ.

All· Amen.

Celebrant: May God, who loves all people, bless all the relatives and friends who are gathered here. In his mercy, may he guard them from evil and give them his abundant peace.

All: Amen.

Celebrant: And may almighty God, the Father, and the Son, ✠ and the Holy Spirit, bless you.

All: Amen.

(d) *Celebrant:* My brothers and sisters, we entrust you all to the mercy and help of God the almighty Father, his only Son, and the Holy Spirit. May he watch over your life, and may we all walk by the light of faith, and attain the good things he has promised us.

Go in peace, and may almighty God, the Father, and the Son,
✠ and the Holy Spirit, bless you.

All: Amen.

77   After the blessing, all may sing a hymn which suitably expresses thanksgiving and Easter joy, or they may sing the song of the Blessed Virgin Mary, the Magnificat.

78   Where there is the practice of bringing baptized infants to the altar of the Blessed Virgin Mary, this custom if observed is appropriate.

Part 4
APPENDIXES

1. The Iglesia Filipina Independiente Rites 1961

These texts are from *The Filipino Ritual, The Administration of the Sacraments and other Rites and Ceremonies of the Church, According to the use of the Iglesia Filipina Independiente*, authorised by *The Supreme Council of Bishops*, Manila, 1961.

The authorization behind these revised rites, as used in the Independent Church of the Philippines, is stated in Part VII of Canon 140, Sec. 1. "The copies of the *Filipino Missal* and the *Filipino Ritual* with Administrations of the Sacraments and other Rites and Ceremonies of the Church, according to the use of the Iglesia Filipino Independiente, together with . . . , accepted by the General Assembly of this Church, in the year of our Lord, 1902, as amended by the General Assembly in the year of our Lord, 1947, and authenticated by the signatures of the Obispo Maximo and the Bishop President of the Supreme Council of Bishops, is hereby declared to be the Standard Book of Divine Office and Ritual of this Church."

The *Filipino Ritual* replaces a former service-book, known as *Oficio Divino*, and now contains, in English, the official texts, to which all translations must adhere. In practice, the rites of baptism and confirmation, as the other services contained in the *Ritual*, are frequently used in English. However, they are more often used in one of the vernacular languages. At least two official translations into local languages have been made; one into Tagalog or Filipino, the official national language, the other into Ilocano.

An examination of the Baptismal text, which is to be used for both infants and adults, reveals a most interesting feature, the fact that a number of "Anglican baptismal features" have been incorporated into an essentially Roman rite. The rite of confirmation also contains material from both the Anglican and the Roman Catholic orders of confirmation.

I THE ADMINISTRATION OF HOLY BAPTISM

2 Holy Baptism administered with the observance of all the rites and ceremonies prescribed by the Liturgy of the Church is called Solemn; otherwise, it is Private.

3 The Priest of every Parish shall often admonish the People, that they defer not the Baptism of their Children, and that except for urgent cause, they seek not to have their Children baptized in their houses.

4 There shall be for every Child to be baptized, when they can be had, one Godfather and one Godmother, who are not the Parents of the Child.

5 The Priest shall be vested in surplice and violet stole and at his discretion a cope; if the Sacrament is administered during the Mass, he shall be vested in amice, alb, girdle, violet stole and cope.

6 Those who are to be baptized, with their Godparents, shall meet the Priest at the Font, if there be one, otherwise in such other place in the church customarily used for the service.

7   ℣. In the Name of the Father, and of the ✠ Son, and of the Holy Ghost.
℟. Amen.

8   The Priest shall address the Godparents on this wise,

℣. What dost thou ask of the Church of God?
℟. Life everlasting.
℣. If you wish for *him* life everlasting keep the commandments.
Thou shalt love the Lord thy God with all thy heart, with all thy soul,
and with all thy mind. This is the first and great commandment. And
the second is like unto it: Thou shalt love thy neighbour as thyself.

9   Then the Priest shall blow softly upon the Child's (Person's) head, saying,

May the Lord impart unto you his Divine Spirit of holiness.

10   The Priest shall then make the sign of the cross on the forehead and breast of the
Child (Person), saying,

Receive the sign of the Cross on thy forehead ✠, and on thy breast ✠,
and may the Lord God help thee to keep his commandments, showing
them and proving them in all your deeds, that you may prove worthy
to remain in the Church of God. This holy sign is the token of the sons
of Christ. Be not ashamed to confess the faith of Christ crucified, and
manfully to fight under his banner, against sin, the world, and the
devil; and to continue as Christ's faithful soldier and servant unto
thy life's end, carrying his Cross with the same meekness shown by
Christ our Lord. *Amen.*

Let us pray.

We beseech thee, O Lord God, mercifully to hear our prayers, and
accept thy Child (Servant) N —— By the sign of thy glorious Cross
may *he* be endued with lasting virtue, and by adhering to thy commandments may *he* deserve the rich reward of thy eternal mercies; through
Jesus Christ our Lord. *Amen.*

11   Then placing his right hand upon the Child's (Person's) head, the Priest shall say,

Let us pray.

Almighty and everlasting God, . . .

CF4, *but* our heavenly Father ⟨heavenly Father⟩—this Child (Person) ⟨this
Infant⟩—the same Holy Spirit ⟨the Holy Spirit⟩

12   The Priest shall take a little salt between his fingers, and shall place it in the mouth
of the Child (Person), saying,

Receive the salt of wisdom: may it be unto thee a pledge to everlasting
life. *Amen.*

Let us pray.

O God of our fathers, fountainhead of all truth, we humbly beseech thee graciously to accept this thy Child (Servant) and grant unto *him* fervent devotion, fortifying hope, and holy joy in thy service, that once purified of all spots of sin in this baptism of regeneration, *he* may, with the company of thy faithful, prove worthy of the everlasting reward which thou hast promised us. Through Jesus Christ our Lord. *Amen.*

13   Then the Priest shall say,

Hear the words of the Gospel, written by Saint John, in the third chapter, at the first verse.

There was a man of the Pharisees, named Nicodemus, ... (John 3.1–8, AV)

Ṙ. Thanks be to thee, O Lord.

14   Then the Priest shall lead the people present in reciting the Apostles' Creed.

THE APOSTLES' CREED

I believe in God the Father Almighty, ... (CF12)

15   The Priest shall then place the left end of his stole upon the Child (Person), saying,

Enter into the Church of God, that thou may share with our Lord Jesus Christ, the everlasting life. *Amen.*

16   The Priest shall speak on this wise to the Sponsors, and to such Adults as are to be baptized.

Priest: Well-beloved, you have come hither desiring to receive Holy Baptism. We have prayed that our Lord Jesus Christ will vouchsafe to receive you, to release you from sin, to sanctify you with the Holy Ghost, to give you the kingdom of heaven, and everlasting life.

Dost thou renounce the devil and all his works, the vain pomp and glory of the world, with all covetous desires of the same, and the sinful desires of the flesh, so that thou wilt not follow, nor be led by them?

Answer: I renounce them all: and, by God's help, will endeavour not to follow, nor be led by them.

Priest: Dost thou believe in Jesus Christ, the Son of the living God?

Answer: I do.

Priest: Dost thou accept Him, and desire to follow Him as thy Lord and Saviour?

Answer: I do.

Priest: Dost thou believe all the Articles of the Christian Faith, as contained in the Apostles' Creed?

Answer: I do.

Priest: Wilt thou be baptized in this faith?

Answer: That is my desire.

Priest: Wilt thou then obediently keep God's holy will and commandments, and walk in the same all the days of thy life?

Answer: I will, by God's help.

17 When the Office is used for Children, the Priest shall ask of the Sponsors the following questions.

Priest: Having now, in the name of this Child, made these promises, wilt thou also on thy part take heed that this Child learn the Creed, the Lord's Prayer, and the Ten Commandments, and all other things which a Christian ought to know and believe to his soul's health?

Answer: I will, by God's help.

Priest: Wilt thou take heed that this Child be brought to the Bishop to be confirmed by him?

Answer: I will, God being my helper.

18 Then the Priest shall anoint the Child (Person) with the Oil of Catechumens, in the form of a cross upon the breast and between the shoulders, saying once,

I anoint ✠ thee with the oil ✠ of salvation, in the Name ✠ of Christ our Lord, that thou mayest have everlasting life. *Amen.*

19   Let us pray.

O merciful God, grant that like as Christ died and rose again, so this Child (this thy Servant) may die to sin and rise to newness of Life. *Amen.*

Grant that all sinful affections may die in *him,* and that all things belonging to the Spirit may live and grow in *him. Amen.*

Grant that *he* may . . . (CF5cd)

℣. The Lord be with you.

℟. And with thy spirit.

℣. Lift up your hearts.

℟. We lift them up unto the Lord.

℣. Let us give thanks unto our Lord God.

℟. It is meet and right so to do.

It is very meet, right, and our bounden duty, that we should give thanks unto thee, O Lord, Holy Father, Almighty, Everlasting God, for that thy dearly beloved Son Jesus Christ, for the forgiveness of our sins, did shed out of his most precious side both water and blood; and gave commandment to his disciples, that they should go teach all nations, and baptize them in the Name of the Father, and of the Son, and of the Holy Ghost. Regard, we beseech thee, the supplications of thy congregation: SANCTIFY ✠ THIS WATER to the mystical washing away of sin; and grant that this Child (this thy Servant), now to be baptized therein, may receive the fullness of thy grace, and ever remain in the number of thy faithful children; through the same Jesus Christ our Lord, to whom, with thee, in the unity of the Holy Spirit be all honour and glory, now and evermore. *Amen.*

The Priest shall change his stole (and cope) from violet to white. He shall cause the Godparents to hold the Child and shall say unto them,

NAME THIS CHILD

The Godparent shall say the name or names of the Child. The Priest shall repeat the name of the Child after them, and shall thrice pour water upon him saying,

N —— I BAPTIZE THEE IN THE NAME OF THE ✠ FATHER, AND OF THE ✠ SON, AND OF THE HOLY ✠ GHOST. Amen.

But note, that if the person to be baptized is an adult, the Priest shall take him by the hand, and shall ask the Witnesses the Name; and then shall pour water upon him, using the same form.

In keeping with ancient tradition, the Priest shall here anoint the Child (Person) with holy Chrism on the crown of the head, saying once,

Almighty God, Father of our Lord Jesus Christ, who hast regenerated thee with water and the Holy Spirit; and who hast given thee remission of your sins, anoint ✠ thee with the Chrism of salvation, that thou mayest have life everlasting through the same Christ our Lord. *Amen.*

Here the Priest shall place upon the Child (Person) the white vesture commonly called Chrysom, saying,

Receive this white vesture, a token of innocency bestowed upon thee, and a symbol whereby thou art admonished to give thyself to pureness of living, that after this transitory life thou mayest be a partaker of life everlasting. *Amen.*

A lighted candle shall be given to every Godparent; to the baptized person, if an Adult, saying,

Receive the light of Christ, that when the bridegroom cometh, thou mayest go forth with all the saints to meet him, and see that thou keep the grace of thy Baptism.

26 The Priest shall sprinkle the Child (Person), the Godparents and other people present with holy water, saying,

Shower thy grace upon us, purge us with hyssop and we shall be clean; wash us and we shall be whiter than snow. Glory be to the Father, by whose omnipotence we were created in his image; Glory be to the Son, by whose mercy our sins have been forgiven; Glory be to the Holy Ghost, by whose wisdom we are given the light of faith.

Ry. Glory be to the Blessed Trinity. *Amen.*

27 Then the Priest shall lead the People present in reciting the Lord's Prayer, all kneeling.

Let us pray.

Our Father who art in heaven, . . . (CF11)

Ꝟ. We yield thee hearty thanks, most merciful Father, that it hath pleased thee to regenerate this *Child (this thy Servant)* with the Holy Spirit, to receive *him* for thine own *Child*, and to incorporate *him* into thy holy Church. And humbly we beseech thee to grant, that *he*, being dead unto sin, may live unto righteousness, and being buried with Christ in his death, may also be a partaker of his resurrection; so that finally, with the residue of thy holy Church, *he* may be an inheritor of thine everlasting kingdom; through Christ our Lord. *Amen.*

28 At the discretion of the Priest, that which follows may be said as an exhortation to the Parents and Godparents.

My beloved Parents, Godfathers and Godmothers of this *Child*.

Holy Church commands me to remind you of your duties to this *Child*; to raise *him* by the teachings of the Gospel, that in due time *he* may willingly ratify the pledge that you have now given in *his* name.

Ye shall keep him far from evil and all possible temptations. "Woe unto those that give scandal to these little children", saith the Lord, because scandal and wrong examples are fatal to tender creatures. Ye shall therefore bring *him* up in the love of God, in charity with *his* neighbours, and in purity of life, because, as saith the Lord,

"Whosoever shall not receive the kingdom of God as a little child, shall not enter therein."

May God bless this *Child*, that *he* may grow into fullness of life; and you, Parents and Godparents, may God reward you for this holy action with richness of life, and strengthen you with the might of his Spirit, that Christ may fill you with the fullness of God.

29 Then shall the Priest ask the Godparents to kneel.

℣. Blessed be the Name of the Lord.

℞. From this time forth for evermore.

THE BLESSING

30 The blessing of God Almighty, the Father, the ✠ Son, and the Holy
Ghost be upon you and remain with you always. *Amen.*

I THE SACRAMENT OF CONFIRMATION
OR LAYING ON OF HANDS UPON THOSE BAPTIZED
AND COME TO YEARS OF DISCRETION

2 Upon coming to years of discretion, the children shall ratify before the Bishop those
things they were bound to believe and do, which were undertaken for them by
their Sponsors in their Baptism. Upon the day appointed, all that are to be confirmed shall stand before the Bishop who, vested with surplice, white stole, cope,
and mitre and holding his staff, shall, after bowing before the Cross, sit in his chair,
and signing himself, say,

3 *Bishop:* In the Name of the Father and of ✠ the Son, and of the Holy
Ghost. *Amen.*

EXHORTATION TO THE CHILDREN

4 Bishop:
My beloved Children of God: Your parents or sponsors being faithful
Christians, brought you to Baptism by which you became the Sons
and Daughters of God and members of Christ's Holy Church. They
did this for your own good and benefit, that your eyes may be opened
to the Faith of the Lord, revealed in the light of the Holy Scriptures
which is the Book given by God, wherein we discover eternal truths,
right conduct in this transitory life, and the way of salvation for life
everlasting. At Baptism you assumed the sacred duty to avoid evil,
which we call sin, and to pursue virtue; you died unto sinfulness and
were born again by Water and the Holy Ghost to righteousness and
innocency of life. Thus, you are duty bound to love God with all your
soul and mind and your neighbour as yourselves. Avoid all occasions
of sin, and beware of evil thoughts which are the root of evil deeds.
We must love God, our heavenly Father, who created us, sustains us,
feeds us, protects us from all perils, and supplies our daily needs. Likewise, we must love our fellow men, even our foes, because we are all
children of God, and as such we forgive one another as true brethren.
  Are you well disposed to ratify publicly the manifest will of your

parents or sponsors to enter into the life of the Church of our Lord Jesus Christ?

Answer: I am so disposed, the Lord being my helper.

Bishop: Do you here, in the presence of God, and of this congregation, renew the solemn promise and vow that you made, or that was made in your name, at your baptism; ratifying and confirming the same; and acknowledging yourselves bound to believe and to do all those things which you then undertook, or your Sponsors then undertook for you?

Answer: I do.

Bishop: Do you promise to follow Jesus Christ as your Lord and Saviour?

Answer: I do.

Bishop: May the Holy Spirit descend upon you and may the grace of our Lord Jesus Christ preserve you from sin.

Answer: Amen.

5 The Bishop, at his discretion, may use the following Exhortation instead of the one above.

Bishop:

Dearly beloved in the Lord, in ministering confirmation the Church follows the example of the Apostles of Christ. For in the eighth chapter of the Acts of the Apostles we read this:

Now when the Apostles which were in Jerusalem heard that Samaria had received the Word of God, they sent unto them Peter and John; who, when they were come down, prayed for them, that they might receive the Holy Ghost (for as yet he was fallen upon none of them: only they had been baptized in the Name of the Lord Jesus). Then laid they their hands on them, and they received the Holy Ghost. Holy Scripture here teaches us that in Confirmation there is both an outward sign, which is the laying on of hands with prayer, and an inward grace, which is the strengthening gift of the Holy Spirit. And, forasmuch as this gift comes from God alone, let us make our supplications to Almighty God, as the Apostles did, that he will pour forth his Spirit upon these persons who in Baptism were made his Children by adoption and grace.

Furthermore, in order that this congregation may be assured that you who are to be confirmed, steadfastly purpose to confess the faith of Christ crucified and to serve loyally under his banner; and that you yourselves may ever have printed in your remembrance what is your

calling and how greatly you need the continued help of the Holy
Spirit, the Church has thought good to order that, before you receive
the laying on of hands, you shall openly acknowledge yourselves bound
to fulfil the Christian duties to which Holy Baptism has pledged you.

6 The Bishop shall say:

Do you here, in the presence of God, and of this congregation, renew
the solemn promise and vow that you made, or that was made in your
name at your Baptism; ratifying the same in your own persons, and
acknowledging yourselves bound to believe, and to do, all those things,
which you then undertook, or your Godfathers and Godmothers then
undertook for you?
Answer: I do.

7 Then the Bishop stands, takes off the mitre, and proceeds with the following:

Bishop: Our help is in the Name of the Lord. . . . (CF14)
Almighty and everliving God, . . .

CF15, *but with ending* . . . increase in them thy sevenfold gifts of grace, through
Jesus Christ our Lord.

Answer: Amen.

8 Then the Bishop shall extend his hands toward those to be confirmed, saying:

Bishop: Receive the Spirit of Wisdom.
Answer: Amen.
Bishop: The Spirit of Understanding.
Answer: Amen.
Bishop: The Spirit of Counsel.
Answer: Amen.
Bishop: The Spirit of Ghostly strength.
Answer: Amen.
Bishop: The Spirit of Knowledge.
Answer: Amen.
Bishop: The Spirit of true Godliness.
Answer: Amen.
Bishop: Fill them with the Spirit of thy Holy Fear, now and forever.
Answer: Amen.
Bishop: Let us pray.

9 Defend, O Lord, these thy children with thy heavenly grace, that they
may continue thine forever; and daily increase in thy Holy Spirit more
and more, until they come unto thy everlasting kingdom.
Answer: Amen.

10 Then the Bishop shall be seated and shall put on the mitre; the children shall kneel
before him; or he, with mitre and staff, shall approach the lines of children, and
lay his hands upon each severally and shall anoint them with the holy Chrism, on
their forehead, in the form of the Cross, saying:

Bishop: I sign thee with the sign of the ✠ Cross, and confirm thee with
the oil of gladness in the Name of the Father, and of the Son, and
of the Holy Ghost. *Amen.*

11 The Bishop shall slightly slap the cheek of each child, right after the signing with
the holy Chrism, saying:

Peace be unto thee.

12 The Bishop shall wash his hands; the Choir shall sing a Hymn or the following:

PSALM 1—Beatus vir qui non abiit.

1. Blessed is the man that hath not walked in the counsel of the
ungodly, . . . (Ps. 1.1–7, BCP)

13 The washing of the hands being done and all devoutly kneeling, the Bishop shall
remove the mitre, and say:

Bishop: Show us thy mercy, O Lord.
Answer: And grant us thy salvation.
Bishop: Lord, hear our prayer.
Answer: And let our cry come unto thee.
Bishop: The Lord be with you.
Answer: And with thy spirit.

14   Let us pray.

O Heavenly Father, who hast imparted thy Holy Spirit to thine
Apostles, and through them and their Successors, Thou dost conduct
thy faithful people towards the paths of righteousness; Have mercy
upon these thy children: confirm and impress in their hearts what outwardly we have impressed on their foreheads with the holy Chrism
in the form of the holy Cross, and grant that thy Holy Spirit may abide
with them that they may be made worthy and living temples of the
same, through Jesus Christ our Lord.
Answer: Amen.

THE BLESSING

15 Then the Bishop puts on the mitre, and taking his staff continues as follows:

Bishop: The Blessing of God Almighty, the ✠ Father, the ✠ Son, and
the Holy ✠ Ghost, be upon you, and remain with you for ever.
Answer: Amen.

2. The Church of South India Rites 1962

These texts are from *The Book of Common Worship*: As Authorized By The Synod of 1962, published by Oxford University Press, London, 1963.

The Order of Service for the Reception of Baptized Persons into the Full Membership of the Church, commonly called Confirmation, was first published in 1950, four years before the Order for Baptism. The second edition of this Order was published in 1960. The first revision of the Order of Holy Baptism provided for the Baptism of both adults and infants, and where variations occurred these were printed in parallel columns. In October 1954 the Executive Committee of the Synod authorized these services for optional and experimental use, whereever their use was desired. Following this authorization the first edition of Holy Baptism was published in 1955, and a second edition in 1960. These services, along with the rest of the material which is now contained in *The Book of Common Worship*, went before the Synod Liturgy Committee in September 1961. After a general revision of all the services, the Synod of January 1962 authorized all services for general use. The first complete service-book, which contained all these services, was published in 1963.

DIRECTIONS TO MINISTERS
CHRISTIAN INITIATION: BAPTISM

I PREPARATION FOR BAPTISM

Candidates able to answer for themselves must be well instructed in the Christian faith and way of life and approved by the minister and the representatives of the congregation before they are brought to baptism. At the beginning of their preparation they may be publicly received as catechumens, according to the service appointed, and commended to the prayers of the congregation.

2 PARENTS AND GODPARENTS

Only those who are baptized and in good standing may bring their children for baptism.

If, however, a husband and wife have been excommunicated, or otherwise disciplined, but still come regularly to church and show a sincere desire to bring up their children in the Christian way, the minister may, at his discretion, make an exception to the above rule and may baptize their children.

The parents or guardians of a child to be baptized must inform the minister some days beforehand that they desire to bring their child to baptism. They must also submit to him the names of the godparents, where it is customary to have them.

As soon as possible after notice has been given, full inquiry should be made and all necessary instruction and exposition of the service given by the minister or some other competent and instructed leader. For this purpose the parents or guardians should be visited in their home, or they should be asked to attend at the church at a convenient hour. Instruction should be regarded as particularly necessary in the case of a first child. If the parents or guardians cannot give the promises contained in the service, the minister may defer the baptism of the child.

The choice of godparents to make the promises at the baptism of children and to share in the responsibility of their Christian upbringing, and the choice of witnesses at the baptism of those able to answer for themselves, are ancient customs observed in many congregations of the Church of South India.

Only those who have the status of communicants are qualified to act as godparents or witnesses.

The parents of children to be baptized make the promises, and the godparents, if any, make the promises with them.

At the time of baptism one of the parents may present the child to the minister and name him, and the other may receive him back.

3 THE CONDUCT OF THE SERVICE

Baptism is as a rule administered at a public service of the church.

It is usual for the ministrant of the sacrament to be a presbyter; but deacons are authorized to baptize, and a layman or woman may do so in an emergency.

If a person or child to be baptized is too weak or ill to be brought to church, he may be baptized at home. The service may be shortened, but must include at least baptism with water in the name of the Trinity and the Lord's Prayer. When a person thus baptized has recovered from his sickness, he comes to a public service of the Church and makes his promises. The minister declares that he has been received into the Church, and the congregation welcomes him, using the forms provided at the end of the service ("The Thanksgiving"). In the case of a sick child, the parents bring him to church after recovery and make the promises for him, and the minister declares that he has been received into the Church.

Where it is the custom to administer baptism during a service of the Lord's Supper, the Order for Holy Baptism may come after the Preparation and be substituted for the Ministry of the Word.

If baptism is administered during Morning or Evening Worship, the Order for Holy Baptism may be substituted for the Ministry of the Word; or it may be added at the beginning of the Prayers (the creed in Morning or Evening Worship being omitted); or at the end of the service.

If it is uncertain whether a candidate has been baptized already or not, the following form of words is used at the baptism:

N, if thou art not already baptized, I baptize thee in the name of the Father, and of the Son, and of the Holy Spirit.

A candidate who has been converted from a faith in which idolatry is not practised (e.g. Islam) is not required to renounce idolatry.

At the discretion of the minister, the questions in the Renunciation, Profession of Faith, and the Promises, and those in the Office for the Making of Catechumens, may be put in the form of statements to be repeated after him by the candidates, or the parents (and godparents). Supplementary questions (or statements) may also be framed in accordance with the particular circumstances of the candidates.

When those able to answer for themselves are baptized together with their children, the minister reads the Order for the Baptism of those able to answer for themselves, with the addition of the promises in the Order for the Baptism of Infants. The parents (together with god-parents, if any) make the promises for their children after they have made their own.

Baptisms, whether public or private, must be entered in the Baptismal Register.

For the combination of Baptism and Confirmation in one service, see the directions on the Confirmation Service.

4   ADDITIONAL CEREMONIES

In addition to the optional use of the sign of the cross, as provided for in the Order, the ceremonies of the light and of the putting on of a white garment may be performed immediately after the Reception into the Church, at the discretion of the minister and with the good will of the congregation. It should be noted, however, that they in no wise add to the efficacy of baptism.

1 # THE BAPTISM OF INFANTS
2 ## A THANKSGIVING AFTER CHILDBIRTH

3 This thanksgiving should be made at a public service of the Church, and the congregation should join in the saying of the Psalm and the Lord's Prayer.

4 The Mother and Father, bringing the newly born *child*, kneel before the Holy Table, or at some other convenient place, and the minister facing them says:

Almighty God has been good to you in giving you the gift of *a child*.
Let us therefore give thanks to him.

5 The minister and parents together with the congregation say the following Psalm responsively:

PSALM 145.1–8

I will magnify thee, O God, my King: and I will praise thy name for ever and ever. . . . (BCP)

6 Minister:
                        Let us pray.

Lord, have mercy upon us:
R. Christ, have mercy upon us:
Lord, have mercy upon us.
Our Father, who art in heaven, . . . (CF11)
Almighty God, we give thee hearty thanks for thy love and mercy in giving this woman, thy servant, a safe and happy childbirth. Grant that she, having in remembrance thy care and love for her, may never cease to give thee thanks and serve thee faithfully; through Jesus Christ our Lord. *Amen.*

O God, our heavenly Father, by whose creative power and love this woman has been granted the gift of *a child*, give to her and her husband wisdom and guidance, that they may know how to train their *child* in the way that leadeth to eternal life, through Jesus Christ our Lord. *Amen.*

7 The parents say:

O God, our Father, we give thanks to thee for the *child* whom thou hast given to us: help us to live together as a family in love, joy and peace; give us wisdom to be good parents, that we may all love and serve thee faithfully; through Jesus Christ our Lord. *Amen.*

8 If the child has died, Psalm 63.1–8 is said instead of Psalm 145.1–8. Instead of the three prayers appointed above, the minister alone says the following prayer:

Almighty God, we humbly praise thee that thou hast saved thy hand-maid from all the dangers of her delivery, so that she can again come to thy house today. Beloved Father, comfort her and her husband in their sorrow, and strengthen them that they may continue in faith, do thy will, and at the end of the days of their journey attain the glory of life eternal, through Jesus Christ our Lord. *Amen.*

9   The minister dismisses them with this blessing:

The blessing of God almighty, the Father, the Son, and the Holy Spirit, be upon your going out and your coming in; upon your down-sitting and upon your uprising; upon your talking and upon your silence; upon your prayers and upon your work; upon your home and upon your fellowship therein, this day, henceforth, and forever. *Amen.*

10 The parents may make a thank-offering, and, if there is a service of Holy Communion, they may receive the Communion together.

THE BAPTISM

11 The minister ascertains beforehand that the children have not already been baptized.

THE DECLARATION OF THE WORD

12 When the people are gathered at, or proceeding to, the place of baptism, a hymn may be sung, after which the minister says:

Our help is in the name of the Lord:
R. Who hath made heaven and earth.

13   Let us pray.

*Almighty God, thou Shepherd of Israel, who didst deliver thy chosen people from the bondage of Egypt, and didst establish with them a sure covenant: Have mercy, we beseech thee, on thy flock, and grant that *these children* who *are* by baptism to be received into thy heritage, may be delivered from the bondage of sin through thy covenant of grace, and attain the promise of eternal life which thou hast given us in thy Son our Saviour Jesus Christ; who liveth and reigneth with thee and the Holy Spirit, ever one God, world without end. *Amen.*

14 The people may sit.

15 Dearly beloved, we are met together to administer holy baptism to *these children*, that, according to Christ's command, *they* may be sealed as *members* of Christ, *children* of God, and *heirs* of the kingdom of heaven.

Hear therefore the words of our Lord and Saviour Jesus Christ:

Go and make disciples of all nations, baptizing them in the name of the Father, and of the Son, and of the Holy Spirit. St Matthew 28.19

Truly, truly, I say to you, unless one is born of water and the Spirit, he cannot enter the kingdom of God.   St John 3.5

* Passages so marked may be omitted.

Hear also what is written in the Gospel according to St Mark:

They were bringing children to him, . . .　　　　St Mark 10.13–16

16　The minister expounds the teaching of Scripture concerning baptism in his own words.

17　Or he says:

You hear in this Gospel the words of our Saviour Christ, when he commanded the children to be brought to him. You perceive how he took them in his arms and blessed them. Jesus Christ is the same yesterday and today and for ever. He loves *these children* and is ready to receive *them*, to embrace *them* with the arms of his mercy, and to give *them* the blessing of eternal life.

These little *children belong* with you to God. In Holy Baptism he establishes *them* in the family and household of faith, that *they* may grow up as *members* of Christ and *heirs* of the kingdom of heaven.

THE PROFESSION OF THE FAITH

18　All stand. The minister says to the parents (and godparents):

It is the duty of those who present *children* for baptism to make confession of the faith in which *they are* baptized and to promise to bring *them* up in the way of Christ.

Do you believe in one God, the Father, the Son, and the Holy Spirit?

19　The parents (and godparents) answer:

I believe.
Let us therefore profess our faith.

20　The Apostles' Creed is said or sung by all:

I believe in God the Father almighty, . . . (CF12)

THE PROMISES

21　Will you, by God's help, provide a Christian home for this child and bring *him* up in the worship and teaching of the Church, that *he* may come to know Christ *his* saviour?
Answer: We will, God being our helper.
Will you so order your own lives that you do not cause this little one to stumble?
Answer: We will, God being our helper.
Will you encourage *him* later to be received into the full fellowship of the Church by Confirmation; so that, established in faith by the

Holy Spirit, *he* may partake of the Lord's Supper and go forth into the world to serve God faithfully in his Church?
Answer: We will, God being our helper.

22   The minister says to the congregation:

Dearly beloved, will you be faithful to your calling as members of the Church of Christ, so that *these* and all other children in your midst may grow up in the knowledge and love of him?

23   The congregation answer:

We will, God being our helper; and we welcome *them* into our fellow-ship.

THE BAPTISM

24   The minister says:

Let us pray in silence for *the children* about to be baptized, that *they* may receive the fullness of God's grace.

25   The people may kneel.
26   Silence is kept for a space. Then the minister says.

The Lord be with you:
R. And with thy spirit.

27   The minister prays in his own words.
28   Or the following litany is said or sung:

Blessed art thou, O Lord God, heavenly Father, who hast created all things and given us the element of water:
R. Blessed art thou, O Lord.
Blessed art thou, O Lord Jesus Christ, the only-begotten Son of God, who wast baptized in the Jordan and didst die and rise again:
R. Blessed art thou, O Lord.
Blessed art thou, O Lord, the Holy Spirit, who didst descend upon Jesus Christ and upon the Church:
R. Blessed art thou, O Lord.
Be present, O God, with us who call upon thy threefold name, and bless this water, that it may signify the washing away of sin, and that *those* baptized therein may be born again to eternal life:
R. Hear us, we beseech thee.
Grant *them* thy Holy Spirit, that *they* may be baptized into the one body, and ever remain in the number of thy faithful and elect people:
R. Hear us, we beseech thee.

Grant that, being united with Christ in his death and resurrection, *they* may die unto sin and live unto righteousness:
R. Hear us, we beseech thee.
Grant that *they* may put off the old man and become a new creation in Christ Jesus:
R. Hear us, we beseech thee.
From darkness lead *them* to light; from death lead *them* to everlasting life:
R. Hear us, we beseech thee.

29 All stand. The minister, having asked the Christian name, pours water upon each child, saying:

N, I baptize thee in the name of the Father, and of the Son, and of the Holy Spirit. Amen.

30 The minister says over each child baptized:

We have received this child into the congregation of Christ's flock (✠ and do sign *him* with the sign of the cross).[1]

31 Then he says for all together:

May *these children* never be ashamed to confess the faith of Christ crucified, but continue his faithful *servants* unto *their lives'* end. Amen.

32 Then may be said or sung:

 * The Lord bless you and keep you: the Lord make his face to shine upon you, and be gracious to you: the Lord lift up his countenance upon you, and give you peace. Amen.   Numbers 6.24–6

33 A hymn of praise is sung. A procession may be made from the place of baptism into the body of the church.

 * THE LIGHT

34 The parents of the children baptized may be given lighted lamps or tapers. When they have received them, the minister says:

Let your light so shine before men, that they may see your good works:
R. And give glory to our Father who is in heaven. St Matthew 5.16

35 Or some other brief forms of words may be said.

THE THANKSGIVING

36 The minister says:

Let us pray.
Our Father, who art in heaven, . . . (CF11)

[1] Here the minister may make a cross upon the child's forehead.

37 · The minister says, or the minister and people say together:

We yield thee hearty thanks, most merciful Father, that it has pleased thee to receive *these children* for thine own *children* by adoption and to incorporate *them* into thy holy Church. And we humbly beseech thee to grant that *they* may more and more show forth in *their lives* that which *they* now *are* by thy calling; so that, as *they are* made *partakers* of the death of thy Son, *they* may also be *partakers* of his resurrection, and finally, with all thy Church, inherit thine everlasting kingdom; through the same Jesus Christ our Lord. *Amen.*

38 The minister says:

Almighty God our heavenly Father, whose blessed Son shared at Nazareth the life of an earthly home: Bless, we beseech thee, the *homes* of *these children*, and grant wisdom and understanding to all who have the care of *them*, that *they* may grow up in thy constant fear and love; through the same thy Son Jesus Christ our Lord. *Amen.*

39 A hymn may be sung, and the thank-offering is taken.

40 If baptism is administered otherwise than at the Lord's Supper or at Morning or Evening Worship, the minister dismisses those that are gathered together with this blessing:

May God almighty, the Father of our Lord Jesus Christ, grant you to be strengthened with might through his Spirit in the inner man; that Christ may dwell in your hearts through faith, and that you may be filled with all the fullness of God. *Amen.*

CHRISTIAN INITIATION: CONFIRMATION

I PREPARATION FOR CONFIRMATION

The candidates are prepared by the presbyter of their own congregation, or someone appointed by him, that in the power of the Holy Spirit they may give themselves to Christ.

2 THE CONDUCT OF THE SERVICE

In the Church of South India Confirmation is administered by the bishop or a presbyter. If a presbyter conducts the service, it is desirable that he should be the presbyter responsible for that congregation, or a presbyter appointed by the bishop.

Before the service, the bishop, or the presbyter appointed by him, may meet the candidates for such examination as he thinks desirable.

The Confirmation Service may be held:

(*a*) as a separate service;

(b) during a celebration of the Lord's Supper (in this case the minister substitutes the Confirmation Service for The Ministry of the Word in the Order for the Lord's Supper);

or

(c) along with Baptism, if the candidates have been specially prepared to be baptized and confirmed at the same time. In this case the two orders may be combined in one service as follows:

Baptism: The Declaration of the Word.
Confirmation: The Vows.
Baptism: The Baptism, the Thanksgiving.
Confirmation: The Confirmation, the Reception.

This arrangement is suitable only when all candidates are being baptized and confirmed at the same time.

I AN ORDER OF SERVICE FOR THE RECEPTION OF BAPTIZED PERSONS INTO THE FULL FELLOWSHIP OF THE CHURCH
COMMONLY CALLED CONFIRMATION

INTRODUCTION

2 A hymn is sung.

3 The minister says:

Our help is in the name of the Lord:
R. Who hath made heaven and earth.

Let us pray.

4 The people kneel, and the minister prays in his own words.

5 If there is no celebration of the Lord's Supper, there is a Confession and Declaration of Forgiveness such as the following:

The minister says:

I will arise and go to my father, and I will say to him, "Father, I have sinned against heaven and before you; I am no longer worthy to be called your son."   St Luke 15.18

Let us examine ourselves in silence.

6 All are silent for a space. After this, the minister says:

Let us humbly confess our sins to almighty God.

All say:

O God, our Father, We have sinned against thee in thought, word, and deed: We have not loved thee with all our heart; We have not loved our neighbours as ourselves. Have mercy upon us, we beseech thee; Cleanse us from our sins; And help us to overcome our faults; Through Jesus Christ our Lord. Amen.

7 The Minister says:

May the almighty and merciful Lord grant unto us pardon and remission of all our sins, time for amendment of life, and the grace and comfort of the Holy Spirit. Amen.

Or he may say *you* and *your* instead of *us* and *our*.

8 All sit.

9 The presbyter reads the names of the candidates, who stand one by one as they are called.

10 The minister says to them:

Beloved in the Lord, in your baptism you were received into the fellowship of Christ and sealed as members of the family and household of God.

Now you come, of your own choice, to ratify the solemn covenant then made, to profess your faith in the Lord Jesus, to consecrate yourselves to him, and to receive the gifts which he is waiting to bestow.

You come that, in accordance with the practice of the apostles, we may lay our hands upon you, praying that the Holy Spirit may strengthen you in every good work.

You come that this congregation may welcome you into the full fellowship of Christ's people, and that together we may worship and serve him all the days of our life.

11 Hear, therefore, the word of God concerning the gift of the Holy Spirit, in the Book of the Prophet Ezekiel:

A new heart I will give you, ... (Ezek. 36.26–8, RSV)

12 In the letter of the Apostle Paul to the Church in Rome:
Brethren, we are debtors, ... (Rom. 8.12–17, RSV)

13 In the words of our Lord Jesus Christ:
If you love me, ... (John 14.15–17, RSV)

14 You shall receive power, ... (Acts 1.8, RSV)

15 Or the minister may choose other passages.

16 The Sermon is preached.

THE VOWS

17 The candidates stand, and the minister says:

I ask you now in the presence of God and of this congregation:

In the power of Christ, do you renounce the pride and vanity of this
world, the sins of the flesh, and all the works of the devil?
Answer: I renounce them.
Do you believe in one God, the Father, the Son, and the Holy Spirit?
Answer: I believe.
Do you accept the Lord Jesus Christ as your Saviour and the Saviour
of the world?
Answer: I do.
Let us therefore profess our faith.
I believe in God the Father almighty, . . .

CF12, *but* Holy Spirit ⟨Holy Ghost⟩

18 Will you keep God's holy will and commandments and walk in them
all the days of your life?
Answer: I will, God being my helper.
Do you promise to join with your fellow-Christians in worship on the
Lord's Day, and especially in the Lord's Supper?
Answer: I promise.
Do you promise to be faithful in reading or hearing the Bible, and in
prayer?
Answer: I promise.
Do you acknowledge yourselves bound to confess the faith of Christ
crucified and risen, and to continue his faithful Servants unto your
lives' end, bearing witness to him both in word and in deed?
Answer: I promise.

19 The minister says:

Beloved, you have confessed your faith in God through Christ our only
Saviour, and your desire to obey him and live in the fellowship of his
people; will you now kneel and pray that the Holy Spirit may enable
you truly to perform that which you have promised?

20 Silence, all kneeling.

21 Then the candidates, led by the minister, say:

O God, my God, Father of our Lord Jesus Christ, I am not my own,
but thine. Relying on thy grace, I give myself to thee, As thy child, To
love and to serve faithfully, All the days of my life. *Amen.*

THE CONFIRMATION

22 The minister calls the congregation to pray in silence for the candidates.

23 Silence is kept for a space.

24 A hymn or lyric praying for the Holy Spirit may be sung kneeling.

25 The minister says the following prayer alone.

26 Or he may invite the congregation to say it with him.

Almighty God, our heavenly Father, who by Holy Baptism has received these thy children into thy family: Establish them in faith, we beseech thee, by thy Holy Spirit, and daily increase in them thy manifold gifts of grace, the spirit of wisdom and understanding, the spirit of counsel and might, the spirit of knowledge and of the fear of the Lord; and keep them in thy mercy unto life eternal; through Jesus Christ thy Son our Lord. *Amen.*

27 The minister lays his hand upon the head of each of the candidates in turn, saying:

Strengthen, O Lord, this thy child with thy heavenly grace, that *he* may continue thine for ever, and daily increase in thy Holy Spirit, until *he* come unto thine everlasting kingdom.

28 The people each time say:

Amen.

29 When all have been confirmed, the minister says:

The Lord be with you:
R. And with thy spirit.

30   Let us pray.

Our Father, who art in heaven, . . . (CF11)

31 The minister prays:

Almighty and everliving God, who, according to the promise of thy Son our Saviour Jesus Christ, hast ordained thy Church to be the temple of the Holy Spirit: Mercifully hear our prayers for these thy children, upon whom we have laid our hands. Let thy fatherly hand, we beseech thee, be over them; let thy Holy Spirit ever be with them; and so lead them in the knowledge and obedience of thy word, that they may serve thee all their days and be with thee for ever; through our Lord and Saviour Jesus Christ, who with thee and the Holy Spirit liveth and reigneth, ever one God, world without end. *Amen.*

THE RECEPTION

32 If the Lord's Supper is celebrated together with Confirmation, the Reception takes place after the offertory sentences, and the Peace is given first to the newly confirmed and by them to the rest of the Congregation.

33 The newly confirmed persons stand and face the congregation, while the minister and the congregation stand and together say to them:

Beloved, we, the members of this congregation, Welcome you with joy As partners in the common life of the Church. We pledge to you our friendship and our prayers, That you may grow in the knowledge and love of God And of his Son Jesus Christ our Lord. God grant that we may all serve him here on earth In the unity of the Spirit, And come to the perfect fellowship of the saints above.

34 The newly confirmed persons turn again to the minister.

35 Each is given a membership card. A Bible, a New Testament, or *The Book of Common Worship* of the Church of South India may also be given.

36 The minister says to them:

In token of our brotherly love in Christ, we give you the greeting of peace.

37 The peace is given, and a hymn is sung, during which the offerings of the newly confirmed and of the congregation are received.

38 If there is no celebration of the Lord's Supper, the minister says this blessing.

Go forth into the world in peace; and the blessing of God almighty, the Father, the Son, and the Holy Spirit, be upon you and remain with you for ever. *Amen.*

3. The Church of the Province of East Africa

Presbyterial Confirmation
Episcopal Laying on of Hands

For some time the Church of the Province of East Africa has been engaged in a re-examination of its rites of initiation. Two major issues have been under consideration, the possibility of presbyterial confirmation at the time of baptism; and the new rite of episcopal laying on of hands as an ordering for Christian service, to be called "Commissioning". A Sub-Committee which was appointed to study these matters has put forward the following recommendations:

1. The reintegration of confirmation and baptism, both for infants and adults.
2. Presbyterial admission to Holy Communion at a service of renewal of baptism vows for children who have reached an age of understanding, and after due preparation.
3. The episcopal laying on of hands for the setting apart of lay workers offering themselves for Christian action in the affairs of Church and Society.

The sub-committee recommended the following form for baptism-cum-confirmation, the words "(with the oil of salvation)" being used only in those dioceses where it is customary to use the Holy Oil at baptism.

N. I baptise thee in the name of the Father, and of the Son and of the Holy Spirit. Amen.
N. I sign thee with the sign of the Cross (with the oil of salvation) and lay my hand upon thee that thou mayest be made strong by the Holy Spirit. In the name of the Father, and of the Son and of the Holy Spirit. Amen.

We receive this child into the company of Christ's Church.

My child, I sign thee with the sign of the Cross in token that thou shalt never be ashamed to confess the faith of Christ crucified, but manfully to fight under his banner against sin, the world, and the devil, and to remain Christ's faithful soldier and servant unto thy life's end.

Thereafter, in those dioceses where it is the custom, the newly-baptized child will be given a white garment and a lighted candle.

The formula for use by a bishop in Commissioning should be as follows:

Defend, O Lord this thy servant with thy heavenly grace, that he may continue thine for ever, and daily increase in thy Holy Spirit more and more;

serving Thee and witnessing to Thee, till he come to thine everlasting kingdom. Amen.

These proposals are not yet in use as they have received no Provincial sanction.

As a member of the East African Church Union Liturgy and Doctrine Committee, the Church of the Province of East Africa has had a very real part to play in the formulation of the revised Orders for the Baptism of Infants and Adults, produced by this Committee. The proposed ecumenical rite, for Infant Baptism, is reproduced below (pp. 317–21). But the rite has received no authorization for use in the Church of the Province of East Africa.

4. *The East African Church Union*

The Service which follows was drawn up by the East African Church Union Liturgy and Doctrine Committee, which is a committee of representatives from five Churches in East Africa—Anglican, Lutheran, Methodist, Moravian, and Presbyterian. The service is provisional and is being considered for use by the Churches involved in its formulation. Some of these Churches have already approved the service in principle, but in no Church is it in regular use. It has received no authorization for use in the Anglican Church.

The text here reproduced is that of the first draft, 1965, and is based on that used in the Church of South India.

1 AN INFANT BAPTISMAL LITURGY

2 This service may be used independently, or in connection with the normal Sunday service.

3 Our help is in the name of the Lord,
  R. Who has made heaven and earth.

4   Let us pray.
Almighty God, thou Shepherd of Israel, who didst deliver thy chosen people from the bondage of Egypt, and didst establish with them a sure covenant; have mercy, we beseech thee, on thy flock, and grant that this child, who is by baptism to be received into thy heritage, may be delivered from the bondage of sin, through thy covenant of grace, and attain the promise of eternal life, which thou hast given us in thy Son our Saviour Jesus Christ, who lives and reigns with thee and the Holy Spirit, ever one God, world without end. *Amen.*

5 Dearly beloved, we are met together to administer holy baptism to this child according to Christ's command, that he may be born again as a member of Christ, a child of God, and an heir of the kingdom of heaven.

6 Hear therefore the words of our Lord and Saviour Jesus Christ:

7 Go therefore and make disciples of all nations, ... (Matt. 28.19–20, RSV)

8 Truly, truly, I say to you, ... (John 3.5–6, RSV)

317

9 And they were bringing children to him, . . . (Mark 10.13–16, RSV)

10 A sermon may be given here if desired.

11 Since in Christian faith you present this child for holy baptism, it is your duty to make confession of the faith into which this child is to be baptized, and to bring him up in this faith. Therefore I ask you, do you believe in one God, Father, Son and Holy Spirit?
Parents and Sponsors: I believe.

12 Let us all profess our faith.

13 The Apostles' Creed is said or sung.

14 In this faith, will you, by God's help, provide a Christian home for this child, and bring him up in the worship and teaching of the Church, that he may come to know Christ, his Saviour?
R. We will, God being our helper
Will you so order your own lives that you do not cause this child to stumble?
R. We will, God being our helper.
Will you guide him, so that abiding in the covenant of his baptism and established in faith by the Holy Spirit, he may come to partake of the Lord's Table, and go forth into the world to serve God faithfully in his Church?
R. We will, God being our helper.

15 Where it is customary for baptismal promises to be made by parents and sponsors on the child's behalf, this form shall be used

Therefore I ask you parents and sponsors on behalf of this child:

Do you renounce Satan and all his ways and all his works?
R. I renounce Satan and all his ways and all his works.

Do you desire to be baptized in the faith of the Church?
R. I do so desire.

Do you commit yourself to Christ, to trust in him and serve him faithfully until you die?
R. I commit myself to Christ, to trust in him and serve him faithfully until I die.

16 The Minister says to the congregation:

Dearly beloved, will you be faithful to your calling as members of the Church of Christ, so that this and all other children in your midst may grow up in the knowledge and love of him?
R. We will, God being our helper.

17   Let us pray.

O merciful God, whose Son by his baptism in the river Jordan identified himself with us sinful men, and revealed our true manhood, grant that the old man in this child may be buried, and the new man be made manifest, we beseech thee.

R. O Lord hear our prayer.

Grant that all evil desires may die in him, and the things of the Spirit live and grow in him, we beseech thee.

R. O Lord hear our prayer.

Grant that he may have power and strength triumphantly to conquer Satan, the world and the flesh, we beseech thee.

R. O Lord hear our prayer.

Grant that each child now to be baptized may receive thy heavenly blessing, and by thy mercy be made an heir of thy eternal kingdom, we beseech thee.

R. O Lord hear our prayer.

18   If it is customary for the water to be blessed, this form, or other customary forms, may be used.

Almighty God, sanctify, we beseech thee, this water, that by thy mercy, this child may receive the washing of regeneration and renewal in the Holy Spirit, whom thou hast poured out upon us richly through Jesus Christ our Saviour, who lives and reigns with thee in the unity of the Holy Spirit, God eternal, world without end. *Amen.*

BAPTISM

19   N, I baptize you in the name of the Father and the Son and the Holy Spirit. *Amen.*

20   Jesus Christ has received you into his flock, ✠ (and I mark you with the sign of the Cross)

Here the Minister may make the sign of the Cross on the forehead.

Be not ashamed to confess the faith of Christ crucified for you, but be a servant and witness of your Saviour to your life's end. *Amen.*

21   Here the Minister puts his hand on the head of the baptized child saying

Lord give to this child —— thy Holy Spirit, and confirm him as thine for ever. *Amen.*

22 If it is customary to clothe the newly-baptized child in white garments, this form shall be used

We will rejoice greatly in the Lord:
R. Our souls shall be joyful in our God;
For he hath clothed us with the garments of salvation:
R. He has covered us with the robes of righteousness.
Put off your old nature, and be renewed in the spirit of your minds.
R. We will put on the new nature, created after the likeness of God.

23 If it is customary for the newly-baptized to be given a light, this form shall be used.

Let your light so shine before men, that they may see your good works,
R. And give glory to our Father who is in heaven.

24   Let us pray.
Our Father, who art in heaven . . .

25 We give thee hearty thanks, merciful Father, that thou hast granted to this child to be born again by thy Holy Spirit, hast chosen him to be thine own, and received him into thy holy Church. We beseech thee to defend and assist him, that he may be enabled to hold fast to those good gifts of thine, which he has received today, and continue with them. Let thy Word enlighten him and lead him in the fear of thy holy name, through Christ our Lord. *Amen.*

26 Or:

We give thee hearty thanks, most merciful Father, that it has pleased thee to receive this child for thine own by adoption and to incorporate him into thy holy Church. And we humbly beseech thee to grant that he may more and more show forth in his life that which he now is by thy calling; so that as he is made a partaker of the death of thy Son, he may also be a partaker of his resurrection through the same Jesus Christ our Lord. *Amen.*

27 Almighty Father, from whom all fatherhood in heaven and earth is named, grant understanding and wisdom to the parents (and sponsors) of this child, that they may bring him up in thy holy fear, that he may ever live to thy glory, and at the last with them and with all thy saints may inherit thy eternal kingdom, through Jesus Christ our Lord. *Amen.*

28 O heavenly Father, grant, we pray thee, that we who have been baptized may not lose the grace of our baptism, but ever remain in it,
faithfully and steadfastly obeying the Word of life, through Jesus Christ,
our Lord and Saviour. *Amen.*

29 Here the service may conclude in any way which is customary; the giving of a
greeting and blessing, or the Holy Communion may follow.